Lost Chance:
Southern Rhodesia
1945–58

Lost Chance:
Southern Rhodesia 1945–58

Hardwicke Holderness

ZIMBABWE PUBLISHING HOUSE

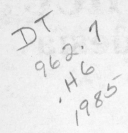

Zimbabwe Publishing House (Pvt) Ltd,
P.O. Box BW-350
Harare, Zimbabwe

© Hardwicke Holderness 1985

First published by ZPH 1985

Front cover photograph by Maggie Steber

ISBN 0 949932 88 4

Typeset by Bookset (Pvt) Ltd, Bulawayo
Printed in Zimbabwe by Zimpak

Contents

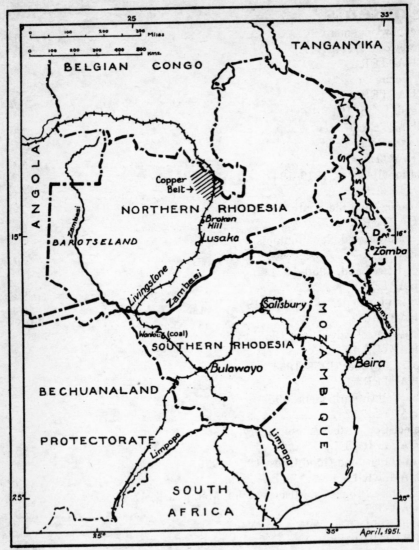

The sketch maps on this and the next page were part of the *Report of the Conference on Closer Association in Central Africa* which took place in London in 1951 — when Zimbabwe was called Southern Rhodesia, its capital Harare was called Salisbury, Zambia was called Northern Rhodesia and Malawi was called Nyasaland.

(The name "Harare" was then used to mean only a part of Salisbury — the part set aside for occupation by "Natives" as defined in the legislation of the time.)

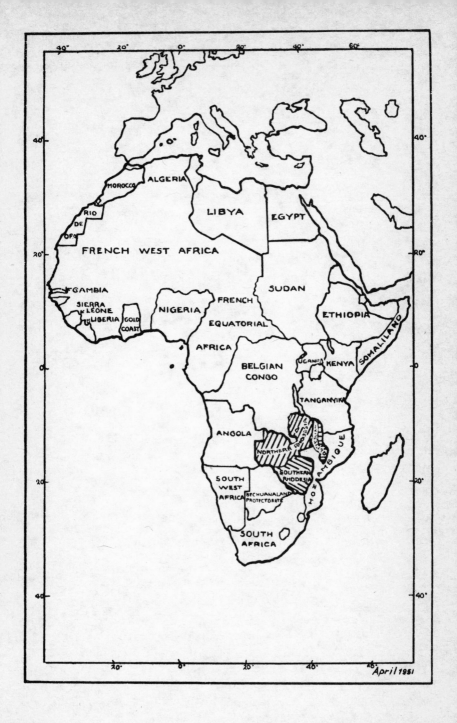

Acknowledgements

I have been greatly privileged to have had access at various stages of the manuscript to highly qualified people who were prepared to read and let me have their thoughts on it. In chronological order: Peter Calvocaressi (who had no obligation of any kind to do it but did, at an early stage); Dr F.T. Russell (who is mentioned in the book); Alan Milton, one–time Professor of Education at what has now become the University of Zimbabwe; Rupert Pennant–Rea of *The Economist* (who is mentioned indirectly); Ronald Robinson, ex war–time chum and now Professor of History at Balliol, Oxford; Professor Terence Ranger of Manchester University. But none of them can be held responsible for any of the book's defects.

My wife Elspeth, apart from enduring what I suppose most wives (or husbands) must have to suffer in the course of a husband's (or wife's) attempts to write a first book, and especially one of an autobiographical nature, has at each stage given unlimited help – as critic, typist and collaborator.

There are others who have given help and encouragement who will I hope be aware of my gratitude to them. And of course there are many not mentioned in the book who played a valiant part in the search for common ground which is part of its story.

If I have committed any breaches of legal protocol, for example in referring by name to my old firm of lawyers or to partners in it who are still in practice, it has been done off my own bat and without any responsibility on their part.

Finally, if there are any readers tempted to feel offended by something which the book says about them, or about someone connected with them who is no longer alive, I ask them to remember that what it purports to be is simply a facet of the truth, as seen from a particular angle.

H. H. C. Holderness
20 May, 1984

1

Foreword

Hardwicke was for ever writing memos and I hoped that one day he would produce a book covering the period 1953 to 1958. I had not expected him to take 25 years to do it but here it is and his notes must have been good for the story is sparkling, sensitive and authoritative. It covers much more than the five critical years at the close of which the opportunity to continue on the road to peaceful political evolution was supplanted by the growing danger of civil war.

Hardwicke spent his early life in the old Salisbury amongst the white community. I spent my first twenty years in Southern Rhodesia in the Lundi 'Native Reserve' with a black community. From such different backgrounds our views were eventually to merge but to the Salisbury background of Hardwicke's experience had to be added Oxford University plus a dis-tinguished war experience in a conflict of ideals — in a war against racism.

This book is largely an account of the experience of a group of men and women who in the forties and fifties attempted to educate their fellow citizens and to inspire such changes in our political life as would bring us all together within a politically viable nation.

1953–58 was a period of hope for those whites who recognised that, in the long term, safety and progress for all depended upon a sharing of political power — theirs for the time being — with an ever-increasing number of blacks. This hope could not have been sustained had there not been black men and women who were prepared to reciprocate in both thought and action. Fortunately the liberal whites were matched by a group of outstanding black men and women, many of whom are today's national leaders and two, Leopold Takawira and Herbert Chitepo, have their honoured place amongst the heroes of the revolution.

I was Prime Minister during the eighth Parliament and my first note to a new MP, Mr Hardwicke Holderness, said, 'I expect you will be a frightful nuisance in the House' and that, as things turned out, was not half the story. Hardwicke, with the limited responsibilities of a Member of Parliament, could afford to be single-minded. As Prime Minister I had to keep a disparate team together to make possible the success of the political and social ideals which he and I shared. I could have appointed a Cabinet who were sympathetic with my ideas on 'Native Affairs' — men like Alan Lloyd, Ralph Palmer, Ben Baron — but I believed that such a group would not last a year in the tough racial climate of Southern Rhodesia. I considered that our only hope of introducing necessary but unpopular change was to make an outstanding success of the economy. The two best financial men were Geoff Ellman–Brown and Cyril Hatty. I decided to give Cyril Hatty the Treasury and to put Ellman–Brown in charge of the spending departments. I was the more humble, at least the less knowledgeable member of the development team. Hatty, Ellman–Brown and I had our successes including changing Lord Malvern's mind after he had decided on Kafue instead of Kariba, but that is another story. All went well until I began to speak of providing better education facilities for Africans, the need for non–racial labour legislation, the desirability of extending the franchise to give the country a safe political base. These matters are, of course, the Hardwicke Holderness story and he tells it well.

This is my chance, though, to clarify two issues. Hardwicke says (p. 124) that I was a missionary turned farmer. I was in fact a missionary turned MP and I thought it wise to drop my missionary stipend because our New Zealand Churches were divided in their views on my entering politics but I remained Superintendent of Dadaya Mission for the next seven years in an honorary capacity. I had to find an alternative way of earning my living. I bought land and this gave me that degree of independence which led to prison at Gatooma, to long–term detention by the Smith government and eventually, when the mists had cleared, to being a Senator for Robert Mugabe. After 50 years I am still chairman of the Dadaya High School Board of Governors.

As regards the second issue, I should explain that instead of presiding over my first cabinet meeting of the new Parliament I sent an apology and flew to the Wankie Colliery where 9 000 miners had come out on strike (p. 141). I recognised two facts: the men had grievances and no adequate machinery to let them be known. Also there was a security problem because every white man seemed to have gone below surface to keep the machines operating. I could not risk an outbreak of violence and so called out the army, not to break the strike, but to keep the peace. At the same time we nominated a Commission of Enquiry which began its work within a few days. The situation was handled safely and fairly.

I am deeply indebted to Hardwicke Holderness for his vision, his tenacity of purpose, his warm friendship and now, for his book.

R.S. Garfield Todd

CHAPTER 1

Prologue

When I think of that once remote country in the middle of southern Africa where I was born, then called Southern Rhodesia and now Zimbabwe, I often think how unique a place it is and how much has happened in the mere ninety-four years of its history since the occupation by Cecil Rhodes' pioneer column in 1890. Annexed to the Crown at a time when additions to Empire had already become unfashionable; administered by Rhodes' chartered company until 1923; a self-governing Colony under the control of a small minority white population from 1923 until 'UDI' (the unilateral declaration of independence) in 1965; from 1965 until 1979 under the rebel regime of the Rhodesian Front and Ian Smith; and now fully independent, under the government of Robert Mugabe. A country more modern and developed than any in southern Africa except the Republic of South Africa itself. And one which until recently most of its white inhabitants, as well as the majority black population, felt to be their permanent home.

Because of the way the changeover from white to black rule has happened I suppose it is doubtful whether many whites continuing to live there will continue to think of the country as the permanent home of themselves and their families, or how many coming to it afresh will find it possible to do so. It seems to me probable that for most the possibility will be found to have been forfeited, as a result of particular choices which the white electorate made when they held power. And that makes me sad, because I once thought that as a country which both whites and blacks felt to be their permanent home it possessed a potential for good unique in history.

Not that I think the passing of political power from white to black hands in 1979 was wrong, or that the way Robert Mugabe's government has exercised it so far has been defective. Once the country got itself set under white leadership on the path which was to lead to white supremacist government under Ian Smith, it seemed certain that when the changeover did come it would be accompanied by widespread acts of hatred and revenge — against whites, and also against blacks who had found themselves supporting the Smith government in one way or another. And the policy of forgiveness and reconciliation immediately adopted by the Mugabe government and the absence of revenge on the part of blacks generally, surely represent a moral as well as a physical victory on their part. But many whites seem to have been too brainwashed by Smith government propaganda to appreciate it; and many have left.

Zimbabwe will no doubt manage without them. But why should the white community as a whole have ended up making such a mess of it?

For much the greater part of their fifty-six years in power the whites had a pretty good record. Economic development was extraordinarily widespread, and achieved without any cost to the British taxpayer or any free handouts from anyone else. Public administration was efficient and entirely uncorrupt. African education and rural development were more advanced than in other, non-self-governing Colonies. The whites' attitude of racial superiority was no doubt arrogant, but there was respect for justice and the rule of law, and no great cruelty. And in the early 1950's, when Southern Rhodesia agreed to join in a Federation with the two British Protectorates to its north (Northern Rhodesia and Nyasaland), the white electorate accepted an underlying commitment to move in a positively different direction from the one to which the Union of South Africa had then become committed with the coming to power of the Afrikaner Nationalist government in 1948.

So how was it that the Southern Rhodesian whites should in the end find themselves resorting to a kind of police state, and involved in a wasteful and brutal war with a black population outnumbering them twenty to one?

I know what the automatic answer tends to be: that it was all part of an inevitable process; that the selfish ambitions of the white settlers were incompatible with, and had to give way to, the legitimate interests of the majority indigenous population. But I think it is an answer based on ignorance of what Southern Rhodesia was really like and how much common ground in fact existed. On the other hand I think it is also a mistake to suppose, as some do who accept that a real chance of achieving something new in fact existed, that it only disappeared at the time when the Rhodesian Front came to power in 1963, or even in the following year when Ian Smith became Prime Minister.

I believe the crucial choice for the white electorate came in 1958, the year in which the then Prime Minister Garfield Todd was repudiated by the Ministers who had served with him in his Cabinet and, at the general election which followed, Todd and his supporters were rejected by the voters in favour of Edgar Whitehead. And as far as I know the full story of what happened then has never been told.

My version of what happened in 1958 and the events that led up to it cannot pretend to be unbiased because I was involved in them — if not in

5

much of a leading capacity, at least emotionally. I was one of a number of people — 'liberals', so-called — who had been deeply committed to politics and political reform during the thirteen years since the end of the war. Of those involved from the beginning I think especially of Pat (C.P.J.) Lewis, whose background was pretty well the same as mine: Rhodesian born, one parent from England and the other from the old Cape Colony, university in South Africa and then at Oxford, and then the Second World War. Even before the end of the war some whites had begun to understand the paradox: that what the whites themselves needed, as a numerical minority in possession of all the political power, was political participation by blacks. Otherwise they would become trapped and incapable of changing with the times — like the South African whites but with worse consequences for Rhodesians, being a smaller fraction of the total population. Younger generation Rhodesians like Pat and myself would have been half blind not to see it, after all the opportunities we had been given to look at the picture from a variety of different angles. The new liberal movement began with a kind of self-education programme in national affairs which Pat and I had a lot to do with. Later, Africans and other non-Europeans joined in; and the movement came to have a crucial influence, we thought, in the formulation during the period of the Todd government of legislation which had boundless possibilities for the future. I found myself in effect spokesman for the movement in the Parliament of that time.

The general election of 1958 put an end to the possibility of the new measures being properly implemented and, as some of us thought, an end to a unique opportunity which white Rhodesians had possessed as a sort of gift from history. Improbably, that small group of people had held in their hands a key to the peaceful evolution of politics in Africa, and at this point they had thrown it away. In less pretentious terms, I remember saying to Elspeth (my wife, and collaborator in all our ventures since her arrival in Rhodesia in 1947), 'this means that Rhodesian whites have condemned themselves to learn the hard way'.

For individuals like Pat and myself the possibility of exerting any further influence in politics disappeared, and under the Smith regime it virtually disappeared even in less romantic spheres of public life. Pat died, sadly, in 1975 before it was possible to see light through the end of the tunnel. Elspeth and I left the country that same year.

In the course of going through old papers and recalling what life was like and the political events of the time as we experienced them, I have often wondered whether it should all be treated as water under the bridge, since the liberal effort we were involved in ended in failure after all; or whether

6

some account of it could be of value to anyone else. I met a young Londoner who encouraged me to think it might be of interest at least to some of the younger generation who had lived there. He was born in Salisbury (now called Harare) the day Elspeth and I were married in 1948 — and so prevented his mother from attending the wedding. His parents were personal friends of ours and had deep roots in Rhodesia. But to them the Rhodesian Front government seemed to have committed the country to such a sterile course that when it came to UDI they felt they must emigrate. He said, 'I was only ten at the time of the 1958 election, but I and friends of mine at school believed in the liberals of your generation and we wanted you and Todd and the others to win. But you didn't. And then we watched what happened to Whitehead, and then the RF government coming to power, and then UDI. And now I, and some of them, have had to make our homes in other countries. We loved Rhodesia and if it had gone right we would have loved to be there. I am grateful I was spared being called up by the RF government. In some ways I have envied Rhodesians of my age who have had the experience of military service and sometimes exploits which, purely from a military point of view, have been brilliant. But I could not have stomached fighting against blacks whom I like at the instance of white supremacist politicians whom I abhor. Why did it have to come to that? We thought you had some influence. Were we wrong? Did you really have none, or did you mishandle it? Could you not have seized the government party machine in 1958 and swept to victory? What went wrong?'

I thought some attempt at an answer was due to his generation, and that there could also be others — some perhaps having no prior knowledge of the country and simply a curiosity about what it was like during its anomalous days as still a self-governing Colony — who would be interested. One possible explanation of what happened in 1958 is, not that white Rhodesians were necessarily less enlightened than any other group of voters, but that under the Constitution granted to the country in 1923 — in effect a scale model of the Westminster constitution — they had been given so much power as to make it impossible for them to change with the times; that it had condemned them, in effect, to commit political suicide in the end. And whether or not there is something in that speculation, perhaps there are some aspects of how constitutions work and how government works which may be deduced from the scale model working in that remote laboratory more effectively than from the full scale article operating in more sophisticated surroundings.

So what I have attempted is simply to give a personal account of what happened as seen through the eyes of two Rhodesians by birth, Pat Lewis

7

and myself; and to give at the same time the essential background information needed to follow the political issues, and enough about our own lives and background to enable the reader to judge for himself what allowances to make for distorted or defective vision.

CHAPTER 2

Small Pond, 1914–1933

At the time Pat and I were born in Salisbury (he in July 1914 and I six months later) it was less than twenty-five years since the Pioneer Column had arrived from the south and selected a site for the town on the Mashonaland plateau. It was on open grassland, alongside a wooded hill or kopje which seemed to provide a suitable look-out and had near it the little Makabusi River to provide an initial water supply. 'The Colony', as people called it, was still under the administration of Cecil Rhodes' British South Africa Company — the 'B.S.A.' or 'Chartered' Company – and its surveyor had laid out the town on a simple grid plan comprising rectangular plots of land or stands divided by wide strips of ground to serve as roads, the ones running east and west being called 'avenues' and the ones running north and south 'streets'. In our childhood the whole grid covered an area of about a mile by a mile and a half, and many of the stands were still empty and covered with tall grass, shoulder high and golden during most of the year.

The southernmost avenue ran along the railway line and gave access to the Railway Station, and from there progressing north, after crossing two or three 'avenues', you would come to the commercial buildings of the town on Manica Road (actually an 'avenue') and First Street (which ran northwards from the centre of Manica Road). A little to the east, on Third and Fourth Streets, were the main administrative buildings and The Salisbury Club, and at the centre of the grid was 'The Park', a large square of still largely uncultivated land flanked by Moffat Street on its west and Second Street on its east side. On the west side of the Park were the Boys' School and the Girls' School and the Library, and the vast Drill Hall and its parade ground. To the north of the Park, after crossing several more avenues, you would come to North Avenue at the top of the grid.

On North Avenue was the Hospital, a proud new one, two-storied but with its operating theatre forming on its own a third storey because, so it was said, it had been forgotten in the original plan. Immediately east of the Hospital was a simple golf course with 'greens' of raked river sand, and then a cricket and rugby ground and a polo ground still innocent of planted grass; then Government House, and finally, at the north-east corner of the grid, the Police Camp. This was more like an establishment for a kind of Colonial Guards Regiment than a civil police force. It was the home of the BSA Police, which had already achieved a high reputation as a mounted force and served, incidentally, as a recruiting ground for settlers, amongst others young Englishmen who might well otherwise have looked for a career in the Guards at home but having tasted life in the country decided to stay permanently. It had a good reputation with the African population, and an excellent military band staffed by blacks — essential feature of all ceremonial occasions. It was all very British, and each morning and at sunset you could hear from far off the echo of the bugles played by a smart detachment of black BSA policemen at the ceremony of the raising or lowering of the Union Jack in front of Government House.

It was a town for whites; the blacks who lived in it, as domestic servants or office messengers or manual labourers, were hardly ever thought of as more than temporary sojourners with their real homes in the Native Reserves. The terms 'blacks' and 'whites' were not much in use then. The official terms employed in legislation and quite generally in conversation were 'Natives' and 'Europeans'. Unofficially it was common amongst whites, and I think generally without any conscious intention of being condescending or contemptuous, to refer to black employees as 'boys' — except, oddly enough, if they were still in fact boys, in which case the usual unofficial term was 'picannin'. The term 'African' was not substituted for 'Native' in the official dictionary until 1957 though it was in general use amongst liberally inclined whites long before that.

Immediately south of the Railway Station and its yards and workshops were 'compounds' for 'Natives' employed on the railways or in the business part of the town. And separate from the town proper were the beginnings of white surburban residential areas which had begun spontaneously with the splitting up of a nearby farm into plots — like Avondale, which started a mile or so north of the Hospital, and Hatfield and Ardbennie on the sandveld to the south of the town.

Salisbury was a long way from the sea. You could go to Beira, about 350 miles to the east, by the railway which the Chartered Company had built from the mouth of the Pungwe River through the swamps and forests of

Mocambique and up to the Mashonaland plateau through the mountains of the eastern border of the Colony and Umtali. But Beira was oppressively hot except in mid-winter, and swampy, malarious and dirty — except for the Rhodesia Railways mosquito-gauzed but rather aristocratic Savoy Hotel — and you would hardly think of going to Beira for a holiday. When you thought of going to the sea you thought of the Cape, where so many Rhodesian whites had come from, mostly before 1910 while it was still 'the Cape Colony' and not yet a Province of the Union (now Republic) of South Africa. This you could do by the railway line linking Salisbury with Bulawayo, and then by the one linking Bulawayo with the Cape railway system which the Chartered Company had completed through Bechuana-land (now Botswana) as early as 1893. The total distance to Cape Town was nearly 1 800 miles and took four or five days in the train through the Kalahari Desert and the Karoo; and when you woke early on the final morning coming through the Hex River mountain pass, and knew that ahead of you were the beautiful mountains and vineyards and huge fir trees and oaks and eighteenth century Dutch colonial architecture of the Cape Peninsula, you felt you could already get a whiff of that extraordinarily powerful smell which the sea gives off crashing on to its rocks and glorious beaches. Besides, the Cape had a relatively gentle social and political tradition as yet not too much affected by the grim influence of the descendants of the Boers who had trekked north in the nineteenth century to get away from it.

Pat's family and mine lived in Cape Avenue, the northernmost but one of Salisbury's avenues, so called because it used to be the beginning of the only road to the Cape until the construction of Beit Bridge over the Limpopo river opened up the route through Johannesburg and Bloem-fontein. It was still the main road to Bulawayo, following the watershed and the railway round in that direction, west and then south, a distance of nearly 300 miles, through Hartley, Gatooma, Que Que and Gwelo, each a small cluster of buildings grouped around a railway station or siding. Bulawayo was also the junction between the line to the Cape and the one to Northern Rhodesia (now Zambia), and the main centre of such industry as the Colony could then boast. Bulawayo whites tended to regard Salisbury, the administrative centre and capital, as starchy and snobbish.

In the language of today we were, I suppose, privileged colonial settlers in a land acquired by conquest. But the colonial era proper had just about ended by the time Rhodesia was born, and any ideas the Pioneers may have had of getting rich quick and lording it soon disappeared. There was gold, but in small inaccessible deposits; nothing like the discoveries on 'the

Rand'. And there was nothing particularly luxurious about our way of living, even in the most respectable part of Salisbury.

The typical house was a small cluster of essential rooms surrounded, or almost surrounded, by a seven or eight foot wide verandah ('stoep' in the language of the Cape) built of brick and roofed with sheets of corrugated iron. The furniture: sparse, some of it home-made out of planks from 'petrol boxes' — the wooden cases which would come each with a pair of rectangular, four-gallon tins in it containing paraffin or petrol, the tins in turn when empty supplying the whole of a family's need for buckets. Water would be supplied initially by hand pump or windlass from a well dug in the back garden and later, in limited quantities, by pipeline from the new municipal dam. It would be heated in 'petrol tins' on the kitchen stove, or later in a drum bricked-in over a separate fireplace outside the bathroom. The garden: a rectangular acre of dark reddish soil still covered with rough veld vegetation except where it had been cleared for beds of vegetables at the back of the house or for flowers in front, or had been eroded by the passage of feet or the tyres of bicycles which formed the standard means of transport, passed down from one member of the family to another.

For 'sanitation' each plot had a self-contained little building known as the 'PK' ('piccanin kia' or small house) away up at the end of the back garden, backing on to a sanitary lane; inside it a wooden seat with a round hole, and under the hole an iron bucket removable through a flap door into the lane to be exchanged for a new one each night during the small hours. This operation was performed by a team of spectral figures wearing for protection sacks with eye-slits over their heads and carrying the buckets on top of them, pad-padding barefoot along the sanitary lane to and from a wagon drawn by a full team of oxen. They were customarily recruited in the Zambezi Valley, and a story of the time told of a lady keen on Shakespeare who, rehearsing late one night on the back verandah declaimed 'Romeo, Romeo, wherefore art thou Romeo?', received the reply from the sanitary lane (in the execrable substitute for a language known as 'kitchen kaffir' which was used for communications between employers and employees): 'Mina aicona Romeo, madam; mina Zambezi boy'.

Other public facilities were limited and families coped as best they could with germs and poisons borne by flies, cockroaches, spiders (fearsome-looking, some lethal but mostly harmless), snakes (various, many lethal but all disposed to mind their own business except when threatened), mosquitoes, and especially the malaria carrying anopheles. In the rainy season — summer — it was essential to use the mosquito nets which would be suspended on rings from the ceiling over each bed, but even so few of Pat's and my generation would escape one or more bouts of malaria and that high fever and its splitting headaches and nightmares and the eerie headnoises caused by the quinine used to treat it.

At the back of the plot, also backing on to the sanitary lane, would be the 'boys' kias', a basic room or rooms and ablution for the family's domestic servants — one to do the cooking, one for the housework, one or perhaps two for the garden and also possibly a 'piccanin' to be general assistant and golf caddie. They earned their rations and a modest money wage and they were, I suppose, our real luxury.

For the greater part of seven months in the year from about April there would be virtually no rain, only glittering clear skies; and from June to August some bitterly cold, frosty nights. Stored water was scarce and the idea that it would one day be possible to have planted, green lawns would have seemed far-fetched indeed. But there were some things which it seemed normal to grow, because they took little water, and perhaps because some of the earlier settlers had happened to hit upon them: bouganvillia and poinsettia and lemon trees, and paw-paws — paw-paw trees with their tapering, papier maché stems and branches at the top carrying leaves like upturned elephants' ears and their yellow fruit jutting from the trunk like a happy parody of human breasts. And there might be on the plot one or two and in some cases even a number, of the indigenous *msasa* — elegantly shaped trees which in advance of the onset of the rains would re-clothe their bare winter tracery with soft foliage in the whole range of copper colours as if from springtime on another planet.

By October the air would become oppressive and hazy with the smoke of veld fires, some ignited simply by a piece of broken bottle happening to focus the sun like a magnifying glass on to the parched grass; and you could watch the build-up during the day of vast, baroque cumulo-nimbus clouds and the play of the light on them, and the spectacular scene towards sunset when the sun's rays, filtered through the dust and smoke of the atmosphere, were charged with amazing colours. And when the time came that a cloud's load of moisture was heavy enough to drop out of the bottom of it, you could see and hear the grey curtain of rain marching towards you and smell before it reached you, the scents released by the rain from the dry earth and foliage. And the lightning and thunder and steady roar of the rain on the tin roof at night was something which you had, like the Ancient Mariner, to learn to enjoy in order to avoid being terrified by it.

The architecture of Salisbury was not all plain and utilitarian. Bicycling round the as yet rough, gravelled roads called avenues and streets, you would be impressed by the character of some of the buildings, though

13

hardly knowing why until much later when you came across in England and Europe the originals of the styles you had seen embodied in them. The premises of Store Bros, 'Milliners and Haberdashers', built at the opening up of Manica Road in 1911, had a Flemish gable and, in front of it, a two-tiered ironwork verandah in an assortment of classical and rococo styles — slender 'Corinthian' columns and, supporting the upper floor and roof, rococo tracery in moulded iron. Many of the single and double storied verandahs along and around Manica Road were of this kind; presumably a staple export from English foundries during the nineteenth century, which would account for a similarity one came to be aware of between Store Bros in the middle of Africa and buildings to be seen in Wild West films. Some roofs, though in corrugated iron, were crowned by a centrepiece in the French style, with oval baroque windows (dummy) and a miniature ironwork palisade. Some buildings, like Chaplin House, had classical facades of real distinction; some heavy, baroque fronts in moulded plaster with little behind them but a single row of rooms under a lean-to roof.

The interior most frequented and enjoyed by both young and old was Pocket's Tea Room — 'Pocket's' — large and spacious, with the tables ranged over the floor area overlooked by others on wide balconies; black waiters in white uniforms who never seemed to resign or be sacked; coffee with cream and anchovy toast; and everyone you knew to be seen there at some time of the day and especially on Saturday mornings. I assumed there must be a similar institution in towns everywhere and was to be sadly disappointed. But the biggest, and in many ways most charming building, was Meikles Hotel, completed in 1914. It was two-storied, covered a vast area, and had along its whole frontage a wide, double-storied verandah supported by Ionic columns below and Corinthian columns above, all in moulded cement. It had many large rooms opening on to the verandah through French windows, and a lounge and vast dining room fit for a banquet or ball in any town or city, with high, festive ceilings made of pressed metal. It was the result, I believe, of a design-construct contract given by the successful transport rider, Tom Meikle, to a builder who had happened in his boyhood to pick up the elements of classical architecture from his Scottish dominie.

———————

My father, 'Jim' Holderness, had come to Southern Rhodesia as a boy of 17 in 1902. He arrived in Bulawayo with a leather trunk and a silver watch and a job as a Judge's clerk, all provided for him by a benefactor who had come to the rescue of his family. His father had been a parson with a parish in Yorkshire and no private means and had died at forty-five leaving his widow, Jim's mother, and eight children virtually penniless. Jim was nearly the youngest, and closest to him during his childhood and holidays from school were two of his sisters, Elsie and May. The best entertainment the family could afford was reading aloud to one another, and the thing which I came to appreciate as something most memorable about each of them (apart from an attractive, boyish way of ragging to make you feel at home) was their love of prose and poetry, sounded in the round, and the habit of reading aloud with enthusiasm but without the slightest affectation, passages from their favourite writers — Shakespeare, Dickens, Browning, Robert Herrick — and sometimes poignant passages from the Bible like the story of Absolom. From his first pay as a Judge's clerk Jim sent some money to Elsie and May, and he continued to do so each month for the rest of his life.

He studied and became qualified as a solicitor — 'attorney' in the terminology taken over from the Cape with the Roman-Dutch common law. He was taken on in the firm in Salisbury established by Sir Thomas Scanlen who, as Prime Minister of the Cape for a brief period, had first appointed Rhodes as a Minister there and had subsequently been appointed by him as Solicitor to the BSA Company with its charter to administer the new Colony. Jim became a partner of Thomas Scanlen's son Arthur.

My mother, 'Con' or 'Connie', came from an English-speaking Cape family called Thwaits and had many relations on her mother's side among people of 1820 Settler stock. Her father was a magistrate and her mother a person with a strong social conscience and high ideals. Con's first experience of Rhodesia was as a single young woman come to help her elder sister, wife of one of the pioneers, to look after her first child in Bulawayo; and in the predominantly male company of that time she seems to have been spoiled a little by impressive people like the senior engineers responsible for the beautiful bridge in the process of being built at that time at the Victoria Falls, over the gorge 500 feet deep, immediately opposite the falls themselves. As a result, and not because Con could be said in any sense to be a tough or masculine young woman, she found herself the first female to be allowed to cross the gorge by cableway, sitting on a plank slung from the cable on a pulley and surrounded by a sack intended, as part of its function, to cut off a little of the over-abundant view below. Later, Con and Jim met and got married and had five children.

In Pat's case it was his father, Vernon Lewis, who came from the Cape, one of the sons of the Principal of the South African College which was to grow into the University of Cape Town. And it was his mother, Amy, who came from Britain, a member of the characterful Jameson clan of which the then most famous member was the wiry little doctor, Leander Starr, friend and associate of Cecil Rhodes, who had done many remarkable things before blotting his copy book with the Jameson Raid. Vernon was a barrister (advocate) and Pat the eldest of their three children.

The Lewises lived next to us in Cape Avenue (later called Montagu Avenue in honour of the foremost promoter of tree planting in the town) and next to them were the Hones: Arthur, a senior civil servant with an English public school background and a number of missionary relations; his wife Olive, a sister of Arthur Scanlen's, and their five children.

This was not untypical of the families in that part of the town: one of the parents coming from Britain and the other from the Cape; several children; the father respectably engaged in the public service or one of the professions, and little or no money in the family apart from his modest earnings. A few had some inherited money in the background which they might use to send a son to school in England. In that case he would in effect disappear for seven or eight years before returning at the age of eighteen or so, since there would be neither time nor money available for holiday visits from England to Cape Town by ship and then several days in the train. More commonly boys might be sent to the 'private' schools — usually Church schools — in Southern Rhodesia or South Africa which were supposed to be the equivalent of English preparatory and public schools. But for most of us, and especially in large families, it was the well-subsidised Government school where one came across children from the whole range of white Rhodesian families of that time.

Thinking of the parental background of some of the boys in my class at the Boys' School, there were people from England and one from Ireland and Afrikaners who were trying to make a living out of farming or 'small-working' (prospecting and mining on a one-man basis); there was a schoolteacher, Scottish as most school teachers seemed to be at the time; an Afrikaans railway worker; a Hollander and a Greek with grocery stores; there were several Jews from central and eastern Europe — one, barely literate who had a mad wife and a small tobacconist shop and another who had a small laundry business and a third, relatively prosperous, who dealt in 'kaffir truck' and grain in the native areas; there was a bricklayer from Yugoslavia, and so on. The boys from out of town were boarders, and the boarders made most of the running in the school. The prevailing approach to life tended to be rough and tough. The standard dress was khaki shirt and shorts — sensible enough in the days before planted grass. And I remember still with some of the original dread the frequent challenges to a 'scrap', and the savage, bare-fisted fights which would follow in the red dust behind the bicycle sheds, out of reach of authority and the rule of law. Rust coloured dust and blood and black eyes, and the taste of being at the mercy of the powerful. Physical prowess was the thing, and in its more refined form on the rugby field. To be interested in what some unfortunate school-master might be trying to get across in the classroom tended to be regarded as 'wet' and to answer his questions as 'creeping'.

There was a contrast between this approach to life and what prevailed at home, and the daily transition from one atmosphere to the other was one of the traumas of being a day scholar.

People like Jim and Arthur Hone and Vernon Lewis seemed to share, without having to be explicit about it, a kind of ethic which placed a high value on fair play, good manners, integrity and deplored boasting, doing people down, questioning the umpire. They saw themselves as English gentlemen, however badly off or modestly placed they might be relative to the social hierarchy of England of the time, and this is the sort of thing they meant by it. It was a tradition still generally current in places like the Salisbury Club, and had been since its establishment by the kind of people whom Rhodes and the Chartered Company had appointed to influential positions in the early days of the Company's administration. I think it must have been an important factor in their relations with the African population; and I remembered it much later in talking to a much-travelled Swiss journalist who said that a thing he noticed, comparing other peoples' Colonies (Switzerland having none), was that British settlers tended to behave better than, for example, Flemish settlers in the Congo, because 'they tried to behave like the Governor'. And looking back at the time of UDI it seemed to me that if my father's contemporaries had been able to visualise this happening it would have been the dishonourable aspect of it — the repudiation of Britain in its role as referee — that would have struck them.

The low, verandahed Salisbury Club building, with its sub-tropical setting and rail for tethering horses by the front door, might seem from the outside to have little in common with a traditional London Club, but inside the atmosphere and prevailing code of manners was distinctly similar. In its approach to the admission of new members it was exclusive, not to say anti-semitic. But it did not follow that outside the Club the members were snobbish in their relations with other white Rhodesians. As between whites it was already a largely classless society, and every day becoming more so.

From the time of his arrival in Southern Rhodesia at the age of seventeen until he was over sixty my father was only able to visit England once, on his honeymoon in 1908, but he continued throughout his life to refer to England as 'home'. This reflected a genuine love and loyalty. But it would have been wrong to deduce that he regarded himself as in any sense only a temporary resident of Southern Rhodesia. He loved its blue skies in winter and its towering clouds in the rainy season; its *msasa* trees, *mnondo*, *mfuti* and *mopani*; the sandveld with its fantastic rock shapes caused by the flaking and erosion of the ancient granite over many geological ages; its individualistic, small wild flowers which would make their appearance like a symbol of faith amongst the black, burnt-out veld grass towards the end of winter, well in advance of the rains.

There was no promise of ever being rich; but for people like Jim and Con, the Lewises and the Hones and others of their generation there was a lot to be grateful for. The kind of house you lived in might be primitive by English standards, but in that agreeable climate you could if you chose live out of doors a lot of the time and, owing to the altitude, even at the hottest time of the year the nights were cool. And you owned your house, freehold, with a great area of garden where, if only you could provide water, plants would grow as quickly as almost anywhere else in the world. Nobody was conspicuously richer than you and simple pleasures were available on a sort of extended family basis: foregathering in one another's houses for 'sundowners' before the evening meal or afterwards for a game of bridge; joint family sorties to some glorious spot, perhaps hardly known to anyone else, with granite kopjes to climb and fast running water — still reckoned to be free enough from bilharzia to be safe to swim in. Tennis, golf, 'tenniquoits'. The occasional glamorous ball, at Meikles or, once in a while, at Government House.

To the younger generation, or perhaps only to less robust specimens of it like myself, there was another side to it. I felt the indigenous trees and rocks and grass and wild flowers were my friends, and I had privileged occasions with them, particularly at the age of about ten and eleven. I used sometimes to be invited, on my own and away from family pressures, to a farm in the Mazoe valley to be company for a blue-eyed Irish creature of the same age who had all the romantic magic for me of a Lorna Doone. She gave me first lessons in riding; and to ride with her over that beautiful farm — especially in the even light before the sunrise, sometimes drenched in dew from the long, coarse grass, sometimes finding ourselves alongside crowded cosmos flowers or a scarlet and black bishop bird — seemed to me a kind of heaven. But I found the full blaze of the Rhodesian sun often oppressive and the atmosphere at sunset, when the sun suddenly disappeared, intensely depressing. And there was a particular place near town where we used to walk sometimes, a mile or two from North Avenue on the kopje then called Hartman Hill with its black ironstone rocks, which seemed to me to have an especially depressing atmosphere. Many years later, in relation to something that happened there, I wondered whether there had been something prophetic about that. Sometimes one would hanker for the sea, experienced at its majestic best on family trips to the Cape which my father was able to organise about once in three or four years by means of raising a mortgage on his house.

School was a nightmare except to the extent that some courageous master would be able to get over to a largely unwilling class some of the magic of literature. This, combined with what came through from Jim's love of the subject and the winter evenings round the fire when he would read to us until we were compelled to go unwillingly to bed, put us in possession of a second home, still in the imagination and not yet visited, but as it turned out, as effectively as if we had been born there.

Pat was a gentle, unselfish fellow and was sent to one of the first of the English style prep schools for whites, first called Cedric and later Ruzawi, and then to St. Andrews College in South Africa.

During the time we were at school the Rhodesian voters (of whom there were 19,000 at the time) opted by referendum in 1922 for Responsible Government instead of union with South Africa, and Coghlan's premiership was followed by Moffat's and Sir John Chancellor's governorship by Sir Cecil Rodwell's. The Moffat younger generation became part of the same large group of young whom we found ourselves bicycling, picnicking and playing tennis with, and the same applied to the Rodwell younger generation when they arrived; and a number of the people trying their hand as M.P.'s would have been familiar to us as friends or acquaintances of our parents, including Dr Huggins who was later to establish a record of twenty five years continuously in office as Prime Minister. However, we were not particularly well informed at that stage about what was going on in politics, and were only vaguely aware of any potential racial problem.

In 1931 — towards the end of our school days — the total white population was just over 50,000 of which more than half lived in the towns. Bulawayo and Salisbury would have had about 10,000 each. The African population was reckoned to be about 1,000,000. There were Native Reserves set aside for exclusive occupation by Africans under a traditional system of communal tenure, and up to 1931 the rest of the land had, theoretically, been open to purchase and occupation by either blacks or whites. Very little had in fact been acquired by blacks. But in that year an Act was passed in Parliament which was to become a sort of focal point for racial discord, the blacks regarding it as symbolic of white supremacy and many whites seeing it as fundamental to their interests. It was the Land Apportionment Act, and what it did was to set aside some of the unreserved land to be held on the same basis as the Native Reserves and some to be held as Forest Land and Game Reserves and then, as regards the rest, it adopted the principle that a limited amount should be 'Native Purchase Area', available for purchase by Natives only, and the whole of the rest should be 'European Area', available for acquisition only by non-Natives. The quantity allocated to the European Area was quite out of proportion to the numbers of the white population and contained all the towns and what is now called 'infrastructure'; but the Act followed the recommendation of a Land Commission which had been set up under Sir Morris Carter, an ex-Chief Justice of Tanganyika and Uganda, and had made a long and thorough investigation of the subject, and it must have seemed to the older generation of whites at the time to be a fair settlement of the land question for the foreseeable future. As schoolboys still we were probably hardly aware of its existence. Nearly all African education was given at remote missions in or near the Native Reserves, and one came across no Africans with a command of English except one or two Court interpreters and the like; and if there existed frustrated political ambitions amongst them there was nothing to make us as whites aware of them. Only a handful were registered on the voters' roll.

Relations with black employees seemed to be uncomplicated. Most of the older generation saw it simply as a matter of being firm but fair and, in the case of the housewife, sufficiently peremptory to exclude any dangers which might result from familiarity. The resulting disciplinarian attitude — which did not exclude a real if feudal kind of concern for health and well-being — seemed increasingly inappropriate as time went on, but it was perhaps an inevitable result of a situation in which, in Con's case for example, there had only been about a thousand white women in the whole country when she first arrived and for a long time afterwards there were only male servants. And in any case the sense of humour which was such a marked characteristic of the Shona people we were dealing with undoubtedly enabled them to take it with a pinch of salt.

I remember my mother recalling how, when she and Jim were first married and still very young, the office messenger, known as 'Scoff', was reprimanded by my father for familiarity with their watchdog — a small, smooth-haired fox terrier called 'Menu'. Scoff must have been taken on as a lad by Sir Thomas Scanlen in about 1896 and was about the same age as my parents, and on this occasion he had ridden on his bicycle from the office along winding paths through the long grass covering most of the intervening stands to deliver some letters. My mother noticed Jim trying to command an imposing and severe presence despite his blonde, boyish looks, and saying to Scoff 'I told you Scoff, that you mustn't talk to Menu'; and Scoff's reply 'Oh it's all right, master, I was talking to him in English'.

Scoff became a favourite with us children, always with a gentle joke for us in his broken English and a wholly disarming smile crinkling his face. He retired as office messenger in 1936, but he lived for another thirty years after that and would appear about once a year at the office to collect his pension (something which must have been fairly unique at the time it was awarded and partly inspired, I would imagine, by Arthur Scanlen who was so attached to his own personal servants that he tried when he died to bequeath to them a farm near the Mazoe valley — with only limited success as it turned out, due to the Land Apportionment Act). It was only when Scoff died and I was invited by his sons to bring Con, now widowed and within a year or two of her own death, out into the Reserve to attend his funeral that we became aware of the other life he had been leading all the time as the gentle patriarch of a whole clan and a Methodist lay preacher certificated as such in 1905. To be shown the certificate by one of the old ladies in the hut where Scoff's body lay in its coffin was a moving experience for Con.

For us of the younger generation it was possible to be on closer personal terms with the staff than our parents, and when African women came to be employed as 'nannies' there was a special relationship with them. Their exceptional patience and capacity for affection and laughter made them in some vital ways the perfect companion for children. And between my youngest brother and Umteru, the boy employed as a golf caddie when both were about ten, there developed an enduring friendship. Umteru was a scallywag in some ways but almost an integral part of the family and he had a droll way of copying, in his version of English, phrases of my father's like 'By Jove' and 'I don't care tuppence' and songs from the gramophone like 'Who tied a can to the old dog's tail?'

As the end of school days came into sight the crucial question was whether one would be able to get away, to university and a new environment. And it is perhaps only in looking back now that I appreciate fully how critically dependent I and others were on there being available at that stage scholarships or bursaries from the Trust which had been set up by Alfred Beit when he died in 1906. This made it possible, provided you could score good marks in the matric exam and your parents could raise just enough to

21

cover clothes, travelling expenses and a little pocket money, to go to university in South Africa (there being none in Southern Rhodesia until much later). If not, it was a matter of getting the best job you could find, such as being a clerk in the civil service or a bank, and hoping by some other means at some later date to get a taste of the big world. In the case of my family the eldest son and the third (myself) were lucky; the second, with brilliant potential as an engineer but little facility at exams and at that stage a deep antipathy to law, became articled in my father's firm, and the fourth, determined to fly aeroplanes, became a civil service clerk pending escape by way of a short service commission to the Royal Air Force. (The tail-ender, a daughter, had no academic aspirations).

If you got to university in South Africa then there was the further possibility, however remote, of a Rhodes Scholarship to Oxford. For that one was supposed to be such an all rounder, and such a potential leader, that nobody with my kind of record at school would have begun to contemplate the possibility save for Rhodes' favouritism to the Colony called after him, which had resulted in no less than three scholarships being available each year for its diminutive eligible population.

Pat went to Rhodes University College ('Rhodes') in 1932, and on to Oxford as a Rhodes Scholar in 1936. He returned to Rhodesia in 1938 with law degrees from Rhodes and Oxford and admitted as a Member of the English Bar; had just time to be admitted as an attorney in Rhodesia before joining up as a gunner for the war; fought in North Africa, was taken prisoner in 1942 and spent the rest of the war as a POW in Italy and then in Germany.

I went to Rhodes in 1933 and, due to understandable doubts on the part of the Selection Committee about my qualifications as a Rhodes Scholar, did not reach Oxford until 1938. By joining the Oxford University Air Squadron I became a member of the Volunteer Reserve of the Royal Air Force, and so found myself serving in it as a pilot during the whole of the war, based in various parts of England, Scotland and Wales.

CHAPTER 3

On the Map, 1946

After his liberation from prisoner-of-war camp during the Allied invasion of Europe in 1945 Pat was brought to England and we met in London by chance, collecting letters at Rhodesia House; and in September we found ourselves on board the MV 'Ruys' together, being repatriated with a number of other Rhodesians and South Africans. There was no alcohol or female company on the 'Ruys' and plenty of time for discussion. We had not met for seven or eight years; and we were surprised to find that our political outlook, conclusions from past experience and feelings about the future seemed to be practically identical.

Looking back, we could see that in our early days as students, even at Rhodes in remote Grahamstown, we had caught something of the disillusionment which must have been general amongst students in Europe following the First World War and the Treaty of Versailles and the great depression. War was intolerable, and even in victory incapable of producing any good — except for the capitalist armament manufacturers. Capitalism bred inequality and injustice: 'food without appetites at one end of the town and appetites without food at the other'. People could be played for suckers by appeals to patriotism. So in 1933 the majority vote in the Oxford Union debate against fighting 'for King and Country' — which scandalised so many of the older generation and, according to some accounts, misled Hitler as to the nature of British youth — was something we could quite understand. But then as students at Oxford we had seen from close at hand the rise of the Fascists and the Nazis, and their intervention in the Spanish civil war. Pat had witnessed the Mosley Blackshirts in action in the streets of London and come across the Hitler Jugend in the course of extensive journeys in Germany which he had made by bicycle during Oxford vacations. I had been in Vienna immediately after the Anschluss in 1938, visiting Austrian students whom I had met on a tour which they made of South African universities. I had seen Hitler driving down the Ringstrasse (or was it Mariahilfestrasse?) and Goering addressing the crowd from a balcony at the Rathaus; witnessed Jew baiting in the streets and heard my student companion, who said she disapproved of it, justifying her acquiescence in the Anschluss on the ground that the alternative Austrian regime was no better and, since the break-up of the Austro-Hungarian empire, Austria had ceased to be viable as an economic entity. Just as the Nazi propaganda said.

I had gone on to Czechoslovakia to stay with Ed Verdier, a Frenchman who had been born of missionary parents in Basutoland, sent to school in South Africa, studied science at Rhodes and was now doing research at the University of Prague. Prague had struck me as a place of unique enchantment and promise; its romantic Bohemian history manifest in the rich architecture and its promise as a parliamentary democracy evident in its then Government and modern industry. But every day through Ed's Czech friends rumours had reached us of the invasion of the Sudetenland by Nazi Germany — chilling foretaste of what was to come the following year.

By September 1939 one had got to the state of feeling that for Britain to have refrained any longer from declaring war on Nazi Germany would have been intolerably shameful. The thought that what the Nazis stood for could come to prevail in the world had made one suddenly see clearly what kind of things it was in the English tradition that one valued fundamentally: parliamentary democracy and the rule of law; the recognition of man's fallibility and refusal to allow any one too much power over others; respect for man's individuality and insistence on his right not to conform; the opening of doors in time before revolution; self-criticism; humour; the deflation of pompousness. (The word 'bullshit' coined during the war had a real and special significance, and all credit to the war-time Air Force for coining it!)

So from being in a sense pacifists we had found ourselves being driven to accept that war was necessary; but still with the gravest doubts as to whether any good could come out of it, and with near certainty that there would be little which unwarlike individuals like ourselves could contribute in the course of it. And again there had been surprises. In some ways things which one had thought of as ideals in peacetime had seemed actually to come to pass in the course of this war. This time it was not a case of the young being induced by doubtful appeals to patriotism to slog it out in the trenches while the rest of the population remained in comparative safety at home. In England everyone was involved, and you knew in your guts what was at stake. For once you could be part of the group without having to compromise your values for it. For once you could be amongst people who were making their maximum effort without thinking for five minutes how much they were going to be paid for it. And if you found yourself with some sort of command it was not necessary to pretend to be a traditional commander or a 'born leader'. You could get better results by making it your business to procure for the people you were supposed to be commanding as much information as possible about strategy and tactics, and cashing in on their capacity to make use of it. Maybe this applied especially in a service like the Air Force because in operating with relatively small and sophisticated machines like aeroplanes (or for that matter submarines or MTBs) there was hardly any room for bullshit.

But then was it not generally true in this war, and at this stage in the spread of popular education, that the best results were achieved by reliance on intelligence and mutual responsibility rather than on formal discipline or a kind of hero worship? Was that not in fact an ingredient of the way even Montgomery had found himself playing it in practice, and the really important one whatever he himself might think? And was there any reason why it should not apply equally in peacetime, at this stage in history, in politics and industrial relations? Could anything else in fact work, at this stage in history?

Talking it over on the 'Ruys' we agreed we would miss England. From the moment of arriving to go to Oxford we had this strange feeling of belonging, and in London in particular of being accepted as legitimate members of her great brood. What could account for it? The holding of a British passport? The fact that one's father or mother happened to be British born though resident elsewhere since childhood? The literature which one had been brought up on, or its capacity to evoke archetypal images in a subconscious stretching beyond one's own lifetime? London had seemed at its best in the time of the bombs and the blackout: people treating them as a joke, and the class-consciousness which we had been disturbed to find so prevalent before the war seeming to have almost disappeared. We would think of the National Gallery Lunch Hour Concerts as symbolising the spirit of it. The Gallery, almost empty of pictures due to the necessity to protect them, put experimentally to this alternative use; and people of all kinds, many of them young, congregating informally over coffee and sandwiches for lunch and enjoying without affectation music which before the war would have been thought too highbrow except for the few. We would remember little Myra Hess, who had promoted the idea without the expectation that it would become a national institution, arriving at the steps in Trafalgar Square to play the Schumann Piano concerto and the affection of the audience for her.

We had been away from Rhodesia for a long time and hardly knew what we should expect to find on our return. But one thing seemed certain: that you could not have parliamentary democracy there and, in effect, confine it to the whites. However uninterested in politics the blacks might have appeared to be in the past they could hardly be uninterested now. The world had shrunk, and Southern Rhodesia could no longer be isolated from its trends. For parliamentary democracy to prevail it would have to be sold in competition with Russian communism and Fascism, both of which after all claimed to be popular movements. And Rhodesian whites could hardly reject the racialism embodied in the Nazi philosophy while practising racial superiority themselves.

But what would today's white Rhodesians think of that kind of proposition? We decided to see if we could get some discussion going among the Rhodesians on board the 'Ruys', and a copy which has survived of a notice typed on the Purser's borrowed typewriter reads:

NOTICE TO RHODESIANS

Programme For Future Meetings

SUNDAY 2nd SEPT.: Recreation Room: 15.30

Lecture	'RHODESIAN AGRICULTURE AND THE PROBLEMS INVOLVED IN ITS EXPANSION'
Speakers	Major Field Lieutenant Goddard
Chairman	W/Cdr Flett.

MONDAY 3rd SEPT.: Recreation Room: 15.30

Lecture	'CIVIL ENGINEERING AND AGRICULTURE'
Speaker	Flight Lieutenant Gibb
Chairman	F/Lt Johnston.

WEDNESDAY 5th SEPT.: Recreation Room: 15.30

Debate	'THAT IMMEDIATE STEPS MUST BE TAKEN IN RHODESIAN POLICY TOWARDS ULTIMATE EQUALITY OF THE AFRICAN'
Speakers	
FOR	Captain Lewis
	F/Lt K. Wilson
AGAINST	Lieutenant Bond
	F/Lt Filmer
Chairman	W/Cdr Holderness.

THURSDAY 6th SEPT.: Recreation Room: 15.30

Lecture	'POLITICAL PERSONALITIES, POLICIES AND PARTIES'
Speaker	Flying Officer Arnold.

The response was quite good, so far as I can remember, and not too hostile to the subject of the Debate. It was Pat's and my first acquaintance with Winston Field, who was to become the Prime Minister replaced by Ian Smith in 1964, and 'Bill' Arnold, journalist, who was to become a staunch ally of ours in the political field within the limits imposed by his job as a civil servant and senior information officer in the pre-Smith days.

The ship reached Cape Town, and the train took us on to Salisbury.

Back home. The brilliant glare of Salisbury station. The gentle and terrible web of family relationships. The sense of slight outrage at finding people eating multi-course meals and steak instead of Spam. The process of adaptation to civilian life.

Since Arthur Scanlen's retirement from Scanlen & Holderness some time before the war Jim had resisted bringing anyone else into the firm so as to keep it open for a member of the family, and I was to join him. Pat agreed to come in with me. We were over thirty, unmarried, each due for a modest war service gratuity and otherwise without assets. Jim had come nearly to the end of his tether trying to run the practice single-handed during the whole of the war. The accommodation was sparse and there had been no time to prepare for us. The staff consisted of one able Scottish lady performing all the functions of typist, book-keeper, office manager and, in effect, proprietor of Jim whom she served with unswerving loyalty. She did not care much for intruders. It was surely a time for single-minded dedication to the career of law, and especially in my case since I had learned little more from the (idle) Professor of Law at Rhodes than the saying 'The law is a jealous mistress', and at Oxford had switched to a differemt course of study. But could politics wait? And had we not in any case as ex-Rhodes Scholars some sort of moral obligation to see what we could contribute in that direction? The duty to make money seemed less obvious, and much less attractive. And so during the ensuing years we found ourselves like jugglers trying to keep a number of balls in the air at the same time: grappling with advanced legal work at the same time as learning it; taking over the running of the firm while still trying to figure out what made a legal firm tick; getting married and setting up home; and politics of a kind. With special emphasis on the last.

———————

There had been great changes in Salisbury since our school days. Some we had seen before the war, on vacations from Rhodes. The gravel streets had been transformed into macadamised avenues lined with fully grown trees, so that in Montagu Avenue for example you could walk for a mile under jacaranda trees which, in about September, would be thickly laden with their mauve-blue flowers each shaped like an elongated bell, and have under your feet, crackling softly, a mauve-blue carpet of fallen blossom; and in Blakiston Street a little later on in the year there would be an equivalent spectacle but in the golden-scarlet colours of the flamboyant flowers (each like a miniature orchid if you looked at them closely). Gardens had been transformed by water from the Prince Edward Dam — so named in honour of the Prince of Wales' visit in 1926. New avenues had been added to the north with new and more pretentious houses getting on towards the formerly separate old hamlet of Avondale. The golf club — 'Royal Salisbury' since the Prince's visit — now had real green greens, and the Salisbury Sports Club properly grassed playing fields and a great new club house with Dutch-colonial style gables. In the centre of the town the first few buildings with lifts had appeared, four storeys high — skyscrapers. To the south the growth of industrial building had gathered momentum, led by the large, up-to-date tobacco auction floor and warehouses. And the African township, Harare, had begun to mushroom, still geared to migrant labour and with hardly any accommodation designed for married men save in an experimental Government village settlement alongside called High-field. Out of town some of the main roads had been transformed by the construction of twin tarmac strips on which you could drive (except while making way for a car from the opposite direction) relieved from the necessity to battle with corrugations and potholes.

After 1933, when the great depression had done its worst and Dr Huggins (referred to by everybody —though not always to his face— as 'Huggie') had become Prime Minister, there had been fairly steady economic progress and increasing respect for the status of the little country in the eyes of politicians and officials in Britain who had occasion to be concerned with it. But still while Pat and I were at Oxford just before the war you would find few people in England who knew anything much about the country and not many who could even locate it on the map with any confidence.

What probably did most to put Southern Rhodesia on the map was the arrangement for it to take part during the war in the Royal Air Force Empire Air Training Scheme. For the RAF this provided, in a country then as reliable for its political loyalty as for its flying weather, eleven air stations complete with runways, hangars, housing and services. For Southern Rhodesia it meant having a population of temporary immigrants who were in effect specially selected — if only for the reason that aeroplanes are an expensive investment and to maintain and fly them you have to have people with relatively high standards of skill and responsibility. At its full development the number of people involved in the scheme — excluding African labour — reached about 15 000 (more than a fifth of the number of the locally-based white population), of whom all but the headquarters staff were supplied by the RAF. So, with the pupil-pilot population changing regularly as courses came to an end and many of the instructors and technical staff being replaced from time to time, by the end of the war a great number of people from Britain and other countries had got to know Southern Rhodesia; and vice versa. Many stayed after the war, or went back and then returned with their wives and families to make it their permanent home.

Amongst the war-time changes in Salisbury which now confronted us were Belvedere, major air station and complete new suburb replacing the old airfield west of the town; and the new air station and suburb of Cranborne south-east of the town where as children we had been accustomed to bicycle through the sandveld to a rocky picnic spot on the Makabusi river. (You would find brightly coloured lizards basking in the sun and if you held one by the tail its body would wriggle off, leaving the tail behind.)

Meikles was still there, holding its own, and so for the time being was Pocket's.

I had been involved in flying instruction during the first half of the war and been one of the original staff of the Empire Central Flying School set up at Hullavington, Wiltshire, in 1942, and had later commanded a squadron of Halifaxes in Coastal Command, and I managed, before being finally demobilised, to scrounge a job with the Rhodesian Air Training Group (RATG). This involved doing a series of flights, some in one of the old Tiger Moths and some in an ancient but immaculate Leopard Moth with a high wing and unlimited vision, to the remote landing strips in various parts of the country which had been provided for emergencies such as engine-failure during a cross-country training flight. I was accompanied by Phil Loots whose job it had been to persuade local Africans to clear and maintain them. He came from a small, badly-off, Afrikaans-speaking community south of Salisbury, was about my age and had been doing jobs in the bush with Africans all his adult life. He could speak fluently and understand a number of their dialects and was on terms of the warmest friendliness and joke-sharing with the people we came across.

We would spend the hot, viciously bumpy mid-day hours on the ground chatting with them, and I remember most nostalgically the original Binga's Kraal, since submerged deep below the surface of the Kariba Dam. The landing ground, so called, was a strip of sand with a young baobab tree and a few giant anthills to negotiate for the landing, and from it one walked almost directly on to a great area of richly-coloured alluvial soil enclosed in a great coil of the Zambezi River. It was patterned by hand-tilled lands and interspersed with huge shade trees, dense with black-green leaves and bearing orange-coloured beans containing oil which the ladies used as a skin conditioner. It was about as remote as you could get from the big towns, but people were not ignorant of the whites' way of life. This man had worked as a petrol attendant in Salisbury, that one as a hotel waiter in Bulawayo.

I remember Phil being amused, strolling into a small town where we had landed, by something I had not noticed in the street. We had passed a group of African girls, one balancing a great load on her head in the poised and graceful way they do. They had been laughing, and Phil repeated the funny and slightly obscene remark one of them had made about us, not dreaming we would understand a word of it. I envied, as I so often have then and since, knowing a language well enough not merely to ask for things but to eavesdrop in it.

The official object of the flights was to inspect the landing strips and to report on them, but of course it was the ideal way to get an overall picture of this country which Pat and I had come back to. Flying at about 80 m.p.h. you seemed to be hardly moving, and at 1 500 feet or so you could see the country intimately and yet displayed for some miles before you, and buildings and suchlike bereft of perspective like toys.

There was the central plateau, between 4 000 and 5 000 feet above sea level, with its red-soil areas favoured by the whites for maize production, and its areas of sandveld derived from the ancient underlying granite, more easily workable and originally left for African occupation but now also in demand by whites for tobacco. There on the eastern border of the country were the beautiful Inyanga and Chimanimani Mountains, overlooking Moçambique. To the north, the escarpment and wild valley of the Zambezi. South-west, between the Victoria Falls and Bulawayo, the indigenous forests, more park than jungle like, on the lower, Kalahari sand soils. South-east between the Limpopo and Sabi Rivers, the torrid but potentially fertile Lowveld. Almost everywhere watercourses, snaking through the bush or, often in the granite country, seeming to drive straight lines through it; some of them dry during the late winter months, others with a few pools or puddles; some still with water but hidden under the sand; and nearly all capable of becoming raging torrents at the height of the summer rains.

You could see the effects of erosion on the older European farms and in many of the Native Reserves; veined furrows leading to 'dongas' and a wasted look as in human disease. But you could also see, already on an impressive scale in some European areas and impressively as a beginning in some Reserves, land protected from erosion and some actually in the course of being reclaimed by a system of contour ridges which in addition lent a special beauty to the scene. You could see some large, prosperous, up-to-date European farms, most of them equipped with tall blocks of tobacco barns, and in the Native Purchase Areas some single-family farms which looked quite promising, and in the Reserves one or two areas where it seemed that something better than bare subsistence might be achieved on a more communal or co-operative basis.

You would come across the slimes dumps and headgear and housing compounds of one of the mines producing the gold which the pioneers had expected to find in greater quantity than they did, or a mine producing one of the wide range of base minerals now beginning to be exploited on a significant scale. At Wankie you had only to make a slight descent from ground level to find yourself inside the vast black gallery where coal from this fabulous deposit had been produced and amongst the massive rectangular columns of it which had been left to support the roof. Shabani was already one of the world's foremost producers of asbestos.

There was something surprising and exciting about the sight of modern power lines marching across wild country in all sorts of unexpected places; and emerging out of the bush in the Que Que area, the modern outlines of furnaces for a steel works; and in the old mining township of Gatooma a new cotton mill, using Africans as modern operatives — nucleus of a whole new industry. It was the more surprising because these three all turned out to belong to public utility corporations: the Electricity Supply Commission set up in 1936 to provide power to users, and particularly mines, which could not be satisfactorily supplied by the municipal power stations in the bigger towns; the Iron and Steel Commission established in 1942 to enable the country to produce steel from its own resources of iron ore instead of only from scrap; the Cotton Research and Industry Board set up to reap the benefit of years of work by a remarkable man, Major Cameron, who had bred a cotton plant proof against the disease which had caused disaster for the earlier cotton growers. How could this have happened in a remote country where, to judge by the declarations of the politicians, nothing but private enterprise could be tolerated?

There was the considerable City of Bulawayo, in the thorn scrub country twenty miles or so north of Rhodes' 'World's View' in the spectacular granite Matopos; and between it and Salisbury were Gwelo and Gatooma, and in a bowl in the Eastern District mountains Umtali, all now considerable towns. And the smaller towns and townships, all growing.

So here was the country of our birth, at the opening of this new post-war chapter of history. In area, three times the size of England. Total population (1.8 million) about a quarter the size of London's and about a twentieth of them (83 000) whites. Rich mineral resources and agricultural potential. A short history of involvement with the modern world — only fifty years since the Occupation and twenty-three since the grant of

Responsible Government; too short to have given rise yet to too many resentments, but a country already fully launched upon an era of industrial revolution. National income £46 million and increasing dramatically. Interesting.

———————————

It was interesting too to reflect that the machinery of government under which Southern Rhodesia had been brought to its present state was still the same, simple one that had been set up under the 1923 Constitution; and that the people running it were, not experts provided from outside, but the same kind of people as had taken over politics from the Chartered Company — local residents without any special background for politics and administration, and largely insulated from the outside world by the country's geographical position and still relatively primitive communications. In a new and remote set-up people find themselves trying their hand at things, be it acting, politics, statesmanship or what-have-you, which in more sophisticated circumstances would never have occurred to them as being within their scope. And sometimes with surprising results.

It was much more like the government of an independent country than of a dependent Colony. And the machinery operated just as if it were a scale model of the Whitehall prototype.

There was Parliament, in this case admittedly consisting of only one House — described in the Constitution as the Legislative Assembly —and only 30 Members, but having basically the same function as the two British Houses of Parliament, namely to debate and pass, with or without amendment, or to reject, draft legislation put before it by the Government (or, very occasionally, by an individual MP). There was the Government, or Cabinet, in this case admittedly consisting of only six Ministers, but having charge of the various departments of the civil service and responsibility for the day-to-day administration of the country's affairs. And as in Britain, there was a non-political civil service, staffed by people resident in the country. There was an independent judiciary, and the principle of the rule of law. There was the Governor, representing the King and performing much the same limited function as in Britain, and in particular the function of appointing the Prime Minister in accordance with British conventional rules.

The 30 Members of Parliament were elected by voters registered on the voters' roll and, as in Britain, there was a single member for each constituency. And there had to be a general election at least once in every five years. The person appointed as Prime Minister must be the Member of Parliament most likely to command a majority in the House, and the other

Ministers must be MPs chosen by him. So that, as in Britain, all the Ministers would, except in the case of a coalition, be MPs belonging to the political party holding a majority of the seats in Parliament. And that Government would control the day-to-day adminstration of the country, and decide on virtually all the draft legislation to be put before Parliament, for five years or until an earlier dissolution of Parliament brought about by a defeat of the Government on a motion of confidence.

So for anyone to get into power and operate as Prime Minister involved very much the same sort of thing as in England. He must lead his party to victory at a general election and thereafter command the support of a majority in Parliament.

There were of course differences as compared with the machinery of government of the 'mother country'. The Letters Patent of 1923 containing the Constitution imposed limitations on the powers of the Legislature related to the country's continuing Colonial status, and ones intended to protect the interests of the Africans: limitations on the power to pass laws imposing restrictions on Natives which did not apply equally to Europeans; limitations on the power to interfere with the Native Department of the civil service and the Native Reserves, and so on. In these areas the British Government held a veto, but in practice it never had to be exercised because, whenever this kind of legislation was contemplated, it would be discussed and agreed with the British Government before being presented to Parliament. The greatest difference in practice as compared with twentieth-century Britain was that in Southern Rhodesia only a small fraction of the adult population were registered as voters. That was not so different compared with Britain before Disraeli's Reform Bill of 1867, and even less as compared with the period before the Reform Bill of 1832. But of course in Southern Rhodesia there was the complicating factor of race. Under the franchise law as it stood at the beginning of the post-war period, to get on to the voters' roll you had, *inter alia,* to own land or mining claims worth £150 or be earning an income of £100 per annum, and this was sufficient in those days to exclude nearly all Africans. There was no actual colour bar, but the roll was in practice nearly all white. Even so, some whites saw the common roll franchise as dangerous. Few thought of it as being unfair to blacks. Most assumed the Natives were not interested in politics; and anyway, was there not a Native Department to look after them?

The way of living of most of the people playing leading roles in politics, business and the public service had nothing in it to distinguish them from, or limit their contact with, other white Rhodesians; and if you happened to have been born in the country and away on war service you would be bound to come across them sooner or later. And the striking thing about the most important of them was their lack of self-importance. Most strikingly so in the case of 'Huggie' — Sir Godfrey Martin Huggins. We had childhood memories of him, as the surgeon liked and respected by everyone and especially by people like our parents who could remember things like the remarkable effect he had had on morale at the time of the disastrous Spanish 'flu epidemic in 1918. But he had not looked or dressed like a specialist or a hero, and would sometimes be at the bedside of us children dealing with a routine complaint in the absence of one of his partners. Lightly built, dapper even, neatly trimmed moustache, nothing pretentious; but with a memorable presence. The main thing one remembered was the cheerfulness he seemed to bring to any situation, and the 'crow's feet' at the sides of his eyes.

Since those days Huggie had become involved in politics, almost by accident, and since 1933 had been Prime Minister and the undisputed leading figure in the country continuously for more than twelve years. Was it possible that here, in 1945, talking to us thirty years his junior at the bar of the Salisbury Club, he could have changed as little? That it should be impossible to discern in him any trace of pompousness or self-importance? He had had for years to use a hearing aid, and even that he would treat as a bit of a joke, pocketing it when he had heard enough and doing so ostentatiously when he wanted to indicate as much. And he would take no precautions to avoid the risk of being overheard which deaf people run because they cannot tell how loudly they are speaking. I was amazed at this first meeting with him of my adult life to have him address to someone like me, with no standing whatever in politics, what seemed to be highly confidential, and even sometimes defamatory, comments on various politicians, including members of his own Cabinet. ('They say I'm a rotten chooser of Ministers. But look at the material I've got to choose from.' Or, 'Poor old Ben. What would he find to do if I didn't give him a job in the Cabinet?' Twinkle of the eyes. Throw-away up-cut with the right hand. This is the kind of thing I remember.) Reflecting on it afterwards, and after I had seen more of him, it seemed to me that if you had been the person concerned and had overheard Huggie's remark you would probably not have been offended by it, and for quite a special reason: the sense of humour which accompanied it, and the fact that Huggie saw himself in no more complimentary a light than he saw other people. Was this not humility in the best sense of the term?

During the war there had been a Cabinet Committee with special responsibility for the country's war effort and it had comprised Huggie, Ernest Lucas Guest and Robert Moffat Tredgold — all subsequently knighted. 'Robbie' Tredgold we had not known previously because he had lived and practised at the Bar in Bulawayo. He was now a Judge in Salisbury and the occasion for getting to know his rare quality was yet to come. But Ernest Guest we remembered from our childhood days, as father of the two daughters and twin sons of our generation and husband of the gentle Edie, who lived in North Avenue a stone's throw away from us. He came from the Eastern Cape, not from England, and his style was different from the self-effacing one of people like Jim and Arthur Hone. He had distinguished himself in the First World War and liked to continue using the title colonel (or in print, Lieutenant-Colonel, M.C.), and he had romantic stories to tell about his exploits which we somehow felt privately that we could not be quite certain whether to believe or not. But here in 1945 was a quieter person whose further achievement in the Second World War told its own story, deeply saddened by the loss of both his sons in the course of it.

At one of the sundowner parties we were invited to soon after getting back to the country, while the discomforts of the readjustment were still being fairly troublesome, I found myself next to an impressive and courteous man who said 'You know I often wonder whether people like you are having any of the same sort of reaction which I remember having getting back to England from the trenches at the end of the previous war. I remember feeling I hated everybody!' He was Andrew Strachan, Head of the Treasury, and I immediately felt a special bond with him. We later came to understand the extent to which the Rhodesian civil service, locally based and largely locally recruited, had benefited from the influence he and one or two others of his kind of quality had had on those under them.

There had to be something of special distinction about the way of living of Sir Ellis Robins, Resident Director of the British South Africa Company which, though it had ceased to be the Government, still owned great assets, including the Railways. He had been one of the first American Rhodes Scholars and become as staunch a convert to the British Conservative tradition as any religious convert to Catholicism; and the official residence at Avondale, June Hill, presided over by him and his Lady from the Cotswolds, remained a sort of second Government House. But he presided also with undeniable business and financial expertise over a variety of companies, and also charities of which he was Chairman.

These were pillars of the establishment, and disposed to be kinder than we deserved to Pat and myself, sons of fellow Rhodesians they had known for years returned from the war. They had proven records of achievement in the country. We had been away almost since childhood. What right had we, then, to question their political views? None perhaps; and yet it was impossible not to feel that in certain ways we were in a better position even than they to understand what would be at issue politically in the future. We soon learned that to try to express in any sort of generalised way how we had come to look at the future would appear to them to be doctrinaire, unrealistic and even perhaps suspiciously left wing. And that was at least as much the case amongst our contemporaries in a place like the sports club where it was normal practice for a great many white Rhodesians to spend a substantial proportion of their time. To express earnest opinions on such subjects as the need to make parliamentary democracy a reality for Africans was hardly the appropriate route to popularity there.

If there was some sort of truth in what we felt to be necessary at the next stage of the country's history, clearly the thing to avoid was trying to propagate it in theoretical terms. The only effective way of promoting it would be to let it emerge from factual studies of particular problems.

CHAPTER 4

National Affairs, 1946–1947

In April 1946 there was a General Election. It had been held over due to the war. At the previous one in 1939 Huggie's United Party had won 23 out of the 30 seats in Parliament, and the remaining 7 had all gone to the Labour Party — a party which relied for the bulk of its support on the votes of white railway workers.

For the 1946 election there were four parties in the field. All of them in practice represented white voters and hardly anyone took seriously the handful of African voters registered on the voters' roll. There were a few people in the Labour Party who did, and who felt there should be provision for Africans to belong to the party, as members of an African Branch. And this had led to a split, so that there were now two Labour Parties calling themselves, confusingly, the Rhodesia Labour Party (RLP) and The Southern Rhodesia Labour Party (SRLP). The latter was the one with an African Branch and a few African members, and it represented the extreme left of that political spectrum. The United Party had no such extreme ideas, and Huggie had been a fairly hard-line segregationist in his time. But he had been capable of changing pragmatically with the times and had consequently done things which were anathema to the die-hards, such as suggesting in 1942 that segregation and white job reservation might not be permanent features of Rhodesian society, and interfering with private enterprise by nationalising the Bulawayo steel works to form the Iron and Steel Commission, and pursuing amalgamation with Northern Rhodesia instead of Dominion Status for Southern Rhodesia. The die-hards had formed a new party which, to crown the confusion of names, they called The Liberal Party.

The result of this 1946 election was a near victory for the right-wing Liberal Party. It won 11 out of the 30 seats; the RLP won 3 and the SRLP 2, leaving the United Party with 13 — three less than an overall majority. The total number of voters registered on the roll was 37 142, and the total number of votes cast 20 551.

In the Salisbury constituencies which Pat and I were familiar with Huggie retained Salisbury North, the one he had represented since he entered politics, and Guest won Salisbury Gardens. Salisbury Central was won by a newcomer to politics, Manfred Hodson, a mild and quite liberal-minded man, Rhodesian born and a barrister. But Salisbury City, Avondale, Highlands and Salisbury South were all won with substantial majorities by Liberal Party candidates, the first two of whom — Jacob Smit and Rubidge Stumbles — we knew quite well. We remembered Jacob Smit as the stolid, cigar smoking Hollander who presided in shirtsleeves and waistcoat at the store where most of our family groceries were bought on monthly account; an honest, deep-dyed conservative who had subsequently risen to be Minister of Finance in Huggie's war-time government and then resigned to become leader of the Liberal Party. His only son, a contemporary of mine known at school as 'Jumbo', had been killed in the war. Stumbles was a solicitor who had lived all, or nearly all, his life in Rhodesia and whose outlook seemed to us to be so confined and his political oratory so laboured that we found it difficult to take him seriously. The candidates we felt most sympathy with, Edward Harben, Gladys Maasdorp and Aitken Draper, all SRLP, lost their deposits. The pleasant surprise was Garfield Todd who made his debut into Rhodesian politics by winning the country constituency of Insiza for the United Party.

Meanwhile a public meeting of ex-servicemen had been organised in Salisbury. It was intended to launch an Association on the basis of a constitution which had been drafted by a group of them still accustomed to the language of the Guard Room Notice Board and described the main object as being —

> With full co-operation of Rhodesian ex-service personnel to keep actively in touch with the Government and by discussion with the elected members in each constituency to show — through the press and otherwise through the Central Committee — the general census (sic) of opinion among ex-service personnel in connection with all points considered to affect the future of Rhodesia.

The name proposed was 'Rhodesian Ex-Service Vigilance Association'. Pat and I attended the meeting and suggested that, before it would be possible to arrive at worthwhile conclusions on 'points affecting the future of Rhodesia', it would be necessary to have a lot of information and discussion, and (as tends to happen if you open your mouth in a small pond) found ourselves elected as members of the first Executive Committee. So did another friend from childhood, Rhodes and Oxford days, Bob (N.A.F.) Williams, who had served in the Royal Navy during the whole of the war and during the latter part of it with a command in minesweepers; outstanding sportsman with a body like a wrestler's and a nice streak of childish hankering in his nature for chivalry and the high life. One of the leading members of the promoting group was Mike (M.J.) Reynolds, a straightforward, unassuming, dependable Rhodesian and son-in-law of the much loved Colonel Nesbitt who had distinguished himself in both world wars. Pat's and my kind of approach was somewhat academic for him, and for many of the rest of the Executive Committee, but we were allowed to get on with it as a sideline. The person elected as first Chairman was Dendy (J.R.D.) Young, a striking and handsome man who had come from South Africa immediately after school to a clerical job in the Civil Service and then, with single-mindedness and ability, accumulated two degrees by private study and finally launched himslf as a barrister (advocate).

An immediate and pressing problem for ex-servicemen, as well as for the immigrants now flowing into the country, was the post-war housing shortage; and the Ex-Service Vigilance Association (soon to be renamed) scored an immediate success with the work of a committee led by Bevis Barker, a young quantity surveyor who was beginning to get himself established in civilian life in Salisbury. He was a dynamic, reddish-haired man with a cast in one eye, freckles and an infectious smile. He had his office in one of the old buildings in Manica Road almost opposite the equally old one which provided crude accommodation for Scanlen & Holderness. And he treated his youthful staff — as we did the ones we recruited — like partners in a war-time enterprise, and work done in office time for the Association as of equal priority with legitimate fee-paying work for clients.

Bevis and his committee ended up with a thoroughly researched and able memorandum on housing and the building industry which was sent to the Prime Minister in September 1946, and its original and far-reaching recommendations came in due course to be nearly all accepted by the Government.

The most original was for a class of temporary housing:

> This type of quarter would be built in Pisé-de-terre with either thatched or asbestos roof on gumpole trusses, with standard doors and windows made from Local Timber with lime and ash concrete floors, W.C. Sanitation with a Septic tank or if possible a central Sewerage system. Labour would be mainly native. It is thought that if enough of these are erected they could be produced for a figure from £350 but not exceeding £500 . . .
>
> The leaders of the Building Trades Unions in Salisbury have agreed to co-operate in the erection of these houses if required . . .

These 'mudde huttes' (as Bevis described them in questionaires designed to obtain the views of the public on sample houses) became an integral part of the post-war scene, and served a vital purpose charmingly.

Meanwhile Pat and I worked on a programme of lectures and debates for the political self-education project we had advocated, and as a start a series of debates, to be held weekly in the evenings, was planned to begin in May 1946, after the general election. A circular designed to sound people's views (or to get them embroiled under the guise of sounding their views) explained:

> The type of motion contemplated is such as will give a reasonable case on both sides and will raise vital issues, e.g.:
>> 'This House favours the abandonment of a feudal system in agriculture for the sake of intensive farming'.
>> 'That private land which is not being beneficially developed should be acquired and developed by the State'.
>> 'This House favours ownership of the Railways at any price'.
>> 'This House favours the Open Door policy for immigration'.
>> 'That foreigners are a liability to the Colony'.
>> 'That aliens as well as British are to be welcomed as immigrants'.
>> 'This House deplores any proposal to disenfranchise the African'.
>> 'This House approves of the proposals to disenfranchise the African'.
>> 'That the doctrine of segregation is no solution to the native problem'.

To Pat and myself the remarkable thing about the general election had been that none of the candidates of the political parties seemed to discuss these or any other 'vital issues' at their meetings. What all the Liberal Party candidates seemed to be saying was that the country's economic problems could all be resolved by simply reducing government spending, taking off all controls and reverting totally to private enterprise; and that the 'Native problem' could be resolved by simply removing all African influence from the white sphere — including the voters' roll — and letting the Natives satisfy their ambitions 'in their own areas' and 'for the good of their own people' and, by acquiring Dominion Status, getting rid of outside influences. It seemed astonishing that a constituency like Avondale, for example, where one would expect a high proportion of the electorate to be intelligently critical, should elect someone like Stumbles advocating this kind of thing, and without seeming to ask either themselves or him the obvious questions. If private enterprise was sacrosanct how could his Party be in favour, as it was, of nationalising the Railways? Would his Party liquidate the Electricity Supply Commission? How could you confine the influence of Africans to their own areas and at the same time be in favour of a more stable and productive black labour force in white industry? And with his Party's policy, how could you hope to acquire Dominion Status? Was there any real difference between its 'Native policy' and what the Afrikaner Nationalists were advocating in South Africa?

But then the situation was not much different with Huggie's United Party and the constituencies where they had been successful. They had just avoided defeat by the Liberal Party, but largely on the strength of Huggie's tactical skill and personal following; not because the voters who opted for them had studied the issues and arrived at thought-out conclusions. That applied even in Huggie's own constituency, Salisbury North, which contained probably a higher proportion than any other of the country's intelligentsia and of whites with nothing to fear from black competition — as well as a relatively high proportion of Jewish people who, if anybody at that stage of the world's history, should surely be capable of taking a long view on racial policy.

What the 1946 election seemed to us to emphasise was not only the stark necessity for a programme of political self-education, but also, looking at it from a hopeful point of view, the unique opportunity which existed for a good programme to be effective. Taking the Avondale constituency as an example, the total number of registered voters in it was 1 517 and of these 1 240 (a higher proportion than usual) had cast their votes. So that even if there had been only two candidates in the field the maximum number of votes required to win the seat would have been 621. (Stumbles had in fact won it with only 567). Dealing with numbers of this order it must surely be possible to get across the facts to voters and for them to arrive at political decisions based on fact instead of merely personal considerations or prejudice. There was not the Poor White problem in Southern Rhodesia which South Africa had been saddled with, and the history of contact between whites and blacks here had surely been too short to leave deep-seated legacies of hatred. Besides, there was the experience of the world which so many Rhodesians had had in the course of war service, and there were all these immigrants with many skills. Surely these were promising factors.

The debates laid on as an initial effort by the Ex-Service Vigilance Association attracted too few people to make a significant impact. They had been held in the evening, and for the main programme of lectures and debates which Pat and I were planning we decided to take a leaf out of the Myra Hess book, and try the lunch hour. The normal pattern of white Rhodesian life was to wake at 6 a.m. or earlier (with morning tea) and be at work at 8 a.m., after delivering children at school. Offices, and in those days shops as well, were closed at the lunch hour. After work, at 4 or 5 in the afternoon, everyone would be off to play some sport or other, usually followed by a 'sundowner' at the Sports Club or at home. Bed by not much later than 10 p.m. — at any rate during the week. So the lunch hour looked like the best bet.

The Executive Committee became quite enthusiastic about the scheme, and eventually approved a draft programme of weekly lunch hour lectures and monthly debates due to begin on 16 August 1946, and a new, brief Constitution and a new name — The Rhodesia National Affairs Association. The opening part of the new Constitution read:

I.   The Association is founded upon the spirit of interest, enquiry and service which was stimulated by experience and travel during the war.

II. The aims of the Association are:

1. To bring home to the individual, irrespective of his race, occupation or religious or political views, the responsible part which he has to play in national affairs.

2. By lectures, debates and other means to enable him to understand and form his opinion on national problems.

3. To give the man in the street the opportunity of making his full contribution to the solution of both immediate and future national problems.

4. As an Association to undertake objective and impartial enquiries into matters of national importance, and to undertake action upon the conclusions resulting from such enquiries.

The draft programme of lectures and debates read as follows:

THE RHODESIA NATIONAL AFFAIRS ASSOCIATION PROPOSES

to hold WEEKLY LECTURES and MONTHLY DEBATES leading up to the formulation of long-term principles of policy for Rhodesia.

THE LECTURES to take place during the lunch hour on Fridays at the Emblem Hall. A sandwich bar to provide sandwiches and coffee; the speaker to lecture from 1.10 p.m. until 1.55 p.m.

THE DEBATES to take place at the Emblem Hall every fourth Wednesday at 8.15 p.m.

A Congress to take place, possibly next Whitsun.

I. GENERAL BACKGROUND

FRI 16 AUG.	The Physical Resources of the Colony: Outline.	D. Aylen
FRI 23 AUG.	— do — : Minerals.	N.E. Barlow
FRI 30 AUG.	The Economic System.	W. Margolis
FRI 6 SEPT.	— do —	F.T. Russell

WED 4 SEPT.   8.15
Race Relations.   J.D. Rheinhallt-Jones

FRI 13 SEPT.	The Racial Set-Up: Europeans, Africans.	
FRI 20 SEPT.	The Racial Set-Up: Aliens.	Minister of Internal Affairs
FRI 27 SEPT.	The Constitutional Set-Up: The Constitution, the Franchise.	W.A. Godlonton
FRI 4 OCT.	The Constitutional Set-Up: Southern Rhodesia and her Neighbours.	W.A.W. Clark

WED 9 OCT.:   DEBATE
E.g. 'This House Opposes Amalgamation with any Neighbouring Territories'

II. AGRICULTURE, MINING, SECONDARY INDUSTRY

FRI 11 OCT.	European Agriculture in Southern Rhodesia.	J.S. Brown
FRI 18 OCT.	Native Agriculture in Southern Rhodesia.	E.D. Alvord
FRI 25 OCT.	Soil Conservation and Afforestation.	P.H. Haviland
FRI 1st NOV.	Land Apportionment.	A.C. Jennings

WED 6 NOV.:   DEBATE
E.g. 'This House favours the replacement of its present regime in Agriculture by a system of intensive farming.'

FRI 8 NOV.	The Mining Industry in Southern	Minister of Mines,
FRI 15 NOV.	Rhodesia: Gold, Chrome, Coal, Mica.	W.H. Ralston
FRI 22 NOV.		W. Gemmill
FRI 29 NOV.		B. Souchon

WED 4 DEC.:   DEBATE on
E.g. Frankel Report

DECEMBER — RECESS

FRI 10 JAN.	Secondary Industries:	Private.	A.C. Soffe
FRI 17 JAN.	— do —	Government.	G. Musgrave
FRI 24 JAN.	Commerce.		S.P. Rowe
FRI 31 JAN.	Protection.		W. Margolis

WED 5 FEB.:   DEBATE on
E.g. The Public Utility Corporation or Protection

III. **NATIVE AFFAIRS**

FRI 7 FEB.	The Native as a Human Being.	Garfield Todd
FRI 14 FEB.	Trade and Production in the Reserves.	W.A. Godlonton
FRI 21 FEB.	The Native in the Towns.	G. Ballenden
FRI 28 FEB.	The Various Two-Pyramid Policies.	N.H. Wilson

WED 5 MAR.:   DEBATE on
E.g. 'The Doctrine of Segregation offers no
Solution to the Native Problem'

IV. **EDUCATION**

FRI 7 MAR.	European Education in Southern Rhodesia.	J. Cowie
FRI 14 MAR.	Education of the African.	C. Drury
FRI 21 MAR.	Adult Education.	
FRI 28 MAR.	The Arts.	V. Hiller

WED 2 APR.: DEBATE on

E.g. A Rhodesian University or Education
Geared to Rhodesian requirements.

V. **HEALTH AND SECURITY**

FRI 4 APR.	Health in the Colony.	Dr. D.M. Blair
FRI 11 APR.	Health and Social Security.	F.T. Russell
FRI 18 APR.		
FRI. 25 APR.	Industrial Relations.	W.F. Baillie

WED 30 APR.:   DEBATE
E.g. 'That the Proposals of the Health Report should
be put into Effect Immediately'
or Social Security
or Native Trade Unions

VI. **IMMIGRATION**

FRI 2 MAY   Immigration and Economic Policy.   E.C. Whitehead
FRI 9 MAY   Immigration and Social Services.
FRI 16 MAY   Immigration and Native Policy.   N.H. Wilson
FRI 23 MAY   External Relations.

WED 30 APR.: DEBATE on
E.g. 'The absorption of Immigrants should be
at the rate of .... per annum'

JUNE 1947

The Policy Committee to submit its Draft of
a Long-Term National Policy to Congress for
Debate and Final Formulation.

Designing a programme of this kind was something very much up Pat's street because his main occupation during his years as a prisoner-of-war had been helping with schemes to turn the time to account by further education; arranging courses, lecturing and acting as adviser and friend (and, as one discovered from people one happened to come across who had been with him at the time, in an unostentatious but high grade way which earned great affection and respect.) Some of this, and in particular studies designed to prepare war-time servicemen as citizens for their return to civilian life, were part of a scheme for South African servicemen which was run by Leo Marquard, impressive representative of that breed of liberal South Africans of Afrikaner background, and it had something in common with the ABCA scheme promoted amongst British servicemen towards the end of the war. In deciding on potential speakers for the programme we had the assistance of people like Frank (Dr. F.T.) Russell, a highly trained economist and statistician in the public service who, after the publication of the Beveridge Report in England, had been charged with producing a miniature equivalent for Southern Rhodesia, single handed, and had in fact done so. He was tall, thin and angular and had to wear spectacles with fairly strong lenses, and this plus a certain abstracted or absent-minded look as he walked along would have qualified him for the description in unofficial Air Force language 'boffin', but he was in fact a political realist with an attractive dry sense of humour, and he seemed to know everyone in Rhodesia, at any rate in the public service.

It soon became apparent that we would have to rely heavily for the lectures on civil servants, partly because there was no university to draw on but also because it was civil servants, dealing with actual day to day administration, who knew at first hand the kind of things the public needed to know in making up its mind about political policies. But would civil servants be allowed to take part as lecturers, or even as members, of the Association? That was a critical issue. Frank Russell and other progressively minded civil servants like Gerald Gardiner, Charles Drury and Neville Bertram had been active members of an association called The Current Affairs Group which had flourished before and during the war. But that had been a small group, and what the National Affairs Association proposed to do was to bring in the public; and for the Government that presented a problem. Was it desirable to have all sorts of subjects thrown open for public discussion? Even delicate ones like Native Policy and the franchise? What sort of people were the promoters? Do-gooders? Long-haired intellectuals? Left wingers? Was it a 'political organisation'?

There was little mystery about most of the Executive Committee. A majority had been born in the country: as well as Pat, Bob Williams and myself, Ralph Newmarch — a member of a well-known farming family who had distinguished himself in the Air Force; Geoff Ellman Brown — chartered accountant and well-known sportsman; Howard Over — heir to the business on Manica Road built up by his father; Herbert Posselt — who had done a key job on the organisational side in RATG (the Rhodesian Air Training Group). Others had lived and worked in the country before the war: as well as Dendy Young, Col. Nesbitt and Mike Reynolds, Vic Salzman — partner in the outfitting business which had grown from the small shop started by his wife's father, Max Mande; Bernard Noakes, life assurance representative and former civil servant; Mike Pearce, still boyish veteran of civil flying with experience going back to the earliest Imperial Airways days in Africa. To complete the list there were Bevis Barker and Pat Bashford — both known for their work in RATG, F.B.W. Lamb and J. Hamilton, and two ladies: Pat Pearce, Mike's wife, and Edna Wattridge, Bevis Barker's secretary, detailed to act also as unpaid Secretary of the Association. It must have seemed a reliable enough body, and we were after all mostly ex-servicemen trying to inform ourselves as well as others about national affairs. We kept emphasising the 'non-Party' as distinct from the political nature of the Association, and fortunately a collision over the question of participation by civil servants was avoided. Enough latitude was given to them for the project to get going and as it did so doubts tended to recede, although for some senior civil servants it always remained a difficult question to decide how far they should allow themselves to be involved.

By 16 August 1946, the planned starting date, arrangements for launching the scheme seemed reasonably complete. We had good speakers lined up for the initial lectures: Aylen of the Natural Resources Board on 'Surface Natural Resources'; Barlow of the excellent Geological Survey Department on 'Mineral Resources'; Miller, first headmaster of the newly-established Goromonzi Secondary School on 'Education for Africans'; Frank Russell on 'The Economic System' (two lectures); Simmonds, a senior Native Commissioner, on 'The African Population'; Beadle, up-and-coming politician, on 'The Aliens Act'; Godlonton, practising lawyer and spare time specialist on consitutional matters, on 'The Constitution'; Arthur Clarke, specially selected first holder of the office of Secretary to the Central African Council, on 'Southern Rhodesia and Her Neighbours'; Jim Brown, presiding genius of the important Farmers' Co-op (European) and Alvord, Director of Native Agriculture, on 'Agriculture'; and so on. The hall we had booked seemed suitable: the Emblem Hall on Jameson Avenue, near enough to the middle of the town to allow most people working in offices and shops to get to it and back without too much waste of time. As for catering, Con had volunteered to put at the disposal of the project her expertise in producing quantities of homely sandwiches acquired in the course of providing for extended family occasions and occasional charity fetes. The entrance fee was to be 1/- for members and 1/6 for non-members of the Association (including coffee and sandwiches).

The experiment was a success. A goodly number of people turned up to the first lecture, and they seemed to enjoy talking over coffee and sandwiches beforehand. Douglas Aylen seemed to communicate in the course of his lecture some of his infectious enthusiasm for natural resources and their preservation and development, and even managed to comply with the plea we made to all speakers to confine the lecture to the limited time available and leave some minutes for questions before the Cinderella hour of two o'clock. More people came to the second lecture, and more to the third, and it was not long before we had to look for a new and bigger hall. The one we settled on was the Cathedral Hall situated even nearer to the centre of town, in Union Avenue. It was in the grounds of the little Anglican Cathedral, which incidentally had some interesting architectural features to it. Its north end was what in a normal church or cathedral would be the east end and had been completed by 1918 in blocks of local granite, and it was to a design by Herbert Baker said to have been partly inspired by the

Zimbabwe Ruins, quite interesting and original — as if after being overawed by the sites of South Africa House in the Strand and the Union Buildings in Pretoria it was possible for him here in this new Colony to be something other than wholly conformist. The rest of the building was still the temporary wood and corrugated iron structure constructed in 1918 to serve as a temporary nave pending the collection of more money for building.

The Hall was a large, general purpose one with a wide verandah overlooking the Cathedral where people could foregather before the lecture, and it was here that the lectures developed into a sort of national institution: Friday lunch-time in the capital city; people foregathering to get information about the country and what was going on and because they found it a congenial thing to do; and as time went on the recognised place to hear and form a first-hand impression, not only of significant local people, but also of visitors to the country who had something significant to say. A national institution, but one which continued to have the flavour of being run by people relatively young and fresh to politics who shared between them on a strict roster basis the duty of acting as Chairman at lectures and the less glamorous one of taking money at the door. The seating was arranged whenever possible in semi-circular fashion, so that instead of the speaker being placed remotely on the stage at the end of the hall he and the chairman would find themselves against one of the long sides of it, with the audience surrounding them.

The original programme provided for a set of 36 lectures which we visualised as covering all the basic ground in logical order, and as the footnote to it indicated, we imagined that by about June 1947 we would be sufficiently in possession of the relevant facts to go on to the formulation of a 'long term national policy'. The idea behind this must have been that in the normal course of events the second general election after the war would take place in about 1951, and if by the end of 1947 work was started on trying to formulate a long term national policy there should be time for the constructive effect of it to have some influence on the election. But the indecisive result of the 1946 election made it almost inevitable that Parliament would have to be dissolved and a fresh general election held long before 1951, which would mean that, for the Association's work to have effect at a general election, it would have to wait for five years after that. In any case there was no lack of material for lectures: particular aspects of problems dealt with generally in the main programme, specialised information from some expert who happened to be available, a bee in somebody's bonnet which we felt he should have the opportunity to let buzz in public or should be exposed to examination by the lunch-hour audience, and so on.

One of the first speakers to take the initiative and himself suggest that he be invited to address the lunch-hour audience was Roy Welensky, leader of the Unofficial Members of the Northern Rhodesian Legislative Council (the nearest equivalent there of Southern Rhodesia's Prime Minister), and the bee in his bonnet was the subject of amalgamation between the two territories. His lecture on 25 November 1946 gave us our first taste of what he was like, and Pat and I found we agreed that, in comparison with the quality which we believed we discerned in Huggie, the impression he made was disappointing. Parochial? Self-satisfied? That would be putting it too strongly. Garfield Todd, who had been asked to give the lecture described in the programme as 'The Native as a Human Being', was one of the first to have to cry off at the last moment, and as we learned afterwards this was because he had been asked to do so by Huggie who thought he would be saying things which Huggie felt would not be 'in the public interest' at that stage. (He was allowed to give it later). Godlonton had made a special study of the franchise in Southern Rhodesia and published a pamphlet on the subject in May 1946. A local character of a different, and somewhat raffish kind, N.H. Wilson, had for some years been propagating his pet theory about Native Policy called 'The Two-Pyramid Policy' which seemed to be regarded with a certain approval even by people like Huggie; and now he had a new theory about 'Capricorn Africa'. The National Affairs audience should have the opportunity of hearing what he had to say about all that, and of putting questions to him. A professor of history, J.P.R. Wallis, who had recently been brought to the country to run an association formed to promote the setting up of a Rhodesian University (Manfred Hodson's baby), would be prepared to give a series of lectures on the Colony's historical background. Arthur Bottomley, Parliamentary Under Secretary at the Dominions Office, was scheduled to make a visit to the country and if he would speak the audience would have an opportunity of forming a first-hand impression to put alongside their existing ideas — mostly hostile — of what a Labour Minister was like.

So the programme of lectures continually changed, widened and extended itself. Also going on were the formal debates — less regularly than envisaged in the original programme and with more modest success than the lectures; and also frequent meetings of the Executive Committee, devoted as much to debating political issues as to the business of running the organisation. In May 1947 the first of the regular Annual General Meetings was held, and the practice begun of changing the Chairman each year and bringing new blood on to the Committee.

Taking stock towards the end of 1947 we would have felt, I think, that the lectures given so far — more than 50 of them — constituted a considerable body of current knowledge about the country and pinpointed many of its problems and possible ways of tackling them. (That was something we asked all speakers to do if they could). They had reached as wide an audience as we could have hoped for, and we had transcripts of nearly all of them which might be used to spread the information more widely in the future. And in at least one specific instance, the issue of the common voters' roll, it had had the effect of bringing the whole question out into the open, and even perhaps of helping to prevent terribly mistaken action being taken as much out of ignorance as out of wrong intent.

———————————

It was too easy for whites to feel that although only a few blacks were registered on the voters' roll now, a great number might soon become qualified to be on it and then the whites might suddenly find themselves 'swamped' and outvoted, and that if blacks had to have some form of political representation (as well as, or instead of, having their interests looked after by the Native Department) it should be in some form which did not represent a threat to whites. And even for whites who could see the other point of view — that having only a few voters on the roll meant that blacks were being inadequately represented — it was easy to think that the proper solution was a separate roll for black voters electing a limited number of special members of Parliament (white) to represent their interests. This was the kind of thing which still seemed to be in Huggie's mind, and it was in fact United Party policy. It was 'liberal' compared with the sort of complete political segregation advocated by the so-called 'Liberal' Party. And taking into account the strength of the Liberal Party in Parliament and the slogan so frequently bandied about by members of both parties that 'Native policy should be taken out of party politics', there was every reason to suspect that a deal might be struck and the country might find itself suddenly committed to the abolition of the common roll. But the lunch hour lectures by Godlonton had helped to put the whole thing in a different light.

He seemed to me to be quite a lone figure, more at home with books than people, having little of Huggie's kind of charm and a certain dryness about his tone of voice which could seem like sarcasm; a solicitor all his life and probably articled straight from school without the intervention of any time at university; and yet an academic by nature whose reading and intelligence put him in a quite different category from someone like Stumbles. In a sense

51

their basic premise was the same: that with the existing franchise the whites could find themselves outnumbered by voters who were 'unfit to exercise the vote' and an easy prey to 'Demagogues' and 'Communists'. As Godlonton put it in his lunch-hour lecture in September, 1946:

> In countries where all the people are of one nation or race, the enfranchisement of large numbers of peoples who are educationally unfitted for the privilege may not cause much alarm or concern, because instinctively and in mode of thought they are all much alike. An educational test which in other circumstances would be quite inadequate is then understandable. But here the position is very different. The vast majority of the population are not only of a different race, colour and standard of civilisation, but they have also inherited from remote times modes of thought and instincts which differ greatly from our own.
>
> Our political institutions have been built up by trial and error over a period of many centuries, and it is a debatable question which has not yet been satisfactorily answered whether the average native, even when given a fair education, can understand them, or, if he can, whether he is willing or able to adapt himself to them not merely in the letter but in the spirit.

But whereas Stumbles and Smit and others of the Liberal Party would see little difficulty, and plenty of political advantage, in concluding that the Party policy should be to remove Natives from the voters roll for Parliament and put them on a separate roll of voters for Native Councils exercising restricted local powers only, Godlonton was conscious of world opinion as it had developed with the Atlantic Charter and UNO and the establishment of the Human Rights Commission, and of

> how careful we must be in making any proposals differentiating between our political rights and those of the natives. Remember the natives have for 48 years been able to register as voters on the same conditions as Europeans. If we want to introduce legislation giving the natives limited political representation different from our own — and there are many who do — we shall be wise to put up a strong case, and that means a just one.

His idea was that, for the time being at any rate, no discriminatory legislation (whether in regard to the franchise or other matters, such as the restriction of occupations open to Natives in the White Area — another plank in the Liberal Party platform) should be passed by Parliament without first having been referred to a special Commission, presided over by a Judge and having as members at least one representative each of the recognised political parties, and Natives amounting to at least a quarter of the total membership appointed by the Governor to represent Native opinion; and he put this forward in an important lecture on 20 June 1947.

We were not sold on the Commission idea, but we felt sure it would be tragic if the principle of the common voters' roll were abandoned as it had been in the Cape; and when rumours reached us that an inter-Party committee being set up might be considering a Bill to this effect, the National Affairs Executive as a whole was sufficiently concerned to send a letter through the Clerk of the House warning them against it and proposing to send a delegation to see them.

No move to change the common roll franchise was in fact made at that stage, and there was to be a change in the United Party attitude towards it after a General Election in 1948 at which the Liberal Party was to suffer a heavy defeat. What actual influence the Association's activities had in all this it was difficult to say, but it seemed fair to assume it had been significant.

We would also have felt after a year's lectures that we had learned some important things incidentally about the Civil Service. It was impressive to hear members of it talking on their subjects — the country's geology and minerals, its climate and soils, timber and trees, its agriculture, economic system, industrial conciliation machinery, or whatever it might be — often without much previous experience of lecturing but with ability and real devotion to the subject, apparently un-envious of people in more lucrative or more publicised jobs, and without resentment that policy decisions would not be for them to make but for whatever politicians might find themselves appointed as Ministers. One began to understand how important an asset it was to have people like this, not just on a transient basis as in many Colonial territories, but domiciled in the country, and what a formidable body of expertise the knowledge and local experience of civil servants represented collectively, however un-significant any particular one of them might appear in the course of tying his particular piece of red tape.

At the same time one came to understand that the part of this Civil Service specifically involved with African administration, the Native Department, formed a little world of its own; that it tended to feel it had, and was entitled to, a monopoly of knowledge about the Natives; that it tended to be accepted by the Government as the ultimate authority in that field, and that some of its members would be amongst the most die-hard of the whites when it came to trying to bring about liberal reforms. This did not apply to all the officials dealing with African affairs, but rather to the ones who had been brought up to be Native Commissioners — in the case of the ambitious ones, with the baton of Chief Native Commissioner in their hands. In the Districts they administered Native Commissioners were like little kings, and their wives like queens, and the Natives were expected to make obeisance to them. It got into the blood of some more than others. The then Chief Native Commissioner, Powys Jones, had been partly immunized by experience of the big world starting as a Rhodes Scholar; but not so his successors in office.

Officials dealing with Africans in a more technical or specialist capacity, in education or agriculture for example, tended to have a much less authoritarian and more man-to-man approach, and the potential conflict between them and the traditional native administrators was an interesting feature of the situation which one was to watch in operation over the years. An early and colourful example of the non-traditional type was D.E. Alvord, who gave one of the early lunch-hour lectures at the Emblem Hall. He was an American by origin, from Salt Lake City, who had the reputation of having been in his youth Pacific Coast Wrestling Champion and looked the part. With a refreshingly shameless disregard for modesty he told the story of a young agricultural missionary who had come to Mount Selinda in 1919 and in 1924 had a booklet published in Boston entitled 'Helping The Heathen to Help Himself', and who had his scheme for promoting agricultural development, better housing and improved water supplies and home sanitation officially adopted by the Southern Rhodesian Government —

> That missionary ... was the first agricultural missionary as such to be appointed in Africa. He had been enrolled for seven years in institutions of higher learning in America, held two Diplomas in Education, a Diploma in Manual Training and Art Crafts and B.Sc. and M.Sc. Degrees in Agriculture, and had been Instructor in Farm Crops for four years at Washington State College, one of the leading agricultural colleges of the United States. He thought he could teach Agriculture to anyone. Fortunately he was past 30 years of age and old enough to have good sense and soon discovered that, in spite of high qualifications and experience, a white man could not teach agriculture to the superstition steeped African, who attributed large crop yields to 'divisi', 'Muti', witchcraft and favour of the ancestral spirits. He concluded that it was impossible to Christianise the Africans without, first of all, intellectualising their agricultural practices ...
>
> He made the discovery that the African 'must see things demonstrated on his own level, within his reach, by Demonstrators of his own black skin and kinky wool'. So, in 1920 he evolved and put into practice a scheme for demonstration work for Natives, which attracted considerable Government attention. He started at the bottom, with

soil worn out by years of misuse, and in three years, using natural fertilisers available to the poorest farmer, he transformed scattered patches of wornout lands into tiny paradises of rejuvenated soil and bumper crops where, on his demonstration plots, maize grew three times as tall and produced six to ten times as many bags per acre as on native lands adjacent to them.

He was discovered in March 1921 by Mr. H.S. Keigwin, then Director of Native Development, and was invited by him to visit Domboshawa in August 1921 and assist in the drawing up of the scheme for agricultural instruction in that newly established Government School for Natives. In 1924 the Government decided to adopt this successful scheme for Demonstration work throughout the country. In 1924 a class of twelve trainees from different parts of the country were enrolled for a two-year course of training at Domboshawa and in 1926 the author of the scheme was asked by the Government to take charge of the work. He assumed duty in October 1926 as Agriculturalist for Instruction of Natives. During the first two years he gave full time to better organising of agricultural instruction in Government and Mission Schools. In 1927 eleven trained Agricultural Demonstrators started work on Native Reserves.

At this point in his lecture he announced dramatically —

That unknown missionary stands before you now, as Director of Native Agriculture under the Secretary of Native Affairs for Southern Rhodesia.

He claimed that Southern Rhodesia was in the lead in the world in its approach to 'agricultural development and economic uplift of rural masses' and gave some convincing details, for example —

Twenty years ago there were no good African farmers in the Reserves. To-day there are more than 400 certified 'Master Farmers' and 14,173 listed 'Co-operators' who, in 1945, secured an average yield for all crops of 9.2 bags per acre.

Fifteen years ago there was no irrigation in Native Reserves. To-day there are 1,173 acres under irrigation in the arid Sabi Valley which give an annual yield of more than 10,000 bags of grain . . .

Ten years ago no soil conservation work had been done. To-day there are hundreds of thousands of acres which have been protected by soil conservation works in Native Reserves.

Twenty years ago no kraal manure was applied to land by Natives. To-day there are entire populations of some Reserves who are putting every available scrap of kraal manure on their land. In some Reserves Natives are stacking all crop residue alongside their cattle kraals to feed to cattle in winter and turn it into kraal compost.

Nearly ten years ago Dr. Tothill, Director of Agriculture in Uganda, while returning from an inspection of methods used in Native

Territories and in the Union, visited Reserves in Rhodesia and . . . later wrote 'Your methods of demonstration work are unique and not employed elsewhere, yet I find you are obtaining excellent results from a minimum of expenditure'.

To-day there is a total of over 9,000,000 acres of Native Reserves which have been surveyed and centralised into arable and grazing areas with residential strips between them. On these Reserves there are now 89 Community Demonstrators assisting and advising on all sorts of community improving enterprises . . .

To-day there is a total of 90,969 improved houses on Reserves which, during the past twelve years, have been built under the direction of our Community Demonstrators . . .'

We felt there was justification for immodesty about the Demonstrator System; but results were slow compared with what whites were achieving in the European Area, with a Natural Resources Board and system of Intensive Conservation Areas created largely on the initiative of farmers themselves. And the traditional Native Commissioner tended to feel that what was needed in the Reserves was more of the stick and less of the carrot.

Some of our wilder ambitions for the National Affairs Association had to be modified. There would be Branches all over the country, we at first thought, and the political conclusions from the material presented in the lectures which seemed obvious to us would be shared by everybody. In fact only Bulawayo found it possible to run a lunch-hour lecture programme, and then in its own way (since Bulawayo never liked merely following in Salisbury's wake). Privately we thought their programme more haphazard and less directional than ours in Salisbury, but bearing in mind our superior access to potential lecturers in government and the civil service the surprising thing, I suppose, was that Bulawayo found it possible to run one at all. And as for shared political conclusions, I suppose we should have anticipated that even amongst our enthusiastic Executive in Salisbury wide differences in approach would persist when it came to interpreting the material in political terms.

CHAPTER 5

Turning from the South, 1948–1950

The near-success of the 'Liberal' Party and slender majority achieved by the United Party at the 1946 General Election turned out to be no great embarrassment to Huggie's Government, but in the latter part of 1948 he decided the time was ripe to seek a bigger majority and found a pretext to call for a dissolution of Parliament.

Should one try one's luck in the General Election to follow? Pat and I must have discussed that possibility, and no doubt wistfully, realising that if Huggie succeeded in achieving a decisive result it would probably be another five years before another opportunity would arise. The chance of winning a seat would be quite good if one could get a United Party nomination. (The SRLP had decided not to contest the election, realising its chances were poor and not wanting to split the anti-Liberal-Party vote). But it was out of the question for us. There was an overwhelming commitment to get more established professionally first and relieve the pressure on Jim; and even if that had not been the case, we could hardly have sought nomination by the United Party while disagreeing with its policy on the franchise. So we must reconcile ourselves to being out on the fringe for a long time.

Dendy Young and Bevis Barker decided to give it a go, as candidates for the United Party. Dendy, who had obvious assets as a politician and whose maverick tendencies had not yet manifested themselves, was offered a constituency which he could be confidently expected to win, and did so. Bevis, with no great claims to proficiency at public speaking and suchlike, was offered the experience of contesting a seat which he could be confidently expected to lose, having as his opponent the Leader of the Liberal Party, Jacob Smit himself. He accepted cheerfully, and resolved that at any rate losing must not be attributable to lack of efficiency or a sense of fun. He roped in his youthful office staff and some of his National Affairs friends in a refreshing and highly organised campaign; and he won too. Pat and Elspeth and I were among his gang of helpers and learned some valuable things about running that kind of campaign.

The overall result of the 1948 election was a resounding victory for Huggie and the United Party. It ended up with 24 out of the 30 seats in Parliament, leaving on the Opposition benches 5 Members of the Liberal Party and 1 Member of the Rhodesia Labour Party.

The result was due, partly at least, to the impact on the electorate of the General Election in the Union of South Africa which had taken place earlier, in May 1948. Smuts and his United Party had lost to Malan and the Nationalist Party. To us the significance of it had seemed clear enough. The attractive kind of South Africanism one had seen embodied in Smuts and in younger generation South Africans, of Afrikaans as well as English-speaking origin, like the ones Pat had come across in the Army and POW camp and I in the Air Force, had lost out, and for the foreseeable future. The government of South Africa had passed into the hands of a Party dominated by the Broedebond; the kind of South Africans who had been most bitterly opposed to the war and most amenable to Nazism; like the Nazis, dedicated to the supremacy of the 'Volk'. How could it have happened? We were inclined to think it was because the South African United Party's brand of enlightenment was so wishy-washy, and in fact hypocritical. They might not care for the word *apartheid* but most of them subscribed to it in practice. In a sense the rot had started in 1935, with the agreement between Smuts and Hertzog to ditch the old Cape common-roll franchise.

But what influence the South African election result would have on voters generally in Southern Rhodesia was not certain. Voters of Afrikaner origin had a strong influence in some constituencies, and of them some were known to have strong Nationalist sympathies. On the other hand a great many Southern Rhodesian voters, including ones of South African but English-speaking origin, would be fearful of Afrikaner Nationalism because of its pro-Volk and anti-British content. How many would there be whose motivation in voting United Party here was that they wanted something better in Rhodesia than either the South African Nationalist or the South African United Party?

It was not possible to give a clear-cut answer to that question, even after the result of the Rhodesian election in 1948 was known; but at any rate it seemed to be some indication of a genuine liberalism on the part of the electorate, and that put Huggie in a stronger position to take further with the British Government the question of amalgamation, or some form of closer constitutional association, with Northern Rhodesia. Meanwhile Welensky had strengthened his hand by winning the Northern Rhodesian general election which had taken place in August 1948.

The question of some form of closer association between the three territories — Southern Rhodesia with its relatively advanced status as a self-governing Colony and relatively large white population and developed economy, and Northern Rhodesia, a British Protectorate but with a significant population of white settlers and great copper deposits beginning to be exploited, and Nyasaland, a Protectorate but with few settlers and little economic development — had already been studied by a Royal Commission under Lord Bledisloe in 1938. There had for years before that been a movement among whites in both Southern and Northern Rhodesia for the 'amalgamation' of those two territories, that is, the substitution of a single, unitary government for the two existing governments; and the Bledisloe Commission had rejected it, particularly taking into account African opposition (which, it said in a footnote, 'it would be wrong to assume . . . is based to a very large extent on ignorance or prejudice or an instinctive dread of change'). The Bledisloe Commission also considered, and rejected, federation of the three territories, that is, the creation of a new, federal government to take over responsibility for specified matters of common interest but leaving the three existing governments with responsibility for the rest. The most it could recommend was the setting up of a body to co-ordinate administration, economic policy and development; and this subsequently came into being, after the war, as the Central African Council, a purely consultative body but with a permanent secretariat based in Salisbury.

Clearly, it was the economic and political dominance of the Southern Rhodesian whites, and the 'Native Policy' reflecting it, which had been the main stumbling block, and no British Government could have ignored the Bledisloe Commission's findings. But now, in the wake of the 1948 elections, was it not time to look at the matter again? Huggins' and Welensky's hands were strengthened to press again for amalgamation, and although the motivation of many of their supporters might still be suspect was it not something different from the racialist, herrenvolk philosophy of the Afrikaner Nationalists? Was there not the possibility of some form of closer association between the three territories resulting in the existence in Central Africa of a stable, prosperous state committed to a more English liberal and democratic philosophy, which might act as a counterweight to a South Africa committed to apartheid?

Huggins' and Welensky's efforts to persuade the British Government continued, and Huggins, sensing that the United Party's intention of abolishing the common voters' roll was one of the current causes of overseas suspicion of its Native Policy, persuaded a Congress of the Party in August 1950 to reverse that policy and to retain the common roll, albeit subject to an increase in the property and income qualifications. And, following a suggestion by Huggins that the discussions had previously been on too high a level, the British Government was persuaded to agree in November 1950 on the appointment of a Conference of senior officials of Southern Rhodesia, Northern Rhodesia and Nyasaland, and of the Central African Council, the Commonwealth Relations Office and the Colonial Office, charged with considering whether it would be possible for them to formulate proposals for closer association which they could recommend to the Governments of the three territories and to the British Government.

In the more remote field of politics which Pat and I were confined to, the National Affairs Association reached a sort of peak of its development by about September 1950, when a resumé of its activities in the four years since the beginning of the lunch-hour lectures was issued as part of an appeal for contributions to a projected Trust Fund. It said —

Lectures

... At the present time a total of some 200 lectures have been held, making an average of fifty a year during the whole period. The Lectures have been given by experts, local people and visitors, to an average audience estimated at 150. Sometimes the number has been nearer 400. Taken as a whole the lectures have maintained that strict political impartiality which the Association requires.

To supply the background of academic knowledge which it is necessary for the layman to have in such matters as economics, philosophy, etc., the Association has imported University Lecturers, who are in daily practice, to give concentrated series of lectures.

Debates

During the period since February 1946 there have also been held some 26 debates, and the average attendance at these is estimated at 70 per meeting.

Broadcasts

In July 1948 the Association started to use the medium of broadcasts. Two series of talks on matters of national importance were held, comprising 25 and 7 talks respectively. At the present time a series of discussions has been started, and 4 of these have been broadcast.

Secretariat

In January 1949 it was at last possible to establish a secretariat, a secretary being found who was willing to serve at a nominal remuneration. An office was obtained and office equipment was subscribed for by the State Lotteries Fund.

Bulletin

In April 1950 a bulletin summing up what has taken place under the aegis of the Association was started and is at the present time distributed to members monthly.

Executive Meetings

Regular meetings of the Executive, and of sub-committees, have been held over the period and these have occasionally been used for the purpose of private discussions with authorities on various subjects.

. . . As for the future, the Association continues to enjoy the support of impartial people willing to work voluntarily for its objects. Lectures have been planned for nearly a year ahead, and plans are in hand for the issue of a publication based on the verbatim reports of previous lectures; further debates are being arranged; broadcast discussions are likely to become more frequent and better . . .

The Executive Committee still had on it some of the original members like Bob Williams and Dendy Young (now QC, MP), and some recruited early on like Hansie Goldin and her husband Bennie (born in Cape Town, now establishing himself at the Salisbury Bar), Jack Howman (Rhodesian born, son of an early and well-respected Native Commissioner, now partner in one of the longest established firms of Attorneys Coghlan Welsh & Guest), Ken Towsey (English born, Oxford graduate, war-time pilot in the Fleet Air Arm, now private secretary to one of the Ministers), Ralph Middleton (war-time army officer, cheerful, helpful and good to be with, one felt sure, during tough times in the desert; now back in insurance), and Jack Humphries (civil engineer with a 'Mr Deeds Goes to Town' look, born in South Africa, London graduate, determined that Rhodesia should avoid South Africa's mistakes). Pat was currently Chairman, and Bob Williams, Bennie Goldin and I had each previously done a stint at it.

The key job of Lecture Programme Organiser had been taken on by Hansie in May 1949, and then and for several years afterwards potential lecturers found themselves dealing with a young woman of extraordinary intelligence and charm. I came to think of her as a bit of a miracle, combining intelligence, fun and extraordinary generosity. Born Hansie Kaplan in remote Mtoko she lost her mother, as I subsequently learned, through cancer at the age of seven, and from then until becoming a university student at Cape Town (presumably with the help of a Beit scholarship) she must have lived for the greater part of the time as a boarder at the Girls' School in Salisbury. I think her Jewish faith meant a lot to her, but so did Christianity; and whatever may have accounted for it her genuine love and concern, not only for family and friends but for beings of all kinds that she had to do with (pet dog included), was a fact. Fortunate National Affairs Association to have such a Programme organiser!

Ken Towsey was editor of the Bulletin and personally made skilful summaries of the lunch-hour lectures to go into it. Edward Harben, witty and attractive man whose accomplishments included cricket commentaries for the radio (and whose nickname 'Bloggy' must, I imagine, have been acquired at prep school in England and somehow stuck to him through Eton and even migration to the wide open spaces) carried main responsibility for the broadcasts.

In the programme of lectures since 1947 there had been included the first one by an African speaker, Gideon Mhlanga, and a series by Ken Kirkwood (then lecturing at Natal University and later to become Rhodes Professor of Race Relations at Oxford) on politics and racial policy in the Union of South Africa, and a series by the Professor of Economics at Rhodes University, Hobart Houghton. And in the pipeline were two further notable series: one on anthropology to be given by Professor Monica Wilson and the other by Hans Holleman (later to be appointed professor at Leiden University) representing the first fruits of the important research into Shona custom which he was then in the process of completing.

It is strange to think now of what an unusual occurrence it was to have Gideon Mhlanga give the lunch-hour lecture on the 16 September 1948. But it was unusual. He in fact was the first Rhodesian African to get himself a university Degree, and still at that time one of only six to have done so. He had been appointed to the staff of a government secondary school for Africans which had been recently set up at Goromonzi outside Salisbury to be a sort of counterpart to boarding schools for whites like Plumtree. But even after Goromonzi was established the total capacity for secondary education for Africans was 120 places a year, and nearly all education previously (provided by Missions of the various denominations, with Government financial support) had been in the earlier primary school classes. So there were still not so many blacks with more than a smattering of secondary education in existence at the time of Gideon Mhlanga's lecture, and we might not have contacted him but for the fact that we had previously known two other members of the staff of Goromonzi, 'Knottie' (A.P. Knottenbelt) and Jasmine Gordon Forbes. (Knottie, a courageous, scrawny, deep-voiced man, we had known from Rhodes days and was to become as much as any white Rhodesian a person trusted by blacks of all persuasions. And Jasmine, who had been a mutual friend of Pat's and mine at Rhodes and afterwards in London, was later — under her married name Rose-Innes — to write a sensitive, prize-winning book about her childhood in Rhodesia which I hope will one day be republished and fully appreciated*.) Anyway, Gideon Mhlanga's lunch-hour lecture was the first occasion that such a public gathering, consisting almost exclusively of Rhodesian whites, had ever been addressed by a black Rhodesian.

There was some concern amongst members of the Executive at the prospect of it. Whites tended to react suspiciously to 'educated Natives' and Missionary influence, and especially whites like Charles Olley — that little Irishman, vituperative, often amusing, dedicated to white supremacy, who had been active even in our childhood with his broadsheet *If I Were King* — and the kind of people who had kept him in office as a Salisbury City Councillor year after year. What would their reaction be when the notice of the meeting appeared in the Press? Would they try to break it up? What sort of audience would attend? How would they react to the novelty of having the speaker amongst them for coffee and sandwiches beforehand? Might he himself be embarrassed? How would he approach the lecture? Might he use it to air a lot of grievances and antagonise the audience? Strange though it may now seem these were relevant questions at the time, and what was decided was that Bob and another ex-heavyweight boxer, Dave Linton, should be standing by for any chucking out that might be necessary, and that we should have the speaker to lunch with us privately beforehand.

As it turned out the occasion was entirely a happy one. The hall was crowded with an audience of about four hundred. Gideon Mhlanga BA was a charming fellow, short, shiny, round-eyed and with a look of great gravity which would suddenly change into a radiant, off-set smile. And he was impressive. We had suggested that he should tell us the story of how he had got his degree, and this is what he did, simply, with humour and sympathy for the susceptibilities of the white audience. It had taken him until he was about forty to do it. He had been born on a farm in the Chipinga area south of Umtali, some time between 1903 and 1905 he thought. He had first gone to a school six miles from his home on the Mount Selinda Mission farm where his father had been allowed to settle, walking to and from school each day and herding goats between times. The area was remote and clothing simple —

> Our attire consisted of cloth which we tied round us, which went down as far as the knee. Our bodies were not covered except on cold days ... One of our playmates was sent a pair of shorts by his father. He could not put them on. We all tried. Try as we would, we failed. We did not know how to do it. We all tried. We tried it all ways and we gave it up as a bad job.

Writing in the Dust, by Jasmine Rose-Innes. (Andre Deutsch, 1968).

In 1914 another school had been built near his home. It was —

> of pole and dagga with a thatched roof and glazed windows, and those
> with benches were lucky. The teacher got his theological training in
> Accra; he was a god-fearing man and he made a deep impression on us
> all. It was an important era in my life history and that was the year in
> which I became a Christian. My father had no objection to my going to
> school. After all it was one of the rules of the Mission that a child
> should go to the school; but he was definitely opposed to my becoming
> a Christian . . .

In 1918 he went to the Mount Selinda Institution where —

> education and industrial training went hand in hand. Most of the
> people who have come from there have not had a white collar complex.
> They all studied carpentry, building and agriculture . . .

In 1922 Gideon Mhlanga and his cousin decided to go to Umtali to get
money for further study —

> We were determined to have higher education. From Mount Selinda
> to Umtali was about 140 miles. You can imagine the two of us twenty
> years ago trudging that distance on foot, on a road winding through the
> mountains in lion country. We were always afraid. What we feared
> most was the people south of Umtali who were hostile to our people.
> They thought we had invaded their country and taken their cattle. It
> was looked upon as enemy territory. We travelled for five days before
> we got to Umtali.
>
> The year 1922 was a particularly bad one. The labour supply
> exceeded the demand. In consequence of that we were not able to get
> work in Umtali and we left for Salisbury where we went to the office of
> the Native Commissioner to get passes to seek work. We could not get
> our passes that day and on the following day we went to look for work.
> We used to go across the Makabusi. We slept outside. We were
> expecting a raid by the Police. In Salisbury we got a job at 15/- a
> month. That would not go very far in study money and we were forced
> to proceed to Bulawayo, but it was the same there; there was no work
> to do. But there were people there in business from Mount Selinda
> and we joined them. That proved to be our salvation.
>
> The location life in Bulawayo was shocking; drunkenness, gambling,
> vice, quarrelling and all the other immoral practices were rife. We
> were not used to that kind of life . . .
>
> One incident occurred there. I was arrested on the ground that my
> pass was lapsed. I told the police I did not renew it because I was going
> away after selling my chairs. I showed him my travelling and town pass
> and identity certificate to prove that I was not a loafer but I was put
> under arrest and sentenced to seven days imprisonment with the
> option of a fine of 10/-. I paid this, but it left a bad impression on my
> mind.

After a year and a half in Bulawayo they thought they had saved enough money to get to Lovedale, a small town in the eastern Cape where many Africans had got their education over the years. They were arrested at the Cape for having no passports and fined, but then released. Gideon managed to win some small prizes and a bursary at school and, by working part time in domestic service, to attain a Teacher's Certificate and get a job as a teacher for two years. In 1930 he decided to return to Rhodesia.

> I had been away from home for nearly nine years and my parents thought I was dead.

He got a job as a teacher at Domboshawa and during the next ten years, as well as teaching with occasional study breaks and supporting his brothers and sisters at school (his parents being now old), he managed, largely by private study, to take the Matriculation exam and eventually in 1944 to complete his Degree.

It would have been easy for him in telling the story to dwell on the contrast between the struggle he had and the virtually unlimited opportunity available to whites for education financed almost wholly by the State or by bursaries of one kind or another. But he refrained from doing this, and ended up —

> 'I would like to pay tribute to the missionaries who gave us the Gospel. They told us we should love our enemies. We never had that kind of doctrine: an enemy was an enemy; we were now told to love our enemies. Further they gave us education; they built schools. They had very little money. They gave us industrial training so that we could become self-reliant. They also put up hospitals and trained us as nurses and orderlies. I should also say a word of thanks to the public for putting up schools like that of the school where I am teaching.
>
> I am glad to find a change of heart on the part of many in the country towards the question of native education and native policy. This is borne out by the fact that the demand for education is increasing every year. We have been pleased to know that the results of the recent election have been what they are. There is a growing need amongst Africans for more schools although they are full to capacity. One school had over a thousand applications and only one hundred could be accepted. All the schools are full up and there is a demand for more education. I am sure this need will be met. We can look on the country as a democratic country in the true sense of the word. The majority of our people are illiterate but I am not a pessimist; I believe things will right themselves. Our being here is not accidental. It is the will of God.
>
> I would like to add that I think it is an honour as well as a great pleasure to be asked to address this gathering. Being an honour, it is also a matter of duty.'

How much we or the rest of the audience appreciated at the time the extent to which he was giving to white Rhodesians generally the benefit of the doubt it is hard to say. The audience applauded enthusiastically, and that seemed fair enough.

CHAPTER 6

Recreation and New Contacts

The pressing need for contacts like the one with Gideon Mhlanga was something continually in the back of our minds, but there was nothing more we could do about it for the time being because of other pressing calls on time and energy not already consumed by the tyrant Scanlen & Holderness.

Elspeth arrived in the country from England towards the end of 1947, and we were married the following January, and about a year later Pat was married to Anne, daughter of one of the country's early Rhodes Scholars, L.R. Morgan, now on the way to being Secretary for Education, the top Government post in that field. Elspeth's father was a quiet-spoken, sensitive man whom you would take to be a pianist or poet and philosopher but whose talents were actually utilised in key positions in British industry — including the planning of the great supply pipeline 'Pluto' used in the invasion of Europe; and he had had to be based in the middle of London during the war, in a flat which Elspeth had shared with him before his death soon after VE day. So it was a change for her to find herself accommodated in the old family bungalow in Montagu Avenue, still much the same as it had been during our childhood but now more cluttered up, with old trunks of belongings and letters of members of the family and suchlike. But what it lacked in sophistication seemed to be more than compensated for by warm-heartedness on the part of Con and Jim, her hosts. Con, small in size but great in sympathy and innocence, was a sort of guru in the minds of many who knew her, and she and Jim had friends of all ages and seemed to treat the ones of six no differently from the ones of sixty.

My bachelor accommodation was 'The Shack' in the back garden, which had started as a 'nanny's' room and been added to by my brother John (laying his own bricks) to accommodate his wife and child during one of his absences overseas in the Air Force. Its pièce de resistance was a Hi-Fi put together for me by one of the ex-Air Force technicians and housed in cabinets of solid local wood. There were few if any LPs and playing the thirty-four sides of Beethoven's 'Choral' on 78s which Pat had bought instead of food during his student days was quite a gymnastic as well as musical exercise. But such things were a great consolation five thousand miles away from London's live music.

The society Elspeth found herself amongst was, in many cases, heavily involved in National Affairs, and in Pat's also with getting going a National Arts Council. But it was not all earnest or puritanical, and less prone than in England to treat men only as fit for some of the best songs and jokes. Pat's younger brother John, who had been two years ahead of his contemporaries at school and taken his matric and first degree with me and then gone on to Oxford and war service with the Army in Somalia, was a man of small build set on a legal career. There was a gloomy, conservative side to his nature which was to become most evident later, in his role as a judge administering the grim security laws of Ian Smith's regime. But in those years after the war it was another, elfin self which often prevailed. He had brilliant natural talent as a musician and raconteur, and could be induced at parties to bring out his old banjulele — relic of student days — and sing wonderful songs from the thirties (golden age of dance music); and others would find themselves joining in. With Elspeth's arrival, and the installation of a baby grand piano bought from the total proceeds of our wedding present money, the range of live music available in The Shack extended to include Beethoven, Debussy, and sad heroic ballads from the Songs of the North. The availability of superb African music, all wholly congenial to the 'western' ear, was something we were then only beginning to appreciate.

We were married in the little Anglican Cathedral — part granite, part corrugated iron, where Con had been accustomed to look in almost every day during the war to say her prayers for her three sons in the Air Force and for all sorts of other people she cared for as well — and the great Meikles Hotel dining room was the place for celebrating afterwards. I had not cared much for the white wedding idea, but in the event there was something impressively tribal and warm about all those families gathered there, with so many common memories. Not that all the guests were old Rhodesians. Already two years after the war the proportion of immigrant to local white population was considerable. By the end of five years it would be approaching equality, reflecting the greatest rate of immigration, if you only took whites into account, of any country in the world except Israel.

The rate of economic growth was impressive and, inevitably, there was inflation. White incomes had kept well ahead of it, but not the minimal wages blacks were getting; and in April 1948 there was a strike of African Municipal workers in Bulawayo. It rapidly spread and developed and soon became what was in effect a general strike of African workers, including even domestic servants, in both Salisbury and Bulawayo. It took nearly all the whites completely by surprise, including officials of the Native Department. Huggie called out the Territorials and the Police Reserve, and at the same time set up a Commission of Enquiry into the strikers' grievances under the Chief Justice, Sir Robert Hudson; and the strike was soon over. But the thought that something like that could happen was a new one with frightening implications for the whites, and in the minds of many the names of Mzingeli and Burombo which began to be heard, as the leaders in Salisbury and Bulawayo respectively of the embryonic African workers' organisations associated with the strike, seemed to have an ominous and even sinister significance.

There was no existing stock of houses to buy ready-made, and building materials were in short supply and planning restrictions tight. And we spent nearly three years living in 'The Shack' while organising the land and the plans and the finance for the house we were ultimately to live in, and waiting for it to be completed. But we came to think it one of the more exciting privileges of living in a 'new' country that, instead of hiring or buying a house someone else had designed, you should have carte blanche to build what you reckoned would suit most exactly your particular way of life and that particular environment, and the odd chance that between yourselves and the architect and the builder — complex and delicate relationship — and despite being severely restricted by shortage of money and building materials, you might even end up with something which was a small piece of real, creative art. Instead of having furniture dominated by copies of masterpieces of another age, or even originals, you could try designing some of it yourself and have it made, beautifully and in beautiful local wood — like Mukwa with its golden-brown colouring and free grain — by a gentle black man whose workshop was a broken-down garage in the back end of the town and who had a home-made notice outside it reading —

S. NELSON
FURNITURE OPERATOR
MT. SELINDA TRAINED
ABOVE AVERAGE

My favourite recreation was flying. You could at that time hire from a small company set up by enterprising ex-Air Force characters the kind of light aircraft which had been designed for war-time spotting purposes and, if you played your cards carefully, at a cost no greater than for a motor car. This was a form of mobility which Elspeth and I thought we should exploit before embarking on parentage, and we had some fascinating week-end sorties. One of them gave us a convincing taste of the southern part of Nyasaland, with its beautiful mountains and Eden-like variety of vegetation, and the southern shores of its great lake, established long enough in geological time to have real beaches, and falling on some of the more exposed beaches, real breakers. Another sortie provided an unscheduled glimpse of the gaol at the historic little fortress town of Tete on the Zambezi in the Moçambique pedicle which separates the countries now called Zimbabwe and Malawi. We had been unable to resist landing to have a look and discovered too late that we should have held a permit.

Over another long week-end we followed the route of the Sabi River from its modest source quite near Salisbury to its junction with the Limpopo in the wild south-east corner of the country, stopping en route at various places. One was Birchenough Bridge where the broad, sandy river bed, with its crocodiles to be seen basking in the sun, is spanned by an immensely elegant silver arc of steel which carries the bridge suspended from it, and beside the road leading to the bridge were many shapes and sizes of that lovable, botanical brontosaur, the Baobab tree, their trunks glazed in a variety of colours — grey, grey and bronze, grey and copper and mauve.

Another was Triangle Sugar Estate. Flying across what seemed to be endless, dry, untameable low-veld in various shades of grey and brown you came suddenly across a patch of brilliant green which turned out to be several hundred acres of sugar cane under irrigation, separated from the dam supplying water to it by a formidable granite kopje. And the story was that for a long time this sort of country had been inhabited only by wild animals and been generally regarded as unfit for human habitation, but it seemed to fascinate some quite unusual individuals. One of them, McDougall, persuaded a small-worker friend of his to help him blast a tunnel 140 feet long through the heart of the kopje, from what he perceived was a superb, natural dam site on the Mtilikwe river to what would be immensely fertile soil if only the water could be got to it. McDougall having made his point but lacking the necessary capital to develop the project himself or keep it going, the Government had felt compelled eventually to take it over. And so the country had found itself with another public enterprise. This was the beginning of huge irrigation estates which were to be developed by private enterprise years later.

We were put up in the house which McDougall had built for himself on the top of another, steep little kopje next to the landing strip where we had landed, and had occasion in the moonlight that night, because of the disturbing influence of something we had eaten, to come across other evidence of his enlightenment. Just off the crown of the kopje and backed by a young baobab tree, suspended over a sheer drop and overlooking endless low-veld, was a 'PK'. It had no door, and the walls curved outwards slightly to disclose the view, like a cell designed for a mystic. And next day we discovered that on the other side of the kopje was a similar PK, suitable for a different series of angles of the sun.

In about July 1949 I was offered the command of an Auxiliary Squadron of part-time fliers which the Government had decided to set up to make use of available war-time experience pending the establishment of permanent squadrons. I decided to accept, with some trepidation. I knew of the reputation Rhodesian pilots had earned for themselves during the war, in operations in North Africa and Europe and also on the instructional side (often at least as exacting); but having come into it myself while still a student in England I had almost entirely missed out on serving with any of them, except one or two like Ted Jacklin. He had come to Hullavington on one of the ECFS courses and impressed everyone, as much by the modest and unselfish nature lying behind his rugged exterior as by his great ability and skill, and was now to be chief of the small nucleus of officers of the post-war permanent force. The ones chosen to constitute the Auxiliary Squadron ranged from youthful veterans like Johnny Deall (DSO, DFC), Don McGibbon (DFC) and Neville Brooks (who had distinguished himself in the Far East and had switched from a civil service job after the war to a job in Scanlen & Holderness) to ones who had little more than completed their training at the end of the war. All of them seemed to share to some extent that attractive combination of modesty and ability; and being in it with them, as well as making good an omission in my contact with fellow Rhodesians (which I seemed incapable of achieving at sports club level), was a wholly congenial experience.

(One of the keenest, Jack Malloch, who was penniless but managed to borrow enough to buy a truck for a self-operated transport service, was later to become the most famous of the country's private enterprise fliers, and a kind of Elizabethan-style buccaneer during the period of sanctions after UDI.)

We were all lovers — of flying; and content to have available aircraft fit for the full range of manoeuvres: the old Harvards which had been used in the Air Training Scheme, and later even some Spitfire XXIIs. We took it responsibly I think, aware of the cost of each flying hour and using it for legitimate, military training purposes; but that did include exercises in mastery of the aircraft — 'limit flying' as we had christened it at Hulla-vington — and this made it legitimate to show off a little sometimes, with the odd display of low-level aerobatics as at the opening of Livingstone Airport in August 1950. And there were of course convivial evenings in the mess. Wives and girl friends were welcome on suitable occasions, and some of the first Sunday mornings in the life of our elder daughter, Dinah, were spent observing the flying from a portable bassinet parked on the edge of the aerodrome.

————————

With all these preoccupations, it was not until mid-1950 that Pat and I found ourselves making further significant contacts with Africans on a political level, and then it came about because of being consulted in our legal capacity by African organisations but concerning matters which were, in reality, rather more political than legal. The Subversive Activities Bill, representing the white Establishment reaction to the 1948 African strike, was about to be put before Parliament, and Charles Mzingeli asked if Scanlen & Holderness would act for the Reformed Industrial and Commercial Workers' Union (RICWU), of which he was the effective leader with the designation of General Secretary, in making an objection to it. And early in 1951 we were asked by Isaac Samuriwo, as Vice-President of an organisation called the Southern Rhodesian African Association, to represent it in preparing and presenting evidence to a Select Committee of Parliament on draft legislation involving, *inter alia*, fundamental changes in the system of land tenure in the Reserves and Special Native Areas, and called, somewhat misleadingly, the Native Land Husbandry Bill.

Pat's superior qualifications, combined with an extraordinary sense of service on his part, resulted in a state of chronic overwork which he bore uncomplainingly all his years in the firm, and it was arranged that I should see Charles Mzingeli. I knew of him as having been on friendly terms with Edward Harben and others of the SRLP, including the staunchest of its leaders, Mrs Gladys Maasdorp, a socialist with roots in the old Cape liberal tradition. But I was pretty certain that in the security files of the Native Department or the Police or both he was classified as 'dangerous'. He must surely have considerable influence to have achieved such prominence in connection with the 1948 strike. He had had little formal education, and none outside the country, but might it be that he had picked up Marxist ideas about the dictatorship of the proletariat and revolution and was ready to appeal to anti-white racialism to promote them? Or that what he was after was the 'self-aggrandisement' with which so many native administrators were fond of labelling blacks who were less than docile? These were questions I could not exclude from my pre-conceived idea of him. And of course for a legal firm at that time it was something new to have this kind of client, and something of a problem to persuade a receptionist to say 'Mr Mzingeli is here to see you' instead of 'A native boy is here to see you', or to know what the reaction would be of clients whom we depended upon for our livelihood to have sharing the waiting room with them a black man, and a black man at that who was *persona non grata* with the Native Department.

The actual person I found myself interviewing was lightly built, bespectacled, earnest, sensitive and — as I came to understand — touchy and probably quite lonely. He brought with him a draft which he had prepared of a memorandum to serve as a basis of discussion, and which read as follows:

Reformed Industrial and Commercial Workers' Union of Africa

SUBVERSIVE ACTIVITIES BILL: The view of the above Union and general feeling of the African people on the bill which has now been amended as the result of strong protest by the European public is this:—

1. Although the bill is non discriminatory, it certainly is intended and will clamp down African workers harder than any other section of the community.

2. It is a product of Hudson's Commission appointed after General disturbances (African strike) in 1948. Hence the form under which it is introduced, although it become dangerous to the non-African section, is done so simple to avoid an interference of the Imperial power of veto against discriminatory legislation.

3. The provisions restricting meetings, passive resistance etc. etc. are definitely aimed at the less privileged section of the community which is African people of this colony, and it is clear to the Government that in order that African people must press for their civil

rights in future as citizens of the colony, a course which must take place in the very immediate future, the only possible weapon for African people or any other under privileged section of the community is strongest agitation, strikes and passive resistance. The Government is well aware that this will be the case and therefor introduces the bill which if it become an act, will give the Government powers to use force against legitimate fight against any measures which have outlived their purposes.

4. We are of the opinion that the Government of Southern Rhodesia is capable of introducing better legislation for the purpose of bringing about mutual understanding between different races of the colony whose future depends entirely on such policy of good relationship rather than using old pattern of notorious legislation of the Union of South Africa.

5. We desire to point out that the colour bar in industry as it exist now under the Industrial Conciliation Act, is one of the strong factor that the intention of the bill in question is intended to keep less privileged section of the community as perpetual drawer of water and hewer of wood. This is complete contrary to the principles of Human Rights the rights which include all those who participated in the battle against nazi and fascism to make the world safe for democracy. We desire to add that the native policy of this country which demand immediate overhauling if co-operation between African people and the Government is to be maintained, has since 1941 deteriorated to a point far below reasonable measure, and the Government is fully aware that African people are strongly opposed to such policy. Yet it now introduce a bill in order to make any protest illegal soon as such bill comes into power.

6. We respectfully ask the Minister of Internal Affairs through the Office of the Minister for Native Affairs to withdraw the Subversive activities bill for the fact that, the purpose for which it is being introduced do not exist at all.

Alternatively: We appeal to Members of Parliament to give serious consideration the fundamental principle of democracy involved in the bill, and to reject its passage through Parliament . . .

There were no guidelines as to the sort of job a lawyer should try to do in these circumstances. I concluded that I should try to redraft the memorandum in such a way as, bearing in mind what I thought I had learned myself about the way the minds of Ministers and MPs were working, would have the best chance of carrying some weight with them; and the outcome was the following re-draft, in the form of a letter from the Secretary General of the RICWU to the Secretary of Native Affairs, Salisbury:

. . . The Bill has met with considerable opposition from the European population and as a result certain amendments have been proposed. But we doubt whether many people realise what the effect of the Bill is upon African opinion, and we feel it is vital that this should be made clear to the Government, to Members of Parliament and to the Public before the matter is taken any further. I therefore respectfully request that you bring this statement — which I am forwarding to the Press — to the notice of the Government as soon as possible.

1. The big question as regards race relations in this Colony is whether we can in fact achieve co-operation between Europeans and Africans or whether we must resign ourselves to working at logger-heads. To achieve co-operation we must overcome the underlying fear which each race has of the other: the fear of the European that the African will 'swamp' him and the fear of the African that the Europeans will oppress him.

2. To the African the Subversive Activities Bill is a most striking confirmation that his fear of oppression is justified. It appears to him as a weapon specifically designed to prevent him from advancing by legitimate means. As such, if it is passed, it will strike a serious blow at his confidence in the European. There are a number of reasons for this:

FIRST, the Bill follows hard upon the Hudson Commission Report which was published as a result of the general disturbances (African strike) of 1948, and although on the face of it it is not discriminatory, it appears to the African to be a discriminatory measure designed to prevent such disturbances, however legitimate, while avoiding any possibility of the Imperial Government exercising a veto.

SECONDLY, the African naturally desires to overcome the limitations which are put on his economic development by the economic colour bar embodied in the Industrial Conciliation Act. These limitations are contrary to the principles of the Atlantic Charter, and it appears quite a legitimate ambition of the African that some system should be evolved whereby he will be enabled to employ his full capabilities in his job. The Subversive Activities Bill which makes illegal such methods as agitation, strikes and passive re-sistance seems to him to be merely a weapon to prevent him making progress in this direction.

THIRDLY, the hope of the African is that in this Colony we will achieve a new and better way of co-operation between the races. But he can see that in the past legislation here has followed closely the pattern of legislation in the Union of South Africa where race policy has become openly repressive and reactionary. Our Subversive Activities Bill is exactly the same in kind (if different in degree) as the equivalent legislation in South Africa, and if it is passed it will confirm the fear that we are going in exactly the same direction.

3. If there had been evidence that dangerous, undemocratic forces were at work among the African people such as to justify emergency measures the African might have been less suspicious of the Bill. But that is not the case, and it accordingly appears to him that arguments based on conditions which exist in some other part of the world are merely a cloak for repressive legislation here.

We do not think the Government will deny the importance of assessing the reaction of the African section of the people to legislation such as this. But there may be a tendency to think of Africans as a homogeneous, ignorant mass. We feel it is essential for the Government and the country to keep in mind the position of the African to whom, by reason of being more advanced than the mass, other Africans look for a lead. It is not always easy for such an African to retain the confidence of his people when he advocates co-operation as the best method of achieving social justice. His own faith, and his position as an advocate, may well be destroyed if it appears that the Government itself has no faith in that method. If the Subversive Activities Bill is passed this will certainly appear to be the case.

It seems to me pretty obvious now that Mzingeli's original was better and more effective than my re-draft; and it makes me smart a little with shame to be reminded that I could have been so insensitive as to have used, even in a letter purporting to come from Africans themselves, generalisations so much conditioned by the whites' way of thinking as 'the African' and 'the more advanced African'. Not that it made any practical difference so far as the RICWU's representations were concerned. For reasons which I came to appreciate more fully later, whatever had appeared in the draft would have made no difference to the Bill subsequently passed by Parliament. But for me the experience of working with Charles Mzingeli made a fundamental difference.

I felt I had got to know him well enough to have a reliable insight into what he was really like, and that this had been possible in so short a time partly because I was in a professional capacity, employed by the RICWU, and to that extent relieved from the opposite, master–servant role customary between whites and blacks. And what I could see was a touching and vulnerable man doing his best to help fellow human beings who were getting a pretty raw deal from white-dominated society, and doing it without any particular malice or racial antagonism towards whites; in a sense a counterpart in the industrial revolution just beginning in Rhodesia of one of the early, groping but dedicated trade unionists at the equivalent stage of English economic history. But what would my impression of him have been if I had been a Police Officer or Native Department official relying wholly or mainly on reports recorded in the files of conduct or statements which might be considered 'dangerous'? And what sort of advice would I have been likely to give in that capacity to a Minister, himself totally lacking any first-hand knowledge of Mzingeli or any Africans like him, and relying on me for information on which to base important political decisions concerning Law and Order? The image which I had been quite prepared to have of Mzingeli before making first-hand contact with him was surely the kind of image most likely to prevail in government for so long as the situation existed in which whites making all the political decisions were acting without the slightest first-hand knowledge of blacks outside the master–servant relationship. And yet to make decisions on the basis of that kind of erroneous image could be disastrous for the whites themselves. However unattractively the point might have been expressed in the last paragraph of my re-draft, was it not true that if whites proved unable to take seriously and sympathetically someone like Mzingeli they would be asking for leaders like him to be replaced by much more implacable ones, and ones who might really have something sinister about them?

I think it must have been this kind of experience that brought home to us how far the National Affairs Association was falling short, despite all its successes, of doing what needed to be done. It had an impressive record. The lectures and debates had reached a surprisingly wide section of the white population and covered an increasingly wide, and sometimes quite specialised field. Its reputation stood high with people in business, the civil service, the professions and politics. But what did this amount to? The original idea was that the basic knowledge thrown up and ideas stimulated by the lectures and discussions would lead on to some enlightened sort of formulation of national policies. Was there not a danger of their being treated instead as an end in themselves, an interesting hobby for a quite large but more or less static body of whites? Was it not just as important that basic facts like the ones contained in the original programme of lectures should be made available to people who had not had the opportunity of hearing them — blacks, and for that matter the white immigrants who had been coming into the country since the lectures began — than that more wide-ranging and specialised lectures should be laid on for established customers? And as for any worthwhile formulation of policies, how could that be achieved except by a body comprising both whites and non-whites who not only possessed the necessary basic information but were also on man-to-man terms with each other?

We decided to see if we could contact in Harare blacks who were young, independent minded, without previous political associations (and especially ones containing any element of Native Department patronage), and who would have sufficient education to participate in English in lectures, debates and the like. We consulted people like Barbara Tredgold, Head of the Anglican Mission called Runyararo which, unlike the earlier missions in remote rural areas, was situated right in the middle of rough, black, urban Salisbury; and Freddie Loveridge, another associate from Rhodes days, who managed to combine being staunchly liberal himself and the husband of Phyllis, a pillar of the SRLP, with being Government appointee as Headmaster of the latest and biggest of its African schools — Harare West School, near Runyararo. And at the meetings which followed the person who stands out most clearly in my memory was Aiden Mwamuka. Short, deep voiced, neatly turned out, he was Headmaster of another of the government schools in Harare and had an air of quiet authority about him; and also another quality which seemed to me quite extraordinary and yet to be quite widely shared by the kind of people we were now coming across. This was a sort of profound courtesy. Not deference arising from a sense of inferiority or consciousness of belonging to a conquered race, and something more than mere politeness, a sort of built-in concern for other peoples' susceptibilities. I wondered whether this was a sentimental observation on my part, a reaction to finding discussion with them so congenial when I had expected it might be difficult. But it was confirmed by subsequent experience; and I later often noticed that when, for example, someone would be speaking in the course of a multi-racial meeting, what a white member of the group tended to be listening for was a cue to enable him to state his own opinion, but what a black listener was doing was trying to understand what was behind the speaker's words, 'in his heart', so to speak. And this seemed to link up with that delightful capacity for discovering the laugh in a situation which seemed to be so common amongst them.

The discussions with Aiden Mwamuka and others resulted in agreement on a proposal for the extension of the National Affairs lectures: a fresh set of basic lectures about the country and its problems, similar to the programme the Association had started with, which could be woven into the lunch-hour programme at the Cathedral Hall and which we would get the lecturers to repeat in Harare each fortnight on Saturday evening. And it must have been in the course of formulating this scheme or in the course of publicising it that we first met people like Lawrence Vambe and Elias Mtepuka, young journalists employed by an independent company, African Newspapers Limited, which published two newspapers — the *African Weekly* distributed from Salisbury and the *Bantu Mirror* distributed from Bulawayo. It produced some other publications as well, for the Government, but the newspapers were surprisingly independent in their approach, and the experience these young journalists were getting — including editorial experience — was much wider than would have been available at their age in a bigger pond. And they were an attractive breed: detached, responsible, humorous, able and modest about it.

The scheme for the new series of basic lectures to be repeated at Harare was endorsed by the National Affairs Executive (with some cajoling) and accommodation made available for them by Freddie Loveridge at Harare West School, and the first one at Harare was arranged to be given on 20 January 1951.

CHAPTER 7

Lectures. Land, 1950–1951

The new series of basic National Affairs lectures were good. There was no difficulty this time about getting the people we asked to agree to give them, including leading civil servants like Victor Robinson, QC, the Attorney General, on 'How Southern Rhodesia is Governed', and the Chairman of the Public Services Board, T.S. Chegwidden, CB, CVO, on 'The Administrative Machine'; the Secretary to the Treasury, Andrew Strachan, CBE, on 'The Financial Administration of Southern Rhodesia' and the Secretary for Native Affairs and Chief Native Commissioner, Powys-Jones, on 'Native Administration'; and the lectures went down well in the Cathedral Hall. But in Harare they were a failure; and we learned a lot from that too.

There was no problem about the first one in Harare. It was a novel occasion and something like two hundred Africans turned up to hear it, including some with evidently only a small command of English. The speaker was Dr Eric Axelson, a person in the best tradition of young South African liberal academic who had accepted an appointment in the embryo organisation of the recently established National Archives (and had, incidentally, become a member of the National Affairs Executive). He had some experience of talking to African students, and the subject of his lecture, 'Rhodesia Before 1890', was uncontroversial. The monthly bulletin 'National Affairs' gave a brief summary of it:

. . . He described ancient mine workings and the evidence for attributing them to the Bantu, the essentially African character of such structures as Zimbabwe and the absence of any evidence that would indicate any greater antiquity. The Inyanga ruins, while having the same basic characteristics, betray less accomplished workmanship. From these and other observations Dr Axelson attempted to reconstruct the chronology of those early days, starting from the early Bantu tribes who arrived here about the 6th century AD and passing to the Arab traders, active from the 10th century onwards, the arrival of the Karanga people from the East of Lake Tanganyika in the 15th century, later to derive the name Shona from their association with the Sena, and including groups of Hamitic origin familiar with the arts of building in stone. Dr Axelson dates the Acropolis at Zimbabwe about the end of the 15th century, the Temple in the 16th and the Inyanga ruins from the 17th to the 18th.

Portuguese penetration took place from the beginning of the 16th century, leading by the middle of the 17th century to the establishment of forts and a garrison and the conversion to Christianity of Mono-motapa, Paramount Chief of the Mashona. Then followed a period of comparatively peaceful infiltration by Portuguese traders with the African tribes asserting themselves from time to time, and finally in the 19th century there came from the south the succession of hunters, adventurers, missionaries, prospectors and concession hunters that brings us up to modern times.

The second lecture, a summary of the history of the Colony 'From the Occupation to the Present Day', was delivered by John Lobb, a school-master reputed to have made a special study of the subject and was reported in 'National Affairs' as follows;

. . . He thought it important that missionaries were the first European settlers in Rhodesia — something more than conquest and exploita-tion. Robert Moffat, who travelled three times up the 'missionaries' road' through Bechuanaland to visit Mzilikazi north of the Limpopo, opened the mission station at Inyati in 1859; and Livingstone Moffat (the first white child to be born in Rhodesia) was born in 1860. Lobengula allowed the London Missionary Society to open Hope Fountain in 1870.

Gold discoveries by prospectors and hunters led to a rush of concession hunters, stimulated by the rich finds on the Rand and romantic tales of workings at Zimbabwe. British public opinion had also been converted to the value of colonies; notably by Cecil Rhodes, dreaming of British occupation of central Africa — 'Cape to Cairo'. But Rhodes had rivals — the Portuguese wanted to link their East and West African territories, so did the Germans, the Transvaal Republic had ideas. 'The scramble for Africa' said Mr Lobb, 'was on'.

Rhodes urged the British Government to declare the Matabele country a British sphere of influence (1887). Lobengula promised Moffat that he would give no territory without British consent and granted the Rudd Concession in 1888 which gave Rhodes' company 'exclusive mineral rights in return for 1 000 rifles and ammunition, £100 per month and a steamboat on the Zambezi'. But the British Government was slow to act.

Rhodes reverted to the old Elizabethan plan of a Chartered Company, backed by the Crown, to open up the territory. He applied for a Charter in 1889 'to open the whole of South Central Africa not yet occupied by a European power'. The Moffat Treaty, the Rudd Concession and the Charter, said Mr Lobb, are the foundation of Rhodesia.

In 1890 the Pioneer Column successfully marched to Salisbury and 'camped on the very spot where we are now sitting' (grounds of the Cathedral). In Mr Lobb's estimation 'The march of this adventurous band is one of the most fantastically daring enterprises in history. Its success was due to the skilful planning and courage of its leaders and the courage and fitness of their followers'. These pioneer troopers became the first settlers. Rhodes next tried to force the hand of the British Government into securing the port of Beira from the Portuguese, but he failed. The boundary was fixed in the Umtali area. Clash is inevitable, thinks Mr Lobb, between a strong civilised government and a wild tribe whose young men want 'to wash their spears in blood'. The Matabele rose in 1893 in a war which ended in the defeat and death of Lobengula. After that the settlement spread rapidly: Bulawayo was laid out close to Lobengula's old kraal. The name Rhodesia was first used in 1895. It was recognised officially by the British Government in 1897.

This development was not without setbacks. 'The ill-starred Jameson Raid' which drew the Chartered Company's Police away from Rhodesia gave an opportunity to the Matabele to rise once more. An army of 2 000 was mobilised; Rhodes himself went, unarmed, into the Matabele stronghold in the Matopo hills, and the Matabele accepted terms. An unexpected rising of the Mashona was more difficult to settle. But these were the last attempts to resist European settlement. Even in these the Africans were divided. As Mr Lobb pointed out there is a stained glass window in the Cathedral to the memory of a loyal native —Bernard Mizeki . . .

The South African War which followed the Raid stimulated progress. After the war the population of SR rose from 1 200 in 1904 to 2 300 in 1911. The railway reached Bulawayo in 1897; the line from Beira reached Salisbury in 1899; Salisbury and Bulawayo were connected by rail in 1911.

Mr Lobb considers disputes with a Chartered Company where free settlers are admitted to open up a country are inevitable. In 1914 the Charter was renewed for 10 years but the fight for self government had begun. A Responsible Government Association was formed in 1917; the Legislative Council passed a resolution asking for responsible government in 1920; an alternative proposal to join the Union as a fifth province was turned down, rightly Mr Lobb thinks, in 1922. In 1923 Responsible Government was granted . . .

Since then, concluded Mr Lobb, Rhodesian history is a story of steady progress, accelerated by the second world war. He believes the history books of the future will head this chapter through which we are living 'The Industrial Revolution' because he considers it is following the pattern of the same change that started in England 200 years ago — expansion of population, increase of national wealth, mechanisation of industry and agriculture, growth of towns, improvement of communications, extension of education and social services, change in the national way of life of all sections of the population. He thinks this year's census will show that SR has reached and passed another great landmark in her national history, and that his audience may see — the completion of the Kariba Gorge project, the acquisition of 'a seaport of our own', the attainment of full dominion status, the formation of a greater Rhodesia of Central Africa. 'These are exciting times to live in.'

In the Cathedral Hall some of the speaker's patriotic enthusiasm communicated itself to the audience. In Harare the reaction was quite different. It soon became clear that some of the events in this period of history which to the average white Rhodesian were part of the heroic story, or at least justifiable in terms of Cecil Rhodes' brand of idealism, in the minds of many of this audience were something quite different — part of a process of deception and bullying as a result of which they now found themselves second or third class citizens. From time to time there would be a kind of grunt or rumble of disagreement, or sometimes that characteristic expression of dissent; a sort of double gasp 'ah . . . ah!' And then at question time the tendency would be, not to ask questions, but to make protest speeches.

Suddenly one could see, from the point of view of both the audience and the speaker, how this business of repeating lectures which had previously been given to a white audience would work out. As one of the speakers you would have to decide, to begin with, whether to use the same words and rate of delivery as before. Surely you must adapt them for an audience with a lower average competence in English? But if you did that you would surely find yourself becoming aware of yourself sounding patronising, or else of a reaction on the part of the audience which indicated that is what they thought. Perhaps you were being patronising. And what about these rumbles of disapproval? And indignant speeches instead of questions? What had these fellows, Holderness, Lewis and Co., let you in for? On the other hand, as a member of the black audience how could you possibly listen to things being talked about complacently which to you were manifestly unjust and humiliating without registering some sort of protest? An occasion like this, when you were invited to say something to the speaker, a person with some real influence perhaps in government, and in the presence of some other whites who themselves might have some influence of some kind, was unique. How could you confine yourself to some dry, dispassionate question of fact?

It became clear that you could not expect the kind of people who comprised this kind of audience to sit quietly at the receiving end of a one-way traffic of information from whites quite unaccustomed to looking at the picture from their point of view; and equally, you could not expect speakers, and especially civil servants, to accept the sort of personal responsibility for the transgressions of the whites which the audience inevitably tended to invest them with at question time. So, after about the seventh lecture, the experiment was called off.

It was disappointing, but it was salutary to have made first hand contact with these people: mostly younger generation black Rhodesians; mostly townsmen; familiar with the tough, if colourful, urban world designed basically for migrant workers; able to cope much more confidently with the modern world than people of their parents' generation; much less disposed to acquiesce in the status of second or third class citizens; and some so hot under the collar about it as to be incapable of remaining silent no matter what risks might be involved of getting into the bad books of the Native Department or the Police. How would our fellow whites react to them, we wondered — even fellow members of the National Affairs Executive who had failed or declined to take the opportunity of attending the lectures in Harare? How would they react to George Nyandoro, for instance? He was perhaps a rather extreme example: small in stature with a big voice which he tended to use incessantly, declaiming against the sins of the white man and making hair-raising threats of revolutionary change; ebullient, voluble — just the sort of person who, if someone you were trying to induce to help bridge the black–white racial gap were to encounter in full spate, would surely be bound to have the effect of sending him or her scurrying off hurriedly in the opposite direction. Except for one thing: the fact that it generally ended up in a laugh.

The job we were asked to do for the Southern Rhodesia African Association early in 1951 put us in touch with Africans of a different kind. It was a bit of an oddity. In fact I have sometimes thought since that it was probably the first and last thing of its kind. The SRAA had apparently been in existence since 1919, and with the benevolent approval of the Native Department at any rate until 1949 (when its annual conference was opened by the Governor); and the voice it tried to speak with was evidently the voice of traditional, rural, black Rhodesia, and in particular the Chiefs who were said to be all honorary members. The situation of the Chiefs, as seen by Powys Jones, was described in his lecture and summarised in the Bulletin —

> . . . Tribal organisation in SR, which had at no time been very developed amongst the Mashona and been considerably disrupted by the incursions of the Matabele, was further weakened by the defeat of Lobengula in 1893 and the action to put down the Matabele and

Mashona rebellions in 1896. The power of the Chiefs was thus largely broken, and it became necessary to transfer their powers of direct administration to European officials. Thus developed the system known as 'direct rule' in distinction to that known as 'indirect rule', which has been the policy in West Africa and parts of East Africa. In practice, this system resulted in the Native Commissioners becoming 'king pins' of Native administration. The chiefs and headmen were used as a medium in the administration, but the real power was vested in the Native Commissioner . . .

With the advance of the African along the road to civilisation, the present tendency is to restore more power to the Chiefs, but with a democratic leavening. This is being done through the medium of Native Councils, which in effect are a form of local government. The policy now is to foster the desire for participation in local and territorial government, and to train both Chiefs and people, through a system of locally elected Native Councils, to play an effective part in their own local government and thus fit themselves for closer participation in central government as they qualify for it.

But the traditional method of selection of Chiefs, combined with a decreasing death rate, had resulted in a high proportion being old and uneducated — as well as dependent on the Government for their meagre salaries — and our inclination was to discount them as a significant influence in the politics of the future. The extent to which the Native Department would in fact allow the Chief-in-Council to supersede the power of the Native Commissioner, as envisaged by Powys Jones, seemed highly questionable, and in any event it seemed certain that in a Rhodesia exposed to modernity the traditional system must give way to an electoral one sooner rather than later.

But early in 1951 the tension which was about to develop between the extremes of traditional, rural conservatism and radical, urban nationalism had hardly begun, and the time when the Rhodesian Front Government would abuse the Chiefs by making them pawns in the game of Divide and Rule was still far off. And there were still some Chiefs who were notably progressive and independent-minded — most notably Chief Mangwende who in addition had an educated and progressive wife. He was later to be deposed by the Government following disturbances in the Mangwende Reserve in 1960, and the Report of a Commission appointed to enquire into the disturbances contains a perceptive and sensitive account of the conflict involved for someone in his position in trying to reconcile the obligation to the Administration as Chief with his loyalty to his people. (It must surely be a rarity for a 'blue book'. It was in fact written by Hans Holleman as one of the members of the Commission, and later repeated without major change in his book *Chief, Council and Commissioner;* and it seems to me to demonstrate how the objectivity normally to be expected from a professional anthropologist can, paradoxically, be combined with the personal insight and feel for language more to be expected from a creative novelist. A combination perhaps only possible for someone as prone as Hans to mental anguish — but that is another story.)

Mangwende took an active part as a member of the SRAA in the preparation of the evidence for the Select Committee on the Native Land Husbandry Bill, including the decision to engage professional lawyers instead of relying on officials for advice — a decision which, quaintly enough, was probably prompted by advice from Dendy Young, soon to become a right-wing opponent of the United Party establishment. Prior to the request to Scanlen & Holderness to act, the National Affairs Executive had been asked to hear Mangwende's representatives and some other Africans on the subject of the Bill and Dendy, with inside information as an MP of the governing party, had told them that the Bill was necessary and they had little hope of making much change in it, and he had added as an afterthought 'But if you want to try to do something about it why not try making representations to your Member of Parliament?' It was quite a revolutionary suggestion at the time.

The Bill was a formidable affair comprising more than 60 clauses and as much as any statute difficult for a layman to feel at home with, even if fully versed in English. A Government memorandum accompanying it explained —

> There is little doubt that the native reserves are rapidly deteriorating owing to over-population, over-stocking, bad methods of agriculture and the misuse of their natural resources. The same deterioration is occurring in other areas predominantly occupied and used by natives.
>
> The object of the Bill is to put a check to this process of deterioration by providing for the gradual allocation of land for farming in the native reserves and other native areas and for the control of farming in such reserves and other areas.

The clauses dealing with 'Good Farming Practice' started with one listing a whole series of things which the Minister of Native Affairs would have the power to make regulations about. This was typical of legislation originating in the Native Department and it was anathema to any lawyers, and especially Pat, who had taken seriously the warning given by Lord Hewart in *The New Despotism* against the tendency of modern legislatures to evade their duty to the man in the street, and reduce the power of the Courts, by handing over to the Executive wide discretionary powers to make law by Regulation. But that sort of objection would undoubtedly be considered academic in the face of the Native Department's argument that flexibility was necessary because conditions differed in different Reserves. Anyway, the concern of Africans about the Bill centred not so much on that as on the, to them, overwhelmingly important aspect of land rights.

The new approach to land tenure embodied in the Bill was largely the brain child, not of officials of the typical Native Commissioner mould, but of one who was more like a bright, backroom boy of the Department, Arthur Pendered, a tautly-strung man of high intelligence with appearance to match — a little like a racehorse. Our legal work on the Bill was time-consuming and not exactly routine. The initial sessions were with a sort of committee comprising Isaac Samuriwo and some sage looking characters in from the country. Samuriwo came from a family which had some claim to being in the line of chieftainship in one of the Reserves, and himself had something of the look of the heavyweight autocrat about him. But his actual authority was derived from being one of the early successful African businessmen. He had made quite a lot of money operating buses into the Reserves, and was generous with his business know-how helping African organisations — in some of which he was to become associated with highly educated people like Stanlake Samkange. He himself had had very little formal education, but he had an engaging sense of humour and would sometimes pass off the lack of education by assuming the role of comic or buffoon. If he agreed with what was going on he would signify assent with a deep, bass grunt of approval; but his English was sometimes almost impossible to follow. The actual Chief, Mangwende, who appeared personally at one or two of the briefing sessions, was of a different mould: in appearance a little like Charles Chaplin off the screen and in personality much more complex and introverted than someone like Samuriwo. But of the briefing committee Samuriwo was the most proficient in English, and himself had to interpret some of the time, and so a lot of time was consumed getting at what they really wanted to say about the Bill. And having eventually got something on paper which seemed to be agreed by the committee, the next step was to put it before what was really more of a public meeting.

In the grounds of Runyararo (again made available by Barbara Tredgold) upwards of a hundred Africans assembled, including a number of Chiefs and Councillors and Headmen; and there under the sky I would present what had been drafted, and it would be interpreted, thoroughly considered and debated, unhurriedly and with frequent striking imagery in the speeches. And then there would be redrafting for discussion with the committee; and eventually we ended up with a Memorandum — eighteen pages of it nicely typed in double spacing and easy to read, signed by 'I.H. Samuriwo' as Vice-President and bearing the rubber stamp (considered at least as valid as a signature) of Z.A. Chirimuta, President of the Southern Rhodesia African Association.

What the Memorandum did was to set out in the second part of it a series of specific recommendations classified as 'Recommendations Which Do Not Involve Amendments to the Bill but do Involve Other Action Being Taken', 'Recommendations Which Involve Additions to the Bill' and 'Recommendations Which Involve Amendments to the Bill'; and these were preceded in the first half by a careful exposition of the reasoning leading up to them. The following are illustrative extracts from the first half:

> . . . The two general principles which we think are of the greatest importance are the following:
>
> (a) That the problem of tenure in the reserves should be considered in relation to the general problem of tenure as a whole.
>
> (b) That it is essential to secure the positive co-operation of the Native people in a measure of this kind.
>
> THE GENERAL PROBLEM OF TENURE.
>
> . . . The reasoning behind the provisions of the Bill regarding grazing and farming permits is as follows:
>
> (a) In the Native Reserves there is a certain maximum capacity of the land for pastoral and arable farming, and if the land is made to work beyond this capacity it will be destroyed.
>
> (b) Already in some areas the land is being made to carry more than its maximum. In other areas it is relatively underpopulated.
>
> (c) All Natives are by law allowed to share in the communal tenure in the reserves, but the Native population is increasing rapidly, and if the process of dividing up the land amongst them continues indefinitely we will reach a state where nobody has an economic holding and all the land will be over used — the same situation which has arisen in the Union where some of the land has become progressively divided up and the 'poor white' problem has resulted.
>
> (d) We will therefore confine the right to share the farming land in the reserves, in the first instance, to those natives who are now living. We will assess the maximum capacity of each area in head of cattle and arable acreage and divide it by the number of qualified applicants for the area. This will provide a basis for permits to be issued to the applicants. If the resulting number of cattle and acres in one area works out to be small we will give the right to move to another area where there is less pressure.

(e) We will impose on a permit holder the obligation to farm properly and contribute labour for communal purposes, and if he does not comply he should not hold a permit.

... We appreciate the logic of this argument ... but we believe the following to be economic facts:

(a) With increasing development in every country a decreasing proportion of the population is employed on the land, and in Southern Rhodesia it is already obvious that not all Natives can be farmers. In spite of this, very few Natives abandon the reserves altogether because they cannot give their families a sufficient guarantee of security in the towns. They therefore leave their wives and children in the reserves, which is detrimental to Native society both in the reserves and in the towns. It is also detrimental to output in industry. (We know of several tragic examples of Natives who have in effect given up their rights in the reserves to live permanently in the town and who after many years have been turned out of their homes for committing an isolated offence. This gives rise to a constant fear on the part of others similarly placed.)

(b) Thus, although there are many Natives who would be prepared to live with their families in the town, when the Bill becomes law every qualified native, knowing it will be his last chance of obtaining some form of secure tenure for his family, will apply for farming rights. The result will be a greater pressure on the reserves than there need be.

Those natives who are not qualified to apply — including, of course, future generations — will lose altogether their chance of getting farming rights in the reserve, as well as those who do not happen to be exercising farming rights when the Bill comes into force and whose applications are turned down ...

... Our main point here is that the Bill attempts to deal with one half of a problem which is indivisible, and we pray that the Select Committee will bring to the notice of Parliament *the vital necessity for providing some satisfactory form of tenure for the natives employed in the European towns* ...

SECURING CO-OPERATION

... If the Select Committee could see into the minds of the Native people they would see that many are afraid that a measure of this kind, coming as it does at the same time as ... the increase in the franchise qualification, may be intended to bring all natives under a more autocratic authority and reduce all their holdings to an equal minimum ... They also fear that the intention may be to abandon the idea behind the demonstrator system — of improving farming by education, example and persuasion — and to substitute a system of punishments under which people may suffer because they are too ignorant to understand what is required of them.

They are afraid, as Europeans are, of officials having too much power over them, and the Bill as it stands puts a great many new powers into the hands of the Native Commissioner who already has extensive powers, both administrative and judicial. On the other hand we realise that many Native Commissioners feel individuals are often too slow to take up suggested improvements, and sometimes that they are obstructionist. We fear, therefore, that there is a real danger of the growth of antagonism between Natives and European 'authority'.

. . . To meet these difficulties we think that two principles are important. The first is that, to the maximum extent possible, in the Bill and in practice, the Native people themselves should be brought in on the administration of the measure. Hence our recommendation that native representatives should sit on the Board of Assessors mentioned in paragraph 8 of this Memorandum, and the many recommendations in Part III to the effect that the Chief-in-Council should be the basic unit for administering the Bill . . .

We realise that local government amongst natives will have to be developed a great deal for this to be generally practicable. But the main provisions of the Bill will take a long time to put into effect and we believe that local government can and must be developed sufficiently in the meantime . . . We think . . . that there should be a Local Government College where natives (and especially the secretaries to Councils) can do courses of instruction in local government; that the Native Commissioner should be the friend and adviser of the Native Council, but not Chairman; that native demonstrators should be attached to the Councils and the land development officers should be in the position of advisers to them. We feel that what is needed is the immediate appointment of a body (to be referred to in this Memorandum as the 'Local Government Board of Enquiry') to go into the whole question of local government in the reserves with a view to making it really effective by the time the main provisions of the Bill come into force, and that the Bill must be administered through the local government bodies . . .

. . . The second principle concerning co-operation is that the 'demonstrator system' should be continually and greatly extended . . .

When the Memorandum was finished and accepted I felt it was about the best that we, as lawyers, could do for our clients, but I was under no illusion about what it had cost them in heart-searching and anguish to settle on the approach embodied in it. Their initial reaction to the Bill had been simply to reject the tenure proposals in toto, and there was more justification for this than either we, or I believe Arthur Pendered himself, appreciated at the time. As Hans Holleman was later to point out in his book the extent to which 'it ignored the very basis of customary land rights' was not fully appreciated, either in the design of the Act or in the application of it afterwards. But what I had to say to our clients about the Bill already drawn up and about to be presented to Parliament was 'Look. I think you can take it as certain that something more or less like this Bill is going to be passed by Parliament. You have two alternatives: to say you think the whole thing is misconceived, and leave it at that, in which case you will have no influence on the shaping of it; or to imagine yourself one of the MPs who has to decide what to do about it and understand the arguments which will be put to him by the Minister as to why the Bill is necessary — arguments which will have been put to him by civil servants he regards as experts — and then see if you can make a convincing case for the Bill to be changed.' They decided this was what they would have to do. I knew the arguments very well, as a result of being in touch with Arthur Pendered through the National Affairs Association, and kept having to repeat it, in the role of Devil's Advocate, in the course of the consultations; and it seemed right to put it in at the beginning of the Memorandum so as to leave no doubt in the minds of the Select Committee that we knew what we were talking about. But it was a hard and self-denying thing for the clients to accept. After all, it would have been quite easy to resort to the short-term argument — that the problem could be resolved by simply releasing vast tracts of land which had been allocated to the 'European Area' under the Land Apportionment Act, and remained unused or neglected.

My own belief was that Arthur Pendered's reasoning was basically right, and it was right that there should be a change in the system of tenure at this stage to prevent a progressive fragmentation of land holdings provided that the other reforms specified in the memorandum were made simultaneously. But was it right that conclusions like that on my part should influence my attitude as legal adviser or draftsman in dealing with a matter of this kind? Was it right that I should have acted as Devil's Advocate in the way I had done? It began to be clear to me how much, if you found yourself acting as draftsman in this kind of matter where no hard and fast legal principles were involved, you inevitably found yourself with a power and influence which you could exercise responsibly or otherwise. (And it was something which I kept being made aware of as time went on, and in other situations — even drafting a mundane business agreement between companies over some deal they were in the process of concluding. If you did the job responsibly the very process of defining what they were agreeing upon would, paradoxically, result in their hardly ever having to look at the agreement again!) If you really tried to understand what the people concerned were feeling you could have extraordinary influence as a sort of catalyst. But once you had put something on paper which could be said to have been broadly agreed everyone was substantially stuck with it, even though it was a defective expression of what they felt. And if you had to start with someone else's draft it imposed frustrating limits on what you could do.

Anyway, the next step on the Native Land Husbandry Bill was to present the 'evidence' in the Memorandum to the Select Committee, and what one had to be aware of here was the probable impact that the Memorandum would have had on the members when they read it. 'What! Elaborate phraseology like this from a body of mainly rural Natives? Words put in their mouth by the white lawyer acting for them? His ideas, not theirs?' So we decided to have quite a large body present at the hearing, comprising the kind of really rural and mostly traditional people who had been involved in the consultations and, with the interpreter, to take them through the Memorandum so as to give the Select Committee the opportunity to question any of them at each stage. And that seemed to work well enough. I particularly remember one occasion when the questions from the Committee — and specifically the Minister of Native Affairs who was Chairman — were obviously prompted by the suspicion that this was not really the voice of tribal people but the voice of the 'clever boys' in the town; and the reply 'The people in the towns are our children, and have our confidence'.

The members of the Committee were courteous enough, but as the hearing went on one realised that, whatever amendments to the Bill they decided upon, the chances of their doing anything effective about the important proposals in our Memorandum, which related to simultaneous action being taken and most essentially the provision of security of land tenure for Africans in the towns, were remote if not negligible. For recommendations of that kind, they could say to themselves, were not really within their terms of reference, were they?

In the event the Select Committee did make a number of amendments to the Bill, and came up with a new one embodying them. Some were in line with what we had recommended, and so it was possible to say that the effort had had some effect. But when you worked it out there was not so much in them, and as regards our important contentions about other action that ought to be taken at the same time there was no evidence that we had made any headway. So was it worth it? Certainly not, from a business point of view. Compared with whites they had so little money, these clients, that when it came to submitting an account I found myself incapable of charging more than a nominal amount — barely sufficient, come to think of it, to cover the cost of typing and stationery. Could that have been wrong in principle, putting professional detachment in question? I think not, because it only happened after the event.

But was it possible to reconcile charging next to nothing in cases like this with one's duty to one's colleagues in the firm? While Jim had kept it going single-handed for some member of the family to come into after the war it was hardly the kind of thing he would have been expecting. And there were now in 1951 others whom we had got to join us, or would soon be joining us, as partners or partners-to-be in the firm: Peter Wigg (Rhodesian born, educated at Plumtree and Rhodes, war-experienced in North Africa and Italy, and whose wife, incidentally, was actually a third or fourth generation Rhodesian, descendant of one of the first missionaries at Hope Fountain), and Basil Hone (youngest of the Hone family, grandson of Sir Thomas Scanlen, recently down from Oxford with a good degree, a half blue for boxing and some flying experience), John ('Ian') McGraw (Rhodesian born, Rhodes Scholar, Capetown University and Balliol), and Anthony Hardy (Rhodesian born, Oxford graduate), and Jack Bennett (Beira born of British parents, graduate of Rhodes), and 'Dick' (W.H.) Turpin (from the Eastern Cape and Capetown graduate). Their future and interests were intricately bound up with the progress of the firm. Could one reconcile doing all this non-paying work with its interests and theirs? What about our competitive position relative to contemporaries who were not dabbling in this kind of thing and more securely placed in other long established firms? But whenever one expressed this kind of anguish to these colleagues the reaction of all of them, including Jim, was always 'If you feel that's the right thing to do, that's all right with us. You must go ahead and do it'.

We could hardly claim success for the effort on behalf of the Southern Rhodesia African Association, or for the experiment outside office time with the lectures at Harare which also took place during the first half of 1951. And yet in a sense both experiences were extraordinarily fruitful. By the time they were over we felt we had begun to establish a powerful bond of trust with Africans who would in various ways have a significant place in the politics of the future, and that we were now able to see and understand what the picture looked like seen through their eyes — at any rate while we were with them, and however much it might fade when we were not. And it was a striking phenomenon: that it did tend to fade almost as soon as you got back into the white orbit. And that in turn was evidence of another phenomenon: that it was quite impossible to explain what the picture was like to a fellow white, at second hand. The only way for him to see it was by being in first hand contact with them.

The lesson from the SR African Association's experiment in the use of the constitutional method seemed to be that you could not expect to get very far by persuasion, however strong your plea or courteous the attitude of the MP's receiving it, without voting power to supplement the strength of your argument.

CHAPTER 8

Design for Federation, 1951–1952

In mid-July ·1951 the Report was published of the officials who had been appointed the previous November to make a further examination of the question of some form of closer association between Southern Rhodesia, Northern Rhodesia and Nyasaland (official title *Report of the Conference on Closer Association in Central Africa*); and that was the beginning of a process which ended with the formal bringing into being in 1953 of a peculiar form of federation between the three territories which came to be called the Federation of Rhodesia and Nyasaland.

In essence what the officials visualised was that the existing governments of the three territories would continue in force, each with continuing authority in its own area; but they would all hand over, to be exercised by a new Federal Government over the area as a whole, certain functions such as general economic development, external trade, external affairs, defence, immigration, railways, civil aviation and trunk roads, electricity supply and distribution, broadcasting and higher education. And they visualised that the Federal Government, which would have a Governor-General and its own civil service, would consist of a Cabinet of about six Ministers drawn from a Legislature or Parliament of quite a peculiar kind. It would be a single-chamber Legislature consisting of a Speaker and 35 Members, of whom 17 would come from Southern Rhodesia, 11 from Northern Rhodesia and 7 from Nyasaland; and 9 of these thirty-five Members (three from each Territory) would be Members specially chosen to represent African interests. One of the nine would be a Minister — the Minister for African Interests — appointed by the Governor-General at his discretion and not, like other Ministers, as a nominee of the Prime Minister. There would also be, outside Parliament, a body called The African Affairs Board which would act as a watchdog for legislation which it considered to be detrimental to African interests, and would have the power to cause it to be held over for possible veto by the United Kingdom Government.

The Report was accompanied by a Geographical, Historical and Economic Survey, and a Comparative Survey of Native Policy in the three

Territories which had been prepared by the three Secretaries for Native Affairs working under the chairmanship of the Chief Secretary of the Central African Council. The Report said that the officials had considered earlier objections to closer association and had come to the conclusion that there had been significant changes during the twelve years since the Bledisloe Commission. In particular, on the question of differences in Native Policy as between the two northern Territories on the one hand and Soutnern Rhodesia on the other, it said that after considering the information and conclusions contained in the 'highly authoritative and objective' Comparative Survey of Native Policy —

> the most striking conclusion which we draw . . . is the degree of similarity between the policies of the three Governments rather than the degree of difference . . . Differences of policy still exist . . . but we believe that these differences, although important, relate largely to method and timing and that the ultimate objective of all three Governments is broadly the same, namely the economic, social and political advancement of the Africans in partnership with the Europeans.

Whatever might be said of possible trends in the development of Southern Rhodesian 'native policy', it seemed to us to be stretching credulity to the limit to describe it in its then state as one of 'economic, social and political advancement of the Africans in partnership with the Europeans'. The officials must surely have had some conflicts of conscience to resolve in arriving at that conclusion — and especially the Colonial Office officials, for whom the underlying principle had for years been that they were holding administrative power as trustees, to be handed over to the indigenous inhabitants when they became equipped to handle it; and particularly as the northern Territories were not even Colonies, like Southern Rhodesia, but Protectorates. Soon after the Report appeared I came across Andrew Strachan, collecting a drink at a party to celebrate some public occasion. He had been leader of the Southern Rhodesian delegation at the Conference, and I said 'You know that contention in the Report just isn't true, is it?' And I remember his reply, which was something like this: 'Well perhaps there are times when you have to assume something is true, in the hope that people will live up to it:'

What seemed to become clear was that, for some of the officials at least, the crucial consideration must have been the new situation brought about by the coming to power in the Union of South Africa of the Afrikaner Nationalists. It was this that must have made it seem justifiable to recommend the setting up of a federation, provided it would be of a special kind — leaving in the hands of the Territorial Governments 'all those matters that are most closely related to the life and ways of the African inhabitants such, for example, as African education, health, agriculture, land and settlement questions and native administration generally'; and having a special mechanism built into the Federal Government and Legislature in case 'action within even the proposed Federal field might at times impinge in some degree on African interests.' There would still be substantial differences between the three Territorial Governments in constitutional status: Southern Rhodesia being almost at the stage of 'Dominion Status', with very little power left in the hands of the Governor; Northern Rhodesia having a Legislative Council consisting partly of officials, partly elected Members and partly unofficial Members representing African interests, and substantial power still in the hands of its Governor; and Nyasaland with all the law-making power still in the hands of the Governor, obliged only to look for advice to a Legislative Council comprising official and unofficial Members all nominated and not elected. Under the federal scheme now proposed each of the Territorial Governments and the Federal Government were supposed to be independent of one another in their own fields, and to treat each other as equals irrespective of the differences between their stages of evolution on the Dominion Status scale. But there was no mechanism which could ensure that, and there was no option but to make an act of faith that Southern Rhodesia, as the most powerful, would play the game.

We got an early indication of the Southern Rhodesian governing Party's reaction to the proposals from a record passed on to us by one of our United Party friends of speeches delivered by Huggie and his Minister of Internal Affairs, Julian Greenfield, at a private meeting of the Matabeleland Executive of the Party held in Bulawayo on 16 July. Greenfield was a lawyer who had been born in Bulawayo and built up a practice at the Bulawayo Bar and, though of a younger generation than Huggie, had become a bit of an éminence grise in the Party. He was able, polite, ambitious, nervous but controlled, cautious, and with a speaking manner a little like a wooden puppet, the jaw moving and the rest more or less immobile. We knew of him as one of the original members of an inner group of the Party which called itself the 'Action Group' and had the reputation of being relatively young, radical and especially influential; but we came to think there was more of the calculating operator behind the scenes than the radical about Greenfield.

Greenfield saw all sorts of dangers in the proposals, and Huggie in his boyish way had evidently said 'You go on and give them the gloomy side and I will follow and try to cheer them up'. Greenfield disliked the idea of a federal as distinct from a straightforward, unitary form of government and thought the trouble was Britain's insistence on bringing in Nyasaland (the most backward of the three territories economically, with the fewest whites). He disliked the proposed Minister for African Interests — the 'cuckoo in the nest' as he had come to be labelled; and he disliked even more the proposed composition of the Federal Parliament. The machinery suggested in the Report for the election or appointment of the 35 Members in the first place and pending the adoption of a new franchise law by the Federal Parliament itself, would result in 14 of the seventeen Members from Southern Rhodesia and 8 of the eleven from Northern Rhodesia being elected by voters on the existing rolls (nearly all of them in practice Europeans) and all the rest of the Members being nominated by one or other of the Governors after certain consultation prescribed in the Report. Greenfield disliked this mixture of elected and nominated members in a single-chamber Legislature, and if you had to have it he thought the 13 nominated members (four of whom must be Africans according to the Report and others could be) was dangerously high relative to the 22 who would be elected by the existing registered voters.

Huggie's speech was a characteristic mixture of more or less diehard Rhodesianism, pragmatism based on exceptional experience and, half hidden behind a joking exterior, a kind of fundamental morality:

> As the Minister told you, one of the greatest difficulties in discussing this matter except in private is that whatever you say that might appeal to the Europeans in Southern Rhodesia or Northern Rhodesia would definitely send the natives in the northern Territories off in the opposite direction and give the Fabians, whom the Imperial Government are still frightened of, all the ammunition to prevent amalgamation taking place . . .

(Odd that the term 'Fabian' which, to someone like Pat signified the achievement of reform by the enlightened process of popular education and persuasion should, even for someone like Huggie, have become such a term of contempt in the white political vocabulary).

> . . . To deal with this cuckoo in the nest as he is called — the Minister of Native Affairs — he is an extraordinary invention because theoretically the Imperial Government have nothing to do with native affairs. And yet one must admit that indirectly they must play a very big part because if there is one thing in this Report that is absolutely definite is that they recommend a very close and powerful federation of the three territories and under the control of a European majority . . .
>
> What I visualise will happen in the Federal Government is that the Prime Minister will appoint his four or five Ministers and will appoint the other one too, and the formality would be asking the

Secretary of State to agree to it. If that were not the case this constitution could not work, and that is what I think must be intended, but too much fuss should not be attached to it . . . He will have an important function all the same because he is Chairman of the Native Affairs Board whose chief function is to look after the interests of the natives in the three territories with a view to getting the policy as a whole unified in so far as it is possible . . . How you are going to get over this difficulty of having nominated Members to start with I don't know although they might, as the Minister has pointed out, function as the old Irish Party did in the House of Commons and make things almost impossible. But why should they? I do not think there is any hope for us in Africa unless we can work with the natives and get them to realise that their friends are not six thousand miles away but here . . .

The most outstanding thing is the distinction between Europeans and natives, and it is going to be extremely difficult to bridge that gap when you realise one set of people represents one class and the other represents another class. We have to ask ourselves how you are going to obviate that. If you mean business you have to find an alternative, and at present I cannot think of any other method of getting the natives represented either in Northern Rhodesia or Nyasaland — and, let us be honest, really in Sourthern Rhodesia because they have a vote but how many are on the register? . . . I think that if we are going to accept any federal proposals we shall find that in the end we have to accept certain nominated members . . .

Huggie was not over-concerned about the powers of the proposed African Affairs Board to cause legislation 'detrimental to African interests' to be referred to the Secretary of State for possible veto by the United Kingdom Government, because of his experience with a similar kind of provision in the Southern Rhodesian constitution relating to 'differential' legislation.

All reserved legislation is agreed to long before anybody in this country or any other country sees it. We take it up with the Secretary of State before it is ever published . . . Once the Imperial Government have granted this constitution to a federal parliament they have lost all control . . . They have already lost all control as far as Southern Rhodesia is concerned by the constitution we have, and nobody knows that better than they do . . . I have argued with these people and I know. They say 'Your reservations mean nothing' and I have to admit it . . . I had a conversation with a well known gentleman named Mr Creech-Jones when he was a back bencher. One evening Mr Malcolm Macdonald asked me to attend a dinner at the House of Commons to meet my 'enemies', and he had them all there. We had a wonderful dinner party and we got on very well and the only one I could not shake was Creech-Jones. After dinner we were leaning against the mantelpiece in the little dining room. I remember it well. He said 'What happens if you insist on carrying out something which is reserved and we don't agree to it?' I said 'We just have a general election and go on and do it. You can't do anything'. He agreed. . . . I think at the worst, and supposing we could not get such modifications as we want, from what we have heard from Mr Greenfield it would be quite a difficult constitution to work as it is. I am one of those people who do not worry about that. Once you have a Parliament with Europeans in charge then you have made an enormous step forward and it ought to be within your capacity to modify it so that it will work. By that time the Africans will realise that whether they amalgamate or not it will not make much difference, although later if they amalgamate they will be much better off than having a small country running along on its own.

For Huggie the ultimate objective was still Amalgamation; and the experience of first-hand contact with 'modern' politically-articulate Africans was still something which had not come his way.

The Secretary of State for Commonwealth Relations, Patrick Gordon-Walker, was due to make a visit to Southern Rhodesia in September 1951, and in August I was asked by Chief Mangwende and Samuriwo to draw up a Memorandum for presentation to him expressing the views of the Southern Rhodesian African Association on the Officials' Report and their recommendations. It was like an extension of the proceedings we had had over the Native Land Husbandry Bill, trying to get at what they really wanted to say.

The reasons for rejecting the contention that 'partnership' was an underlying objective of Southern Rhodesian policy were many and obvious in their eyes, and the Memorandum mentioned a number of them: the land and land tenure situation; the fact that, immediately following the United Party's decision to maintain the common voters' roll — cited in the Comparative Survey of Native Policy as evidence of the underlying 'partnership' — a Bill to raise the franchise qualifications had been introduced 'for the express purpose, according to a statement by the Minister for Internal Affairs in the Legislative Assembly — of keeping Africans off the roll'; official hostility towards 'the younger Africans who have had experience in the towns and to whom the older people look for a lead'; and so on. It mentioned a recent warning 'to the native people' given by the Minister of Native Affairs 'against belonging to associations such as ours' and urging them 'to express their grievances through councils of chiefs which he proposed setting up'. (Evidently the SRAA effort on the Native Land Husbandry Bill had not pleased the Native Department; and Mangwende could hardly be expected to be popular for taking a leading part in preparing this memorandum for a Minister of the United Kingdom

Government). I wondered if a catalogue of objections to existing policy was all that was wanted, but the Memorandum ended up as something more than that. It concluded —

> In view of the above we are afraid of the motives for federation. We think that many Europeans look to federation primarily as a means of providing a bigger supply, and therefore cheaper, native labour, and others are afraid of the political advancement of the Africans in the North and want federation so as to be able to stop it; and we think that if federation took place Southern Rhodesia would be able to do so notwithstanding the safeguards contained in the Constitution. We have seen in the Union how, despite the safeguards in the Constitution, it has been possible to establish separate voters rolls and to take other action inconsistent with the spirit of the Constitution . . .

> We are afraid that, even though under a federation scheme native administration were left to the Territorial Governments, the functions of the Federal Government would nevertheless have a decisive influence on it, and we think that Southern Rhodesia's influence would prevail in the Federal Government. We approve of the principle of Africans and Europeans being on the same governing bodies and having access to each other's point of view, but we do not think that the machinery of the African Affairs Board and the Minister for African Interests would be able to prevent the Federal Government, led by Southern Rhodesia, from doing what it liked in the last resort. We think that the next step would be Dominion Status, and that the advances being made by Africans in the North would come to a standstill.

But the final paragraph left the door slightly open —

> We think the time will not be ripe for closer association until there is some real evidence of partnership in Southern Rhodesia's native policy, for example in regard to the economic colour bar, the qualification for the franchise, tenure in the towns and local government. Some evidence of the possibility of such a change would be provided if the Government showed signs of making use of African opinion to help in solving the problems underlying these matters.

I could not be totally certain that this was how they wanted it, but I think it was.

The African reaction to the proposals in the northern Territories, according to reports, was uncompromisingly hostile.

Gordon-Walker's visit to Southern Rhodesia corresponded with one being made to the northern territories by his Labour Government colleague James Griffiths, successor to Creech-Jones as Colonial Secretary, and those visits were followed by a Conference at the Victoria Falls held in the famous hotel which had been built in the early days (and with great good taste) by the Chartered Company. But at that stage the Labour Government fell from power in the United Kingdom, and whatever Griffiths and Gordon-Walker might have thought of the representations made to them ceased to be relevant. In the new Conservative Government Huggins and Welensky had powerful friends, and in April 1952 at a further Conference in London they were able to secure significant changes in the scheme as proposed in the officials' report; and the amended Constitution which emerged from the London Conference was, except for a few details, the one which came to be finally adopted a year later. The main changes that they achieved were the abolition of the 'cuckoo in the nest' Minister for African Interests and the conversion of the African Affairs Board from being a body of ten including officials outside Parliament to a standing committee of Parliament comprising six of the nine Members for African Interests.

———————————

As public opinion developed over the 1951–1952 period we got a pretty comprehensive view of it through our involvement with the National Affairs Association's weekly lunch-hour lectures and periodic public debates in white Salisbury, and with a series of monthly meetings arranged by a new body called the National Affairs Discussion Group to take place in black Salisbury — Harare — from September 1951 onwards. And an unexpected opportunity of getting to understand what was being discussed amongst rural Africans living on land remote from Salisbury opened up as a result of coming into contact with a remarkable newcomer to the mission scene called Guy Clutton-Brock.

The National Affairs platform at the Cathedral Hall had become fully established by this time. In fact a bit too much so in the eyes of some MP's when we arranged for lectures on the content of the Officials' Report on Closer Association to be presented by some of the officials themselves soon after its publication. That, some MP's thought, would be usurping the functions of Parliament. Parliament should hear about it first. So we had to get that part of the job done by members of the Executive. But later, lunch hour lectures on the federation issue were given by most of the leading protagonists, and the lunch-hour audience was to hear as a matter of course (though not always on the federation issue as such, which was a prohibited subject for some speakers) eminent visitors like Patrick Gordon-Walker and his successor Henry Hopkinson and, after their respective retirements as Prime Minister of Great Britain and Principal of the London School of Economics, Clement Attlee and Carr Saunders.

The National Affairs Discussion Group was a small phoenix risen from the ashes of the lecture programme we had tried to get going in Harare. The lectures had had to be called off, but the multi-racial committee which had come into being refused to die, and a new venture was decided upon: discussions introduced by a leading speaker instead of lectures, and the sponsorship of a new body, still connected with the National Affairs Association in its title and in having one of the members of its Executive nominated by the Association, but otherwise autonomous. Its first Executive was chaired by Aiden Mwamuka, with Jack Humphries as vice-chairman, and it attracted an active membership of about ninety comprised almost equally of Africans and non-Africans (mostly Europeans). It held monthly meetings and a high proportion of the membership were regular participants. The venue was a large classroom in the Harare West School. Discussion was uninhibited, and sometimes heated, but generally constructive; and at the conclusion of the discussion proper informal contacts would continue over coffee, sometimes late into the night.

Guy Clutton-Brock was based at St Faith's Mission about 120 miles from Salisbury beyond the small town of Rusape on the road to Umtali. I first met him early in 1951 when he came to Scanlen & Holderness about a legal problem concerning fencing on the common boundary of the Mission land and one of the neighbouring farms. He had the weatherbeaten look of someone totally involved with the land who pays no attention to what he wears, except that for this visit to town he had put on an old tweed jacket and tie — his only ones as we afterwards discovered. He had shaggy eyebrows, and a missing tooth because he could not be bothered with dentists, and a boyish smile. I suppose I would have guessed that his background included being at an English public school and Cambridge, but the striking thing was a sense of immediate familiarity and friendship with him and a total absence of any sanctimoniousness on his part as a missionary (if that was what he was). It was as if we had shared the no-bullshit atmosphere of war-time flying, and I think we probably had a beer together across Manica Road at the Posada Bar which still existed then (nostalgic survivor of the early days, with elaborately engraved mirror glass behind the bar like a classic London pub, but outside, a colonial-style verandah where in earlier days rickshaws had been used to wait to take home gentlemen in need at closing time).

But the feeling of being at home with Guy was something nearly everyone seemed to experience who came into first-hand contact with him; and we discovered that the job he and his wife, Molly, had in fact been doing during the war was living and working in one of the worst bombed areas of

London with the kind of young people to many of whom society and the police seemed natural enemies, and that they had enduring friendships with many of them. Guy had previously been Chief Probation Officer for the Metropolitan Area and, after the war, head of the Youth and Religious Section of the Control Commission in Germany for a while; and then he and Molly had retrained themselves in agriculture (Guy by working as a farm labourer) in order to help bring people into closer, touch with the land.

Guy talked about a co-operative and community development which had started at St Faith's, and after our meeting sent me a copy of a periodical report which he had prepared for the benefit of the people involved in the project and also to send to the donors of money for it which was being raised by friends and former associates of his and Molly's in England (amongst them a body called the African Development Trust, by-product of the Africa Bureau). Later came a copy of a twenty page document entitled 'Memorandum from St Faith's Mission Discussion Group on the Report of the Conference on Closer Association in Central Africa'. What seemed to be happening on St Faith's Mission land was something brand new: an experiment based on the principle of maximum participation by the people there in everything affecting their social and economic lives — food production, conservation of natural resources, community life, and even politics.

The twenty page memorandum was a highly articulate document which could only have been produced after detailed study of the Officials' Report and the two Surveys accompanying it. It took the general line that federation should be supported provided the principles of partnership were made a reality in Southern Rhodesia's native policy by the adoption of a number of reforms spelt out in the Memorandum. It was evidently a product of Guy Clutton-Brock's draftsmanship and embodied some of his philosophy, and one could easily have discounted it as comprising words put by him into the mouths of unsophisticated people; but it would have been wrong to do so, as I discovered on a visit to St Faith's to attend a conference arranged by the Discussion Group at the end of 1951.

St Faith's was a historic mission situated high above sea level on open sandveld broken here and there by picturesque kopjes (weathered granite brilliantly decked with lichen, tawny grass, beautiful indigenous bush) and verging on the increasingly granite-kopje landscape which led on to the Inyanga Mountains. The traditional centre of the Mission was marked by a plantation of old, towering gum trees, wide-girthed, tall and a little gloomy; and amongst them stood the old brick church, in more-or-less Gothic style, and the equally old brick homestead of the Priest-in-Charge; and nearby was the school. These had been the principal activities of the Mission over the years: religious services in the Church, and school education. Like a number of other missions of various denominations in various parts of the country, St Faith's had had allocated to it when it first started extensive lands where African families attending the Church and school could live, growing crops and keeping a few cattle, under simple tenancy arrangements; so that there had come to be villages — groups of small houses, round, with pole-and-dagga walls and thatched roofs. It was a hand-to-mouth kind of agriculture, wasteful of natural resources, and it had become more and more so as the population increased, and the men had tended to head for the towns to find work there, leaving their wives and children behind. It was this deteriorating situation which had led to the appointment of Guy as Agricultural Adviser to the Anglican Church and his installation at St Faith's, where the then Priest-in-Charge Donald Stowell was a pleasant, broad-minded man.

Some distance away, in an area which contained some ancient farm buildings and a barn-like old meeting hall, was the new development: a co-operative store and mill; a new, common farm intended to be also a demonstration farm applying and evolving methods most suitable for small scale agriculture; 'the C-B's house' — a couple of interleading rooms apparently open to all comers at all times, where Guy and Molly and their small daughter Sally lived with the minimum of luxury and on basically the same diet as the African villagers. Molly, a gentle and courageous person whose way of expressing herself was more telegraphic than Guy's, had learned a special physio-therapy technique for the treatment of paralysed, spastic, deformed and polio-affected children, and behind 'the C-B's house' was the first stage of a building later to become famous as the 'Mukuwapasi Clinic'. The farm manager was John Mutasa, a stocky, able and engaging character who had turned his back on the bright lights of Johannesburg to return to the country and take part in the revival; and at all levels the fee ing of belonging and being involved in the decision-making seemed evident. On the old mission land the villagers had begun to adopt better methods, and even to apply a new, selective-cutting procedure in the indigenous woodland which had been evolved by an enlightened white farmer called Willoughby.

One of the striking things about the St Faith's Discussion Group conference, held in the old meeting hall with people representative of all sections of the mission population as well as some visitors present, was the perceptiveness of the comments of some of the older villagers who, although their children were getting some schooling, had had little if any themselves. In Southern Rhodesia's two-worlds situation Africans had got into the habit of speaking with two voices, and this was the one usually reserved for discussion amongst themselves. The 'C-B's' seemed to have established a rare line of communication with both generations, and that must surely, we thought, be an invaluable asset in whatever attempt there was going to be to make a reality out of 'partnership'.

As the national debate progressed it became increasingly clear that a substantial majority of whites would vote in favour of federation. For them the economic argument in its favour would seem decisive. Southern Rhodesia with its area of 150,000 square miles now had a population of about 2 million of whom (according to the latest figures available at the time of the Officials' Report) 129,000 were whites (representing an increase of 55% over the last four years!) and about 9,000 were Coloureds and Asians, and it now had a national income of more than £73 million (representing an increase of 37% over three years); and with federation it would, in the field of operations of the Federal Government, find itself part of an area three times that size having a total population of 6 million, including a further 40,000 whites (36,000 in Northern Rhodesia and 4,000 in Nyasaland) and a further 8,000 Coloureds and Asians (3,000 in Northern Rhodesia and 5,000 in Nyasaland) and a total national income of more than £113 million, and vast additional untapped resources, including the copper and other mineral resources of Northern Rhodesia. It would make an impressive economic bloc, and most whites seemed to be confident that the business drive and expertise which had produced demonstrable results in Southern Rhodesia would surely come to prevail in the management of it, in government as well as in business.

As to the controversy about 'Native Policy' and the concept of 'partnership' which the Report seemed to regard as crucial, there were many different ways of looking at that. One thing nobody could really do with any plausibility was to reconcile the term 'partnership' with the kind of system the South Africans were after, designed to prevent blacks from ever sharing political power with whites. And for that reason a certain proportion of Southern Rhodesian whites, probably including a high proportion of those of Afrikaans origin, would be opposed to Federation whatever its economic charms. If it was important that the country should belong to a bigger economic grouping they would prefer it to be with South Africa, except that, for the English-speaking amongst them, that would mean being on the wrong side of the tide now running strongly in South Africa against English-speaking dominance in finance and business as symbolised by the Rand Club. A section of white opinion would be in favour of Southern Rhodesia remaining on its own and, as well as rabid right-wingers like Charles Olley, that would include most of the so-called Liberal Party and amongst them people like Stumbles and even, despite his significant position in the world of finance, Geoff Ellman-Brown.

But a fairly typical attitude of whites towards the question of black participation in politics was that it would have to come and should, provided it could come gradually. The Africans must first learn to handle political power in local government 'in their own areas', and then little by little the ones who had learned to be industrious and 'responsible' should be allowed to become registered as voters for Parliament. This approach was often allied to an idea about the creation of an 'African middle class' consisting of Africans who, through the skill and responsibility they had learned, would have come to own property and so have 'a stake in the country' and come to feel an identity of interests with whites and therefore to be no longer a threat to them as voters. Some whites who had this kind of approach seemed to feel it could be reconciled with the concept of partnership — especially if you looked to the analogy of partnership in business, starting as a junior partner and gradually working your way up. Whether in that context one was supposed to be identifying the whites as a group with the senior partner and the blacks as a group with the junior partner, or to be talking about individuals, was usually left rather vague.

Anyway, it seemed to become certain that a majority of whites would accept Federation, with some kind of 'partnership' as part of the package.

African opinion in Southern Rhodesia seemed remarkably reluctant to reject federation entirely. In April 1952, when the London Conference called by the new Conservative Government was to take place, Huggie managed to get two Africans to agree to go along to it with him, and one of them was Joshua Nkomo. We had not seen much of him because he was based in Bulawayo, but we knew of him as someone who had been an original member of a branch of the African National Congress movement which had come into existence earlier on in Southern Rhodesia and later become dormant, and who would be likely to be a dynamic leader if it, or something like it, should arise again. The other was Jasper Savanhu, one of the early journalists of African Newspapers whom we had got to know quite well, and who had, I think, over-influenced us in the direction of supposing that the most important element of the political problem was the frustration experienced by the as yet small group of educated and 'advanced' Africans as distinct from the growing resentment amongst Africans as a whole against racial discrimination.

We were quite surprised by Huggie's decision to extend the invitation to Savanhu and Nkomo, as well as by Nkomo's decision to accept it. The SRAA had earlier asked for African observers to be sent to the Conference and for the request to be put before the Prime Minister, but the Minister for Native Affairs — a job which Huggie had some time previously handed over to 'Ben' Fletcher — had interviewed them and said that the delegation to the Conference would be composed of members of the political parties represented in the Southern Rhodesian Parliament who would speak for the people as a whole. He had refused to listen to the argument that, however much in principle they might be representative of the people as a whole (because of the common voters' roll), they were not representative of Africans in practice. In a letter confirming the interview the Secretary for Native Affairs had said with suitable severity 'You should therefore explain to your Association . . . that the interests of all people, of whatever race or colour, will be adequately represented by the representatives chosen to attend the London talks.' However, Bevis Barker had apparently suggested to Huggie that that was a silly line to take, and Huggie had agreed. I had happened to be seeing him about something soon afterwards and he had said he had an African in mind and was looking for another; had I any ideas? And in a note which I wrote to him after thinking about it I had said incidentally —

> I can think of several Africans who I am confident will — if they come to feel Europeans really want their co-operation — have a lot to give. What I cannot guarantee is that in these circumstances and at this stage they would do what you want, which I gather is to express an unqualified and well reasoned conviction that federation is the thing. I think they would probably say — with a number of Europeans — 'if we could feel that the temper of the Europeans is such as to make a living reality of the partnership principle which turns out to be the principle behind Huggins' policy then we would be entirely in favour of federation'. And I can't think of one African I know who *might* not feel it his bounden duty to his people to use a rare opportunity like this as an opportunity of expressing their *misgivings* on that score. The occasion would be a terrible tight-rope for most of them — stretched between real desire for co-operation and the fear of being played for suckers. (Incidentally I don't know a single African, even among the more sophisticated, who is even slightly infected with the doctrinaire revolutionary attitude to which the left wing in Europe were driven by the beginning of this century). . . .

In the note I mentioned Gideon Mhlanga as someone Huggie might think of approaching, but added the caution that over the last three years I gathered his 'optimism about racial co-operation has decreased'.

After the London Conference and the changes in the federation proposals made there at the instance of the Southern Rhodesian delegates, and after publication of the kind of arguments subsequently used by politicians, from Huggie downwards, to persuade the Southern Rhodesian voters (who for practical purposes would all be whites) to vote in favour at the promised referendum, it was out of the question for any African leader like Joshua Nkomo to do other than oppose Federation. But even then one felt it was a kind of conditional rejection — conditional on African suspicions being confirmed that the 'partnership' which the whites were supposed to be accepting was hypocritical and a fraud. Even then the possibility seemed to exist of the rejection being withdrawn if it should turn out to be otherwise.

CHAPTER 9

Multi-Racial Adventure, 1953

During the first half of 1953 a major attempt at defining a genuine policy of partnership was embarked on by a multi-racial collection of people from a variety of backgrounds; and in July the Interracial Association of Southern Rhodesia was launched to continue the work and bring what influence it could to bear in getting agreed policies implemented.

Of the people originally involved some (like Pat and myself) were from the National Affairs Association/National Affairs Discussion Group milieu, some belonged to or were in touch with the Clutton Brock/St Faith's Discussion Group venture (including a number of the more radical Africans), and some (specifically Edward Harben, Charles Mzingeli, Phyllis Loveridge and Nathan Zelter) were former members of the old Southern Rhodesia Labour Party which had taken a beating at the 1946 Election and since petered out. Pat and I were invited by 'Bloggy' Harben to a meeting at his house with some of his former SRLP colleagues and an enlightened and impressive lady from Marandellas, Mrs McLintock, and two contrasting young men whose names had become familiar recently as authors of progressive letters to the paper about politics: Fred Lacey (spontaneous and generous chap, English working class and proud of it, war-time aircraft engineer in the RAF and now proprietor of a small bicycle business, social democrat of the solid English kind), and Brian Cole (small statured, shyish schoolmaster, faithful Roman Catholic).

Bloggy Harben's mildly socialist approach when he stood as a candidate at the 1946 Election had resulted in a bit of a smear campaign of the McCarthyist kind against him, and he had never quite got over it; but the situation was now so critical, he felt, that he must do whatever he could about it even if it meant only trying to get others more acceptable to the electorate to take some action. What could be done? It was no good looking to the United Party, was it? There was Huggie, but he was just not in touch with current African opinion; and there was a promising newcomer like Garfield Todd. But the Party as a whole was hardly distinguishable from the United Party in South Africa which, by trying to be all things to all white men, had ended up laying out the red carpet (well, not exactly red) for the Afrikaner nationalists. The SRLP had tried and failed. Could the National Affairs Association do something about it?

What emerged from the meeting was the proposition that, if the kind of reforms we had in mind were ever to be brought about, it would only be through the emergence of a new political movement, within or beyond the governing party, relying for its influence on clear-cut principles and policies rather than individuals; and the best we could do about it would be to try to formulate a statement or declaration specifying the reforms we considered essential and the reasons for them and the principles behind our thinking. I undertook to try to produce a first draft to get the discussion going. Elspeth and I had had our first long holiday since the war earlier in the year and spent it in England, and I felt quite strong and with some time free from office commitments coming up over Christmas and the New Year. A sub-committee was appointed comprising, as well as Phyllis Loveridge, Cole and myself — Nathan Zelter; and that, we realised, would be a problem. Zelter was of Hungarian origin; must have arrived in Rhodesia about the time Pat and I had left school and gone to Rhodes, and since then had been a staunch supporter of all the more left-inclined intellectual movements. When you got to know him you found him to be a generous, innocent sort of chap; but he still spoke with a fairly strong accent and much of the doctrinaire terminology of the Central European socialist, and took life very seriously indeed. To any rugger-playing white Rhodesian, and probably the whole of the Special Branch, he would appear dangerously communist. But between him and Charles Mzingeli there seemed to be a genuine friendship and mutual respect, and not many other whites possessed a relationship of that kind in politics.

A few days after the meeting at Bloggy Harben's another one took place, comprising National Affairs Discussion Group people and Guy Clutton-Brock and one or two other members of the St Faith's Discussion Group who were in Salisbury at the time; and that meeting asked itself similar questions and came to a similar conclusion, and appointed a sub-committee consisting of Guy, Aiden Mwamuka, Lawrence Vambe and myself to produce the draft document which was to be the basis for further meetings. And so it turned out that the cockshy which I was to produce came to serve both purposes.

In the course of tackling the preliminary draft a specification for the kind of document we should be aiming at seemed to formulate itself. First, the political conclusions embodied in it must rely for their validity, partly at least, on their having been arrived at by agreement, after thorough consideration and discussion, between people representative of the various sections of the population, and in particular the two main racial groups, Europeans and Africans. Secondly, the essential reasons for proposing each course of political action recommended in the document must be stated, so that any reader would in effect be compelled, before rejecting a proposal, to think carefully about it and to state his reasons for rejecting it. Third, the drafting and presentation must be such as to give a reader no excuse for disregarding or misunderstanding it because of long-windedness or ambiguity or messy or unattractive layout. Fourthly, despite being clear-cut, the document must not purport to be final; it must remain a draft open to further debate and discussion. As important as its conclusions must be its power to attract participation in the process of reaching agreement.

Work on the document — drafting, amending, redrafting, typing, making copies, getting them to the members of the sub-committees, discussing, amending, circulating to the wider groups — became a paramount commitment of both Elspeth and myself in the small but, as we thought, attractive little house which we had now had built for us amongst the rocks and tawny grass and msasa trees of a wonderful plot of land about five miles from the centre of Salisbury in Orange Grove Drive.

The two original groups merged and brought in several members of the small 'Coloured' and Asian communities to constitute an informal assembly of about thirty-five people to consider a draft document which had by this time come to be called 'Notes for Possible Non-Party Declaration on African Affairs in Southern Rhodesia to be Agreed by Liberal-Minded People of all Races'. Freddie Loveridge agreed to put a large classroom of the Harare West School at our disposal, and marathon meetings took place over several week-ends.

It was sometimes painfully slow going, and for unexpected reasons. The representatives of the Coloured community held strong and conflicting views which they seemed determined to express at length. For some the question of whether they should be referred to as 'Coloureds' or 'Eurafricans' was a burning issue. At first it seemed exasperating to have the time of the whole meeting taken up with this kind of debate; but then one came to see how it revealed another facet of the Rhodesian reality. Some of the Coloured community were, or saw themselves as, descendants of the Coloureds of the Cape who should identify themselves as much as possible with white society. Some were children — mostly illegitimate — of a black mother and a white father who either disowned them or took some responsibility for them clandestinely. In that case should you be ashamed of your black mother who had looked after you and brought you up, or should you be proud of being 'Eurafrican'?

The other small minority group, the Asians, contributed a powerful antidote to chips on the shoulder in the form of V.S. Naidoo. The Asian community were mostly traders and 'V.S.' (as he was generally known) was the schoolmaster who had the kind of special role as teacher, counsellor and friend which I believe the dominie once had amongst communities in Scotland. He was a big, dark, lovable man, deeply interested in Tagore and Ramakrishna and all the trends of contemporary philosophy concerned with the common element in the great religions, and had a pervasive sense of humour. He had been born in Natal in a community where Ghandi's leadership had first manifested itself, and had married a daughter of one of Ghandi's then colleagues, Sita, also a teacher who had a nice line in mild scandal and engaging appreciation of the idiosyncracies of Salisbury's various racial communities. (She would tell with wide-eyed animation of how, for example, an Indian child would come to school with a note asking for him to be excused for being late and signed with a firm's rubber stamp 'Ashabhai & Co' or 'Patel & Co). As a government servant and headmaster of one of the few schools for Asian and Coloured children in the country, V.S. was really at risk taking part in a political venture of this kind; but I remember his background influence as a kind of peace maker and personal friend being one of the special features of it, then and afterwards.

The main body of those present at the week-end meetings were of course 'Europeans' and Africans, excluding right-wing whites. At the white end of the scale it started with a National Affairs Executive member like Jack Humphries, and even a Native Commissioner (though hardly a typical one) Fitzpatrick, and extended through whites a bit more to the left like Pat and myself and at the other end of the scale, Zelter, and thence to blacks who found little difficulty in collaborating with whites, like the older-vintage journalist Jasper Savanhu and young schoolmaster, Chad Chipunza, to radical or potentially radical Africans like Leo Takawira, James Bassopo Moyo and Nyandoro. And that spread of opinion was sufficient to produce some fireworks. In a part of the draft document leading up to the statement of 'Basic Principles' there was a passage reading —

> Racial fear may mar the development of Southern Rhodesia. The Europeans and Africans, who form the majority of the population, had hardly mixed until about sixty years ago when the Europeans first came here. African civilisation had a well developed family and tribal system but had been little exposed to contact with the rest of the world, and it was still primitive in other spheres such as industry, commerce and literature. The Europeans brought with them the

113

knowledge and skills of European civilisation, and took control of the development of the country. The danger is that the Europeans who hold the power may abuse it, by exploiting the African and attempting to make their civilisation exclusive to themselves. The Africans who are in the majority, may expend their energy in opposition to the Europeans instead of working constructively to acquire the gifts of their civilisation. The Europeans may become 'Herrenvolk' and the Africans 'Black Nationalists.'

Jack Humphries thought it was dishonest in the context to use the phrase 'African civilisation'. 'African culture', yes, but not 'civilisation'. That would merely make people think there was pandering by whites to blacks on our part, and not a genuine coming together on the basis of candour and no-bullshit. George Nyandoro's hackles erected themselves instantly; and I am not sure that the difference in approach as between people like him and people like Jack revealed by that part of the debate was ever really fully resolved. Fortunately it was much easier to reach agreement on less academic subjects and unnecessary deadlocks were avoided, partly by wise chairmanship on the part of Guy Clutton-Brock who had been elected to act in that capacity at the week-end meetings. And I believe it is true to say that the draft document which emerged out of those meetings did in effect define, as reliably as it was possible to do at the time, the then available common ground: the minimum reforms which you could expect a self-respecting, potential 'Black Nationalist' to accept as adequate and the most that you could realistically expect the potential 'Herrenvolk' to concede.

The proposed reforms were specific and limited. The first was to do with land and the provision of satisfactory residential areas for Africans in the towns and the conversion of business and industrial areas in the towns into multi-racial areas. The second was to do with the industrial colour bar and promoting the growth of responsible trade unions on a non-racial basis. The third was to do with the opening up of the common voters' roll and establishment of responsible local government in the African urban areas and Reserves; the fourth, with personal and official attitudes and the fifth with the social colour bar. The sixth was to do with differential legislation and reform of the pass laws and liquor law. The approach was diplomatic. For example, the proposals concerning land tenure in the towns would certainly necessitate making changes in the Land Apportionment Act but the document did not say, 'We advocate changes in the Land Apportionment Act'. To have done so would have been to invite many whites to reject the proposals without even studying them and many blacks to reject any proposed amendment of the Act in favour of total repeal. What the document did say about land will serve as a sample of its approach to the other proposed reforms as well:

THE MOVEMENT TO THE TOWNS

A. African Residential Areas:

The Problem:

19. One of the most pressing problems is that of 'urbanisation'. An industrial revolution is in progress. The establishment of industries by the Europeans has given rise to a mass movement of Africans into the towns for employment in those industries. This is very similar to the movement in England at the beginning of her industrial revolution which caused chaos enough. But the problem here is aggravated by the fact that hitherto most Africans have come in only for temporary periods as 'migrant' workers, leaving their families in the Reserves. The Africans have been on suffrance in the towns, living in 'compounds' or 'locations', their only claim to be there lying in the fact that they were serving the interests of the Europeans, and they have lacked the incentive to become steady, permanent workers in industry.

This system of migrant labour has been condemned by various authorities, including the Fagan Commission in the Union of South Africa, and some attempt has been made in Rhodesia to convert the compounds into proper townships. But the position is still extremely unsatisfactory.

Some Africans do live permanently with their families in the townships but there is little encouragement for them to do so:

The bulk of the inhabitants are still migrant workers temporarily released from family obligations and family discipline and without a social discipline to replace it.

Many of the women are 'temporary' or 'town' wives and the children are easy victims to delinquency.

There is acute insecurity of tenure: any lease can be terminated on a month's notice and the residents know that the authorities have nothing to lose by giving notice because there is an absolute shortage of housing and in any case rents are often sub-economic. The residents themselves bear no responsibility for the management and good order of the township except as members of an Advisory Board.

The results of such a system can be seen in the older African townships which exist in the South.

The position in the country is equally bad. The broken home presents a serious problem in the Reserves, where the 'real' wives and children are left for long periods. Agriculture suffers. The Native Land Husbandry Act, which was passed recently, adopts the principle that the land in the Reserves must not be split up beyond the point where holdings are economic, and that Africans must choose whether to be farmers or townsmen. But no African will willingly uproot his family from the Reserve and give up his rights there unless conditions in the town offer a prospect of a secure and respectable life.

Conclusions:

23. It is clear from all points of view — that of the African who wants to live a decent life, that of industry which requires a stabilised labour force, and that of peace and good order — that urbanisation of the African must be on the basis of permanently settled family units.

24. In the situation as it is this can only be done by providing special African residential areas which comply with the following essentials:

i. The areas must be *adequate in size* to allow for the increasing standard of living of the Africans in it, so that as individuals advance they can improve their residential circumstances just as Europeans do; and they must be planned to serve the real needs of a permanent community of human beings.

ii. *Secure tenure* must be available. Long leases have been discussed but they have proved an embarrassment in England when numbers of them have come to an end simultaneously and in Rhodesia they are seldom used. We consider freehold tenure the only satisfactory form.

iii. The areas must be *accessible to the place of work* of the inhabitants. The African must be able to travel daily between his place of work and his home. The fewer the areas the greater will be the distances from the places of work of some of the residents, and transport will have to be provided. Few people realise what the cost of adequate transport would be but a good idea is given by the fact that in other parts of the world, for economic reasons, the workers who can least afford transport live nearest to their work. In Rhodesia the heavy cost of transport would be a burden which the country would have to bear in the form of an increased cost of living. The logical solution is to have enough areas for each to be close enough to the part of the town it serves, but not so many that the areas will be too small for the provision of proper amenities. The Europeans must realise that if they conspire to prevent adequate areas being established *close* to places of work the country will suffer. If proper provision is made the townships will be law-abiding and respectable; if it is not they will be a menace however far away they are — as can be seen in Johannesburg. It is a worthless argument that Africans can be accommodated on employers' plots; for some it is suitable, but there is no security of tenure and therefore no basis for a settled labour force.

iv. There must be *responsible local government* on democratic lines and a spirit of civic responsibility in the townships, and we must get away as soon as possible from the system of running them primarily by means of officials of the European municipality. Only the inhabitants themselves can effectively control their own people and if we fail in this we will have the juvenile gangster element, out of control of its own parents and leaders which, we are informed, is largely responsible for the recent riots in the Union and the Mau Mau activities in Kenya.

B. BUSINESS PREMISES:

25. Under our present legislation it is illegal for an African to occupy business premises in the town, except in the 'African urban area'. This is based on the false assumption that the African urban area is both a residential and a business area, but it is in fact — and will remain — primarily residential and therefore only suitable for certain businesses. It is assumed that the African should serve the African, but during working hours the African consumer in fact makes his purchases in the commercial area of the town which is part of the 'European' area.

26. Although residential areas of a town may be separate we believe it is false to assume that business and industrial areas can be duplicated, and we consider that present legislation should be amended so as to leave what are at present European business and industrial areas open to the operation of normal economic forces, irrespective of race.

There were still many whites who found it really offensive to see a fellow white associating on other than master–and–servant terms with a black man — a defiance of the proper order of things, irresponsible, dangerous. We could not escape being aware of it whenever we found ourselves talking in the street with one of our new-found friends. So the spectacle of a body comprising about fourteen blacks and the same number of whites and about seven Coloureds and Asians assembling to fraternise over politics during almost the whole of Saturday and Sunday of successive week-ends was still

117

a strange enough one at the time to have excited a lot of comment and publicity if the meetings had been held in the middle of white Salisbury. Having school premises available across the way in Harare — the part of the town reserved for African occupation — enabled the meetings to proceed in reasonable privacy. But Charles Olley got wind of them, and wrote letters of protest to *The Rhodesia Herald* and to the Minister of Internal Affairs. For whites to discuss politics with blacks could only have the effect of creating 'mental turmoil, discontent and a sense of oppression' because 'even those with education and semi-education have never enjoyed the essential background which enables them to understand all that is involved in the onward march of civilisation'. It was preposterous that the meetings should be permitted to take place in Government-owned property.

The Minister of Internal Affairs referred the complaint to the Ministry of Native Affairs and, fortunately, we had a friend at court there in the person of the official who had been asked to comment. He (in common with others) had taken the complaint to relate to the regular meetings of the National Affairs Discussion Group, and one of his contentions had been that they were not harmful; on the contrary, they were doing a lot of good providing a safety valve for the expression of African grievances. Which was fair enough, but quaintly similar to the reason which George Nyandoro would give for decrying the Interracial Association when he was feeling in a hostile mood. He would refer to it as a 'cooling chamber'.

Soon afterwards we were informed by the Municipality's Director of Native Administration, George Hartley ('Colonel' George Hartley) that in terms of the new Salisbury Native Urban Areas Bye-Laws a whole series of permits were required for meetings attended by whites to take place in Harare. We had a look at the bye-laws and were appalled, not only by this but by many other aspects, and I felt it warranted exploiting the contact which I had established with Huggie, the Prime Minister. I said in a memo to him 'To read through the bye-laws is like reading rules for the management of a ghetto in Hitler's Germany and fills me with anxiety when I consider their possible effect on race feeling at the present time'. Huggie got the Minister of Native Affairs to twist Hartley's arm, and a letter from Hartley eventually arrived in effect excluding the meetings at the school from the operation of the bye-laws. It was not something he really had power to do and it must have gone against his grain. He was a big man with a rather squeaky voice, and he enjoyed wielding authority and holding the rank of colonel in the Territorial Army. He had fitted well into the niche of authoritarian Native Commissioner before moving from Government service to take up his present job with the Municipality; and a passage from his Report

118

for the year which was to appear later expresses his attitude to the embryo Interracial Association and illustrates what his style and psychology were like —

> To those who have studied the problems of race relations, and in the course of doing so have acquired some small experience of the approach thereto of the African in particular, the time would seem to be ripe for some plain speaking if a nucleus of persons of high principles are to avoid being led by their ideals to disillusionment merely from lack of better understanding of the psychological make-up of certain of the individuals with whom they seek to fraternise. While this may be due to the policy under which his every need is provided for him either by the employer or by benevolent Government, the majority of the Africans of this Colony are at present congenitally incapable of recognising the fact that they have any contribution to make if race relations here are not to deteriorate.

The Municipality of Bulawayo, too, had its Director of Native Administration, but he was a different kettle of fish — Hugh Ashton, former Rhodes Scholar and a highly civilised man.

By about May 1953 the statement of principles and policy — now entitled 'Draft Declaration on African Affairs' — seemed reasonably complete, and we decided to have a thousand copies printed, and to send them to people we thought would be interested, asking for their comments and asking also whether they thought a new Association should be formed to do work of this kind. One of the principal objects of an Association would be (in the inevitably earnest wording of a draft constitution which we also sent with the circular) —

> To examine the problems of the country's development and to work out solutions based on: (a) the aim that fullness of life, both spiritual and material, shall be available to all its inhabitants, and (b) the means of utilising fully the capacity of each individual to contribute, irrespective of race, creed or colour . . .

More than 300 people replied, some with unqualified approval, some expressing personal approval but doubt or pessimism about the reaction of the majority of whites, a few rejecting the Draft Declaration as being unrealistic or premature. I sent a copy to Huggie for information and got a note in reply saying 'I am interested in your work but for the present am keeping very quiet on the matter as the Europeans have accepted a lot lately and I must not give them an overdose until I have the Federal machine working'. (Coming across his note again recently reminded me of another aspect of white concern at that time: a growing suspicion in the wake of India's recently acquired independence that the Asian population of central Africa might be a potential instrument of subversion, and be suddenly expanded by further migration from India. Huggie's other brief comment in his note to me was 'Our Indians are for the most part all right but Nehru and his Indian Imperialism is a menace to Africa'; and this idea was said by some to have been an unpublished but influential motive for adopting Federation, since the only way of controlling immigration into the northern territories was to change their status as Protectorates by making them part of it).

The response of the people we had approached made the formation of a new Association inevitable, but we knew the whites amongst them were not a typical sample of the white electorate and that belonging to an inter-racial association would be something 'normal' white Rhodesians would tend to keep clear of as being cranky or too left-wing or 'likely to get into the wrong hands'. So it was important to get it launched under the best possible auspices; and we decided to approach Robbie Tredgold — Sir Robert, now Chief Justice of the Federation — to speak at the inaugural meeting and give it his blessing.

Robbie Tredgold was a Rhodesian of special quality. He had been born in Bulawayo at about the turn of the century, his father Attorney General in the Chartered Company administration and his mother a descendant of Robert Moffat. He was a Rhodes Scholar at Oxford immediately after the First World War, and during the Second World War was Minister of Justice and Defence until his resignation to become a Judge in 1943. There was probably no white Rhodesian who had a greater knowledge of and sense of identification with the country and its flora and fauna, and particularly the Matabeleland bush, and some of the unusual characters who lived in it. The shy English girl he married soon found herself familiar with it too, travelling to remote parts in a Ford half-ton truck and sleeping amongst the kopjes under the stars. But there was nothing rough about Robbie's style. He was a scholar and philosopher by nature and spoke a classical brand of English, and was universally respected as a person of absolute integrity. Differences in approach between him and his contemporaries, in regard to the Land Apportionment Act for example, had been a factor in his decision to leave politics for the bench, and I wondered how fair it was to ask him to risk further isolation by getting himself mixed up with a new inter-racial association. But he had no hesitation in agreeing to speak at the inaugural meeting, and persisted in it despite the publication, not long before it was due to take place, of damaging and misleading articles about it in *The Sunday Mail* (weekly counterpart of *The Herald*) and in a publication called *New Rhodesia*.

The inaugural meeting, held in the Cathedral Hall on a Saturday afternoon in July, seemed to go well. There were more than 300 present, including some 'normal'-seeming whites and even one leading member of the sporting establishment in the person of Bob Williams, God bless him. The Interracial Association of Southern Rhodesia was born; and for the next five years or so it was to provide a basis for multi-racial co-operation in a number of enterprises: further detailed investigations of some of the problems covered by the Draft Declaration, and in particular industrial relations and the franchise; evidence to Select Committees and other investigating bodies; monthly Forums leading to the formation of a Parliamentary Debating Society; the production of an original and attractive quarterly journal called *Concord*; innumerable committee meetings and periodic general meetings for members and guests. Its political approach was almost invariably logical and pragmatic rather than dogmatic or doctrinaire, but it could never quite escape the suspicion of being extremist in the minds of white voters. Simply being multi-racial at that stage placed it on the left of white politics, with nothing to be to the right of. We realised that was something it would have to live with as long as there were too few black voters to make it necessary for 'normal' whites to take them seriously as a factor in party politics.

CHAPTER 10

Politics Proper, 1953–1954

Not long after the launching of the Interracial Association on the fringe of politics a new prospect opened up of getting a foothold in politics proper — in Parliament itself.

The final version of the proposals for the Federation of Rhodesia and Nyasaland had been approved by Southern Rhodesian voters by nearly a two-thirds majority at the Referendum held in April 1953, and the implementation of the scheme was to begin in September with the setting up of an interim Federal Government, to be followed by a Federal general election in December to provide occupants for the seats in the first Federal Parliament. A new political party, called the Federal Party, had been set up to operate in the federal field with Huggie as its leader and Welensky its deputy-leader. This meant that Huggie would be appointed interim Prime Minister of the Federation, and a new leader of the Southern Rhodesian United Party would have to be chosen to replace him and to become Prime Minister of the Territorial Government of Southern Rhodesia. And there was to be a Territorial general election towards the end of January 1954 of members of the Southern Rhodesian Parliament, now to become the Territorial Parliament of Southern Rhodesia. There seemed little doubt that a lot of the members of the existing Southern Rhodesian Parliament who wanted to carry on in politics would choose to 'go Federal' and contest the seats allocated to Southern Rhodesia in the Federal Parliament, and that would leave a lot of seats in the Southern Rhodesian Parliament (where most of the business we were specially interested in would be conducted) open to newcomers. Should people of our way of thinking contest them? That was the question.

If we did decide to try for Parliament it looked as if we would have to do so as independents. A new opposition party had to come into existence with the intention of operating in both the Federal and Territorial fields and calling itself the 'Confederate Party'. It was a home for members of the old, mis-named Liberal Party most of whom had opposed federation because they wanted nothing to do with 'partnership', and a home also for the kind of new Rhodesians who saw in the country a last haven for white supremacists — and especially those lacking the qualification of Afrikaner origin now requisite for political advancement in South Africa. There was a fair number of blimpish ones in this category who had made their appearance after the war, from Tory circles in England or from other parts of the Empire where colonialism was on the wane; and Dendy Young of all people had accepted the leadership of the party. How could he have done it? Because of disgust at the two-faced attitude towards 'partnership' of some of his former colleagues in the United Party? Possibly, because he himself was an engagingly forthright fellow. Or because, as some scandalmongers had begun to suggest, he was really an Afrikaner at heart who had changed his name from de Jong? Anyway, the Confederate Party was clearly not for us. But neither was the United Party on its showing to date, and partly for the reason that the attitude to federation and 'partnership' which had been evidenced by many of its leading members in the course of the federation debate had seemed to us to be in fact shamefully two-faced.

But in August the picture suddenly started to look different. At a congress of the United Party held in Bulawayo Garfield Todd was elected to take Huggie's place as leader of the Party and hence, in effect, to be the interim Prime Minister of Southern Rhodesia. It seemed to us an astonishing decision when we heard about it, and greatly encouraging. Not that we thought it would necessarily lead to an immediate liberalisation of policy. There was nothing particularly radical that one could point to in the speeches which he had made in Parliament since coming into politics in 1946; and in some ways he had seemed to us to be still quite paternalist. But that was of little importance compared with the dynamic and refreshing quality which we had sensed in him ever since contacting him first to give one of the early lunch-hour lectures; and as time went on we were to get to know him and Grace, his wife, as close personal friends, and to learn more about their background.

They had both been born in New Zealand and completed their education there, Grace as a teacher and Garfield as a member of the first course of theological students to be trained in that country (and doing part-time jobs as a labourer in brickfields and the like to provide the money for it). It was the time of the great depression, and because of their combined qualifications they were chosen to be sent to Southern Rhodesia to take charge of the Mission there sponsored by the Church of Christ in New Zealand. They must have been in their early twenties and the Mission, Dadaya, was situated in remote bush in the rugged, low-rainfall, south-eastern part of the country; and they had spent the next twenty years or so working at it as missionaries. Then, about the time the war was coming to an end, they decided to make a change and managed to acquire a ranch in the same area which was going for little money, and Garfield decided to become a student again and do a short course at the University of the Witwatersrand — in medicine, because he had been so often called on to act as doctor or midwife at the Mission. So they had become officially ranchers, but with still an overall responsibility for Dadaya Mission, to which they allocated some of their newly-acquired land. And at the time of the general election of 1946 someone suggested to Garfield that he should stand for Parliament; and he did, and got in.

So in 1953 he had been a backbencher for seven years. But he had never held office as a Minister, and he had never become 'one of the boys' in the sense of being accustomed to fraternise with fellow whites in the Club or Sports Club manner; and he was not the kind of man who could be relied on to pay only lip-service to Christian principles. So how had he, this ex-missionary, come to be elected as leader of a party whose whole membership comprised white Rhodesians, and in preference to Julian Greenfield who we heard had been the other candidate in the election? That, surely, must signify a readiness for change in a liberal direction on the part of at least a substantial proportion of the white electorate.

Soon after his appointment as leader we learned that Garfield Todd had been approached by some of the former members of the old Liberal Party (which had for a time changed its name to 'Rhodesia Party') who, after being vanquished at the Referendum, had decided to make an approach to him instead of joining the Confederate Party. Amongst them were Ellman-Brown and Stumbles, and it had evidently been agreed that the United Party would change its name to 'United Rhodesia Party' (URP) and that they would be accepted as members of it and would disband the Rhodesia Party. It was difficult to know exactly what to make of this, but it was reported to have been an integral part of the deal that the URP would be committed to the common voters' roll and some liberalisation of the franchise, and that seemed to be consistent with the image of Todd as a leader committed to a genuine interpretation of 'partnership'.

Pat thought it was time to try for Parliament, and that the right thing to do was to apply for a URP nomination as a candidate in the Territorial election. Our commitment to Scanlen & Holderness prevented us from both doing it and he proposed — with typical unselfishness — that I should be the one to try, and if I were successful, he would come in on the running of the election campaign. If the campaign were to end in success there would be the risk that one's commitment as a URP Member of Parliament would turn out to be inconsistent with one's other, and in a sense prior commitment, as chairman of the Interracial Association; but that was a risk one must accept.

I had been invited earlier on by the chairman of the United Party, C.D. Dryden, to put my name on the party's panel of possible candidates for Parliament, but that was before the public launching of the Interracial Association and publication of my connection with it, and I was not at all sure that I would still be welcome. And if I was, must I not also think about what the position would be if, having put my name down, I was awarded the nomination for a particular constituency in preference to members who, unlike me, had given the party long and faithful service and if I were then to be rejected by the electorate for being 'too liberal'? As well as letting down the party which had adopted me as a candidate might I not be letting into Parliament some diehard with a pernicious political influence?

I spoke to Dryden and to Garfield Todd and put out a feeler to several friends and associates. Fred Lacey, who by this time had become a close associate in the course of work in the Interracial Association, thought it was a rotten idea and went to the trouble of putting his reasons into a letter penned at 3 o'clock on a Sunday afternoon —

... Whilst admitting the progressive outlook of Garfield Todd (and his sincerity) I fear that the UP as present constituted is as reactionary right-wing as it ever has been — so much so that if you succeed in obtaining a seat on a UP ticket yours will be a voice crying in the wilderness ... All you can hope to be in this new version of the UP is an ineffective backbencher effectively stifled by the Party whip (plus 90% of the other MP's) ... My amateurish, immature but sincere feelings are as follows —

(1) Forget your political ambitions at the moment and stand aside. On the other hand do nothing to embarrass the UP by standing as an Independent ...
(2) Let's (as reasonably young people) dedicate ourselves to the future and immediately after the elections get down to work to build up a Progressive (I will forego the word Labour) Party from the bottom up so that in 1958 we can enter the political arena with the right policy and party ...

Don't choose the easy way — it is not the way for a real Democrat like yourself — it is not the way to extend the benefits of Democracy to the non-European. It is not the way to victory for our British Democratic ideals. Let's try the hard way over the next five critical years. Let's convince the non-European that the only alternative is NOT COMMUNISM or MAU MAU but *co-operation* ... The answer is,

Hardwicke — to build a Progressive Party during the next five years strong enough to ask for a political alliance with the UP . . .

I respected Fred's view and would not have discounted it if African associates in the Interracial Association had been as emphatic; but they were not, and my impression was that so far as they were concerned the proof of the pudding would be in the eating. So I decided to put my name in the hat; and on 5 December I learned that it had come out. I had been nominated as the URP candidate for Salisbury North — the very constituency which Huggie himself had represented over the years.

Fred was conciliatory —

'Congratulations to a b***** good type of a Conservative from a typically tub-thumping Socialist . . . You know how sorry I am — however that doesn't matter a damn . . . I know you will do everything possible within the framework of the UP.'

Garfield was encouraging —

Dear Holderness,

I am delighted to hear that you have been made candidate for Salisbury North. My heart was in my mouth once or twice this morning at the way things were going for I was afraid you were about to miss out ... I expect you will be a frightful nuisance in the House, but by the list of people we have got we are going to have a number of strong men and Sir Godfrey always reckoned that strong men are a nuisance ...'

Later a touching letter from Dryden arrived. This had been his great opportunity of getting into Parliament and I knew he had set his heart on it. He was an unheroic looking man with a close-knit family and had built up a little family group of companies, and I learned from Tredgold afterwards that in his younger days before coming to Rhodesia he had been distinguished for courageous conduct — in the Indian Army I think it was. But for some reason he was not much appreciated by the Salisbury Club establishment and was a bit of a loner in that respect. He had put his name down for nomination, with Salisbury North as his preferred constituency, and he had lost out. He must be bitterly disappointed, but he wrote —

Dear Hardwicke,

Now that the nominations for the Southern Rhodesian general election are fixed I would like to give you my congratulations on being chosen for Salisbury North, and I wish you the very best of luck ... .

You have got to contend with the fact that your prominence in the programme of the Inter-Racial Association is going to deter a number of people from voting for you (but I do not think they would vote against you) . . .

You will inevitably find that if you are to advance your cause effectively you will need to take things gradually and be patient . . .

You will find much scheming and axe-grinding which may horrify you from time to time but the majority of people who get into Parliament are, unfortunately, not always guided by high ideals, but by their own ambitions and interests . . . Consequently it is often rather a disappointing confused kind of job for the man of ideals. However, that is the set-up and you have to take it as it is and do the best you can with it, and not expect too much too soon.

I think it might be valuable to you if you could get Mrs. Rixom on your side. Strictly confidentially she has looked askance at some of your 'inter-racial' activities. She is, however, a grand old soul and 'the' organiser for election purposes in Salisbury North . . .

Mrs Rixom. Yes, I must face her; and not only her but others of the United Party establishment in the constituency, and in particular the branch chairman, Major H.G. Mundy CMG. I had not planned to ask them to run a campaign for me. Pat was to be my official election agent and Elspeth and Anne Lewis my unofficial ones, and we had mobilised canvassers and helpers who were mostly already personal friends as a result of past collaboration in the National Affairs Association or in legal business or the Auxiliary Air Force. Attractive people mostly in their early thirties or younger, like Pauline Pennant-Rea (happily married to Peter, ex-Air Force aeoronautical engineer) and Auxiliary fliers Don McGibbon and Ray Wood and Don's fair and beautiful wife Joe (ex WRNS); Basil Hone and his old school friend Barney Pycroft; bachelors Sidney Sawyer (himself politically ambitious) and Marcus Orpen (who had been on the 'Ruys' with us); Neville Brooks and his wife and Bloggy Harben's son Anthony (still a student); new Rhodesian lawyer Eric Heaversedge, and a few of the older generation — staunch Huggie loyalists Mrs Rezin and Mrs Buckland, and Con and Jim; nearly all newcomers to politics. And we had planned a rather unorthodox programme of meetings, including two lunch-hour meetings at the Cathedral Hall which I suppose were partly designed to cash in on any goodwill available from the National Affairs Association connection. And then there was The Manifesto.

It was the thing to have a manifesto — in this case quite a brief pamphlet containing a letter to voters on one page and a photograph and brief curriculum vitae on the other. The latter had caused me some heart searching, relating to the war record part of it. During the war three 'gongs' (as the Air Force called them) had come my way, but what I felt about them (knowing how much they owed to the grace of God and team work, and how little to fearlessness) was so different from the *popular conception, especially amongst people who had been five thousand miles away from the scene of that war, that it was a subject best forgotten for most purposes. But for this one purpose, of trying to carry weight in a liberal direction amongst people susceptible to prowess in sport, it seemed legitimate to exploit gongs and any popular illusions that went with them. So there it was in the curriculum vitae: 'Held the rank of Wing Commander and was awarded the DSO, DFC, and AFC.'

The letter-to-voters part of the manifesto said —

On Wednesday, 27 January, you will be called upon to cast your vote for a Member of the Southern Rhodesian Parliament.

At first sight this may appear a less important matter than the Referendum or the Federal Election, but I believe it is every bit as important. Under a federation the Territorial Government is not a subsidiary body like a municipality or a provincial council. Within the Territory it has sovereign power, except in those matters which have been allocated to the Federal Government. The Southern Rhodesian Parliament will be solely responsible in Southern Rhodesia for some of the most important and most difficult of all our problems, including the whole sphere of 'native policy'.

I believe that Southern Rhodesia has the best, and perhaps the last, chance in Africa of finding a lasting solution to the special problems of a multi-racial community such as ours. I have tried to make a special study of these problems and tried to understand the minds of people in the non-European communities who are also interested in national affairs. In this way I have become a member of the Interracial Association. We have a wonderful combination of resources in this country, but I believe that abundance and harmony can only be achieved if individual people who are capable of taking an interest in national affairs work together, irrespective of race, to examine the problems and find solutions for them.

However, I understand some people have doubts about this approach, and what I would appreciate is an opportunity of being 'cross-examined' on it, and discussing any other matters in the Territorial sphere . . .

The prospect of presenting myself to the official pillars of the party in the Salisbury North Constituency, who had had the proud task of keeping it safe for Huggie over the years, was intimidating. My mental images of them were still formidable semi-caricatures derived from childhood. Major Mundy, impeccable senior civil servant living with his severe wife in a gloomy, immaculate residence not far from Government House; bow tie, polished shoes, clean car; respectable. And living even nearer to Government House, the Rixoms: she large, bass-voiced, like a jovial ogre or a Queen out of Alice in Wonderland, and her husband Frank, small, precise, ladylike man of integrity on the way to being the head of the leading trust company ; contented couple with an only daughter, Mary, of my age.

I called on Major Mundy in the nick of time, the day before receiving a letter from him saying —

Dear Mr. Holderness,

Following your selection as the URP candidate to contest the Salisbury North seat in the Territorial election I have been expecting that you would get in touch with me or with the Secretary of the Salisbury North Branch of the Party, Mr Theo Bourdillon of 160, Rhodes Avenue.

Instead, I have read your somewhat unusual notice in to-day's Herald.

It is customary for candidates to discuss their election campaign with the Chairman and Secretary of the Branch and indeed to ask for an opportunity to meet Branch members and seek their support as canvassers and for duties at polling stations.

Such action is of course not obligatory and you are quite at liberty to make all your own arrangements in these directions. But, the Branch is gravely concerned in holding the seat for the Party and the Executive Committee of the Branch is entitled to know what your plans are so that they may assist in whatever directions appear desirable. It would probably be best in the first instance if you could meet me at this address on Thursday next for a preliminary discussion . . .

I had next to present myself to a branch meeting called by the chairman, and the first item on the agenda was a resolution — duly passed nem con — expressing discontent with the method which had been applied in selecting and nominating the party's parliamentary candidates! However, one of the members of the committee, Colonel W.M. ('Mac') Knox (actually a son of the Mrs McClintock who had attended the meeting in Bloggy Harben's house preceding the formation of the Interracial Association but, as it was to appear with increasing clarity, of quite a different political inclination from his mother's), was good enough to arrange a gathering of constituents in his house to meet me, the candidate. Major Mundy was present at the meeting, and I got a note from him afterwards, more friendly but nevertheless quite austere —

Dear Hardwicke

. . . I was glad to be able to come to the Knoxs for your meeting there.

Now I am going to be quite frank. I felt . . . that you were hedging on the question of relationships between Europeans and Africans. I know you are an idealist and a courageous one at that. But, in my opinion if you are to win the seat your statements of policy must be more explicit and less equivocal. If you feel able to do so I suggest you

> declare yourself in favour of the purity of the white Race in S. Rh. and
> opposed to inter-marriage between Whites and Coloureds or Africans
> and equally of course against illicit intercourse between Whites and
> the darker races. These statements to apply to the foreseeable future.
> No one can tell what public opinion will be towards these matters 3–4
> generations hence. I cannot see anything in these statements at
> variance with your movement for close and better relations between
> Europeans and civilised Africans. Unless you can give these assurances
> I for one could not vote for you and I think many other URP supporters
> may also refrain.

My heart sank a bit. Could it really still be the old story in slightly altered
form — 'Would you allow your daughter to marry a kaffir?' Obviously the
logical answer ('Whoever my daughter chooses to marry will be for her to
decide, not me') would not be acceptable, and the pill had to be swallowed;
and in my follow-up letter to voters just before polling day there was this
paragraph —

> Election time brings its usual crop of rumours, and I hear the one
> about me is to the effect that my object is to bring about social mixing
> and — believe it or not — inter-marriage! Like most rumours of this
> kind, it is completely untrue.

I wondered what my friends in the Interracial Association would think
about that. In fact I did quite a lot of wondering. How could it be that,
within ten years of Hitler and Goebbels still emitting their poison about
racial purity, someone like Mundy — who was really a nice man and very
kind to me in the end — could bring himself to talk about 'the maintenance
of the purity of the White Race'? And what about this 'idealism' mentioned
by both Mundy and Dryden? If as a member of a governing white
community outnumbered 14 to 1 by blacks, and destined to be increasingly
outnumbered in the future, you tried to establish common political ground
with black leaders of the future, was that being 'idealist' or pragmatic? But
of course it could not be as simple as that for someone who had no way of
knowing how much steam was building up in the Rhodesian kettle — no
way, that is, except second-hand from an 'idealist' who must no doubt seem
to be that much obsessed, and probably priggish into the bargain. Vicious
circle.

For us and our congenial — and largely uninitiated — band of helpers,
and even for the four children ranging from four months to three years who
were now sharing our lives (Grizelda — carrycot campaigner — and Dinah
belonging to Elspeth and me, and Annette and Christopher to Pat and
Anne), the campaign was largely a cheerful experience. The constituency
was virtually home ground, with the house where I had been born and where

Con and Jim were still living situated in the older part of it, and Pat and Anne's house in the middle of the newer part. A high proportion of the residents were well established and educated people, less prone than poorer and unskilled whites to being frightened by talk of African advancement, and better placed perhaps to adopt a new and progressive approach than immigrants. (When you came to think of it one of the things immigrants wanted most was to be accepted and so they would be much more likely to conform to existing racial attitudes and patterns of behaviour than to be dissenters). Quite a number were intellectuals of Jewish origin, who might be expected to react as we did in the aftermath of Hitler to talk about 'purity of the White Race'. Our organisation, under Pat's command as election agent and based on his and Anne's house, was efficient and good — making capital out of the fact that, with only some 1800 registered voters, you could get on to one large piece of cardboard a square for each of them and then, by appropriate markings on it, eliminate the ones whom canvassers reported that it was no good pursuing. So towards the end of polling day you could see instantly which of those you calculated would vote for you had not yet been to the poll, and so pursue them and bring them in. But our most important advantage, I suppose — though I think we underestimated it at the time — was having the party nomination.

In the Federal general election the previous month the Federal Party had won twenty-four out of the twenty-six seats allocated to elected members in the Federal Parliament, and the only candidate of the Confederate Party to win one had been Dendy Young himself; and now in the election for the thirty seats in the Southern Rhodesian Parliament the Confederate Party was only fielding sixteen out of a total of twenty-nine opposition candidates (the other thirteen comprising 10 Independents, 2 Independent Labour and 1 Independent Rhodesia Party). In five of the constituencies there was to be no contest and the five URP candidates were returned unopposed. In Salisbury North there was one opposition candidate, Dr Olive Robertson.

Olive Robertson would have been about 44 then but looked younger. She possessed concise and durable good looks, with a deceptively childlike aspect to her face, and was able and ambitious. She was the kind of person I would hate to have lost to. Not because she was a woman in a context in which women were still a novelty in national politics. One of them was soon to become one of my favourite chums. The Independent candidate for Salisbury North seemed to me a dominant lady with an illiberal outlook convinced of the virtuousness of it and making use of her femininity to get under her still youthful-seeming thumb the ladies of the Womens' Institute and whoever else would submit to it. Her opinion of me was equally uncomplimentary. The Womens' Institute was a formidable force in the country, and she had been a leading member of it, as well as a member of the City Council, in Bulawayo where she and her husband had been living before coming to Salisbury. She had spent her childhood in Canada and trained, and practised for a while, as a doctor, and married a Rhodesian (a gentle man to whom Elspeth and I were to come to feel a lifelong sense of gratitude for being Superintendent of the Salisbury Hospital when Dinah was rescued from the jaws of death there three years later). She had been a staunch member of the right-wing Liberal Party, but instead of joining the Confederate Party had decided to contest Salisbury North as an Independent. My weaknesses were her strengths. I was reluctant to knock on people's doors for fear of invading their privacy. She conducted a tireless and determined campaign of individual interviews, and in the end scored 540 out of a total of 1318 votes cast in the constituency. In those days it was still customary for candidates and their helpers doing battle with each other to be on easy and friendly terms. But after attending the counting of the votes when the result became known there was no shaking of hands. She said with some venom 'If only I had another two weeks I would have won'.

It was a relief to have won and not to have let down all the people who had helped me. But I suppose it was a bit odd to have done so on the basis of an approach to voters which said in effect 'Please vote for me, not so much to express your views as to try to get across to the House the views of blacks which are not now being sufficiently understood'. Maybe she was right, and could have won given another two weeks!

The performance of the URP as a whole in the election was impressive. The party manifesto — traditionally a document full of generalisations and not a few platitudes, but important because of being quotable against a successful party after an election as defining the limits of the mandate given to it by the electorate — had things in it which Pat and I did not care for much. But on the whole it seemed much better than previous ones and, on the sensitive issues which would have to be tackled during the coming five years, if not unambiguous at least adequate in relation to the mandate. Under the section 'Principles', incidentally, there were two which had been traditional manifesto items for years —

'Loyalty to the British Crown'.

'English as the sole official language'.

There was also a new one which we were not so keen on —

'To press for Dominion Status for the Federation'.

(In due time, perhaps, but surely not before the party could claim to have won the confidence of blacks). Under 'Native Policy' there were these passages —

Political Development

The basis of the United Rhodesia Party's policy is gradual development while maintaining the principle of one Parliament for the Territory. This avoids the undesirable principle of separate representation on racial lines.

The United Rhodesia Party plans to set up a Commission or Select Committee to consider qualifications for the franchise and consider the best means of ensuring that the government of the territory will remain for all time in the hands of responsible and civilised men.

Education

The emphasis in African education should be on character, and the inculcation of a sense of responsibility and pride in work efficiently performed.

The Party's policy is to continue the expansion of educational services through State schools in the towns, and under the control of the Native Education Department in the country.

And under 'Industrial Relations' —

The maintenance of industrial peace through the machinery of the Industrial Conciliation Act and the corresponding provisions of the Rhodesia Railways Act is a principle of the Party.

The United Rhodesia Party is determined to maintain and improve the standard of living of the European and will give protection under the Act against unfair competition based on wages which do not allow of a civilised standard of living.

Can it be that these were statements of a new-look party, more to the left than its predecessor and rivals? I find it hard to believe myself now, until I remember how potent and pervasive was the underlying fear that whites had of the consequences of opening doors to blacks, in either politics or the economic field. We thought at the time such statements were the kind of thing you had to accept and, thankfully, ambiguous enough to permit the kind of interpretation we would want to put on them.

In matters of economic policy the manifesto was quite positive and good, and it had this promising passage about Housing —

Proper accommodation and security of tenure in African urban areas are the foundation of sound industrial and economic development. With schools and recreational facilities, they are the chief bulwarks against slum conditions, discontent and delinquency.

At the public meetings arranged by the party at various centres in the country the attendance was much better than anyone had expected in an election held so soon after the recent general election for the Federal Parliament and at a time of year usually avoided as being at the height of the rainy season. That was partly, if not mainly, due to the remarkable performance of Garfield Todd as the principal speaker at nearly all of them. He had a commanding platform presence — tall, clean-cut, powerful build; shock of dark hair — and a command of the English language and delivery which no doubt owed a lot to his training as a preacher but, adapted to dealing with the whole range of national affairs (and, incidentally, still spoken with a discernible New Zealand accent), seemed to be sufficiently down to earth and appropriate for politics; and heckling and hostile questions usually provided fuel for the best part of the performance — highly intelligent, instantaneous and humorous. It was a delight to listen to.

The overall result of the election was a Parliament — officially the Eighth Parliament of Southern Rhodesia — comprising twenty six members of the United Rhodesia Party with Todd as Prime Minister and four miscellaneous opposition members: Stewart Aitken-Cade (the one Confederate Party candidate to win a seat, who had endeared himself over the years to the voters of Hatfield — many of them little privileged and a number of Afrikaans origin — by assiduous attention to their welfare at local government level), Jack Keller CBE, Independent Labour (veteran member of the Railway Union, still discernibly cockney, who had actually held ministerial office for a while under Huggie during the war), Ray Stockil, Independent Liberal (a live-wire, witty man who had been born in sugar-producing Natal and studied agriculture in America and then come to Southern Rhodesia and created in the rain-starved lowveld an irrigation estate which was in a sense the natural successor to McDougall's little miracle at Triangle), and Robert Williamson, Independent (ultra conservative Scottish accountant from Gwelo).

The spread of occupation and background amongst the twenty-six URP Members was fairly wide — accepting the basic limitation that all were white: seven farmers (one an ex-missionary), ten businessmen (seven involved in commerce and industry and three in accounting and finance), a mining expert, a housewife (traditional description), a doctor, an ex-newspaperman and five lawyers. The average age of all thirty Members was quite low: five would have been around sixty, two (including myself) still in our thirties, and of the remaining twenty-one about half would have been in their forties and the rest in their fifties. Only six out of the thirty had experienced being in Parliament before — of the Opposition Members, Keller and Stockil, and of the URP Members, Todd, Stumbles (who had got in unopposed for Avondale), P.B. ('Ben') Fletcher and Davenport (the mining expert). Apart from Jack Keller, only Ben Fletcher and George Davenport had held office as Ministers. So we were nearly all new boys.

CHAPTER 11

The Eighth Parliament, 1954

The Eighth Parliament of Southern Rhodesia — to use the official description of it given in Hansard — must surely have been the most agreeable parliament in all history to be a member of.

The debating chamber was a high, unpretentious room with a certain historic atmosphere about it; part of an early-vintage, double-storey building overlooking the jacarandas of Cecil Square at right-angles to the Salisbury Club. The building must originally have had a two-tiered period verandah round three sides of it and some of this was still intact, despite later extensions of the building, so that from the library upstairs you could walk out on to the old wooden flooring boards supported by its ironwork frame. It was a good parliamentary library, and had two highly-trained and live-wire librarians (one of them now designated 'Federal'), and there was a small, well-brought-up parliamentary staff, helpful and devoted to the job. In the chamber there was room for each of us as Members to have an individual writing table and round-backed, cushioned chair, both elegantly executed in oak and green leather which I imagined must have dated from the Chartered Company days since the materials and workmanship were reminiscent of the beautiful early coaches of the Rhodesia Railways. Behind and above the Speaker's throne was a small press gallery, and below the Speaker the Clerk of the House and shorthand-writer, then the Ministers and Opposition Members facing each other, and then the rest of us facing the Speaker; and behind us a small, two-tiered public gallery. The formalities were strictly observed under the supervision of William Addison — retired newspaperman who had been a cub journalist in Scotland at the outbreak of the First World War and MC, DCM by the end of it — who found himself elected as Speaker and, being unfamiliar with the job and elderly, having to have his hand held strongly by the Clerk of the House. We referred to each other as 'The Honourable Member for So-and-So' and had the line of parliamentary language drawn at a decorous level. But in many ways it was the ideal debating set-up, in which we all got to know each other so well that in thinking out how best to try to get something across in debate one could pretty well forecast each Member's likely reaction to the various possible ways of approaching it.

The business which had to be dealt with in full session only took up about a fifth of the year, but Garfield Todd decided from the beginning to hold regular caucus meetings. In that simplified set-up the term 'caucus' was in use to mean simply a meeting of MP's belonging to a particular party, and the term 'Cabinet' to mean all of the Ministers forming a government and not a special, inner group of them as in England. Garfield had suffered as a backbencher in Huggie's administration from the feeling of being kept in the dark and so, each month when the House was not in session and more frequently when it was, all the backbenchers of the governing party were brought in on what the Ministers were doing, and enabled to question them. With a maximum complement of twenty-six we could all fit quite well into a committee room, round one large table; and this was our privileged contact as MP's of the governing party, not only with the actual Cabinet but in effect with the whole executive branch of government. What a particular Minister would be discussing with us was not simply his brain child but something which had been worked on for him by the experts — the civil servants in a Ministry or Department who were experienced in dealing with that kind of matter from day to day and represented a continuity of administrative experience over the years and over the lifetimes of successive governments. So here in these caucus meetings we backbenchers were being given a chance of influencing government policy in the process of formation. That was the important thing, and put us in a privileged position even relative to those other Members of Parliament who were not members of the governing party.

A wide range of political views was represented in the Eighth Parliament (accepting the basic limitation that there were no blacks in it, and that the left end of the spectrum was about where I stood) and there was plenty of scope for hostilities, and in fact some quite effective, and sometimes quite witty, insults were exchanged from time to time in the course of debate. But the remarkable thing about that Parliament as a whole, and not only Members of the governing party but including the four Opposition Members, was the degree to which an underlying feeling of personal friendship and shared jokes seemed to develop.

If I had been required, after individual attitudes had begun to emerge, to classify them relative to Pat's and my kind of outlook, I think I would have produced something like this (in decreasing order of congeniality) —

Potential allies: Ben Baron (Bulawayo solicitor). Ralph Palmer (public spirited farmer married to an enlightened wife). Paddy Lloyd (Bulawayo barrister). Abe Abrahamson (thirty-two year old darling of a Bulawayo industrialist family).

Broad-minded and potentially sympathetic: George Davenport (former mine manager and Minister in Huggie's government). Muriel Rosin (wife of a leading surgeon, enlightened but with hampering commitments to white womens' organisations). William Addison (touchingly congenial but neutralised as Speaker). Cyril Hatty (pleasant man with the up-to-date, then novel, qualification of industrial consultant but perhaps cautious as a new Rhodesian).

Middle-of-the-road (Rhodesian): Ralph Palmer's brother Eric.

Conservative: Geoff Ellman-Brown and 6 other URP Members. Ray Stockil (Opposition).

Die-hard: Ben Fletcher (veteran, one-time Minister of Agriculture and later promoted to Minister of Native Affairs in Huggie's administration), Stumbles and the remaining 6 URP Members. All the remaining Opposition Members — Keller, Aitken-Cade and Williamson.

So the governing party was not dependent on the opposition for diehards. We had plenty of our own.

I suppose one of the reasons for the underlying family feeling which seemed to exist was the fact that we were mostly new boys. ('New girl' I suppose one would have to say in Muriel Rosin's case, and yet there was something about her which was boyish without being unfeminine — something quite different from Olive Robertson's style. I remember once questioning her about it, and her saying that as a child she had been sent to a co-educational school in London — something quite unusual at the time — which seemed to have resulted in a certain difference in outlook as compared with most female contemporaries, and a strange sense of familiarity if occasionally she came across one who possessed a similar background). Another reason may have been the fact that the 'partnership' mandate had in effect been endorsed twice since the Referendum, at the Federal Election and the Territorial Election, tending to induce in the die-hards a certain resignation on the lines of that old advice to ladies 'if rape is inevitable you might as well lie back and enjoy it'. But I think the principal reason was a high level of recognition amongst that particular collection of thirty people that it is possible for political discord and personal harmony to co-exist.

There was a lot to be grateful for about the Eighth Parliament, but looking at it from the outside, in company with Pat or other friends in the Interracial Association like Stanlake Samkange or Nathan Shamuyarira, what became clear was that great changes were going to be needed during its lifetime; and the question was whether it would be capable of making them. Where people of our kind would have to exert all the influence we could muster would be in the areas of the franchise and the industrial colour bar. Putting oneself in the shoes of the kind of Africans we were now increasingly coming across it was easy to see that if this Government and Parliament should fail to open sufficiently the door to the franchise and the door to the acquisition of skills in industry, the brand of civilisation which the whites were supposed to be offering would appear to be nothing but a sham, and anything — black nationalism or even the Russian brand of communism for that matter — would seem to hold more promise. But there would be few Members of even this new and younger Parliament in a position to see the picture from that angle, and it would be up to us to do what we could.

Initially, Garfield Todd appointed only four other Ministers apart from himself: Ben Fletcher, CMG, as Minister of Native Affairs; George Davenport, CMG, as Minister of Mines, Lands and Surveys; Cyril Hatty as Minister of the Treasury and Geoff Ellman-Brown as Minister of Roads and Road Traffic, Minister of Irrigation and Minister of Housing. Todd himself acted as Minister of Justice and Internal Affairs as well as Prime Minister. Then something happened which I found agonising at the time and still hate to think about even now. Todd summoned me to his Prime Minister's office and asked me if I would like to be the sixth Minister, with the portfolio of Justice and Internal Affairs. It was the last thing I had expected, and I thought he was taking a great risk in making the offer, and I felt overcome by it. But how could I accept? The Justice part of the portfolio would be largely concerned with the administration of law in the courts, and particularly in the criminal courts, and I felt hopelessly half-baked as a lawyer because of the way I had come into the profession, and particularly in that field. But more important: most of the Internal Affairs which I felt I might make a useful contribution in dealing with would still come under the Ministry of Native Affairs, and Ben Fletcher as Minister. It had been impossible for Garfield to do otherwise than appoint the old hand, Ben, to that office, or at that stage to remove from the scope of the Native Affairs Ministry things which badly needed a fresh approach; and while Ben would undoubtedly see himself as the elder statesman in full control of everything falling under his command, I had seen enough of him to be satisfied that there would be little distinction between what he did and what the traditionalists in the Native Department wanted to see done. As Minister of Justice I would not only be precluded from operating in his field, but would have to share responsibility for what in effect the Native Department decided should be done, and in particular on the question of Africans in industry. It would surely limit my chances as a liberal of influencing the necessary legislation in that field, and in the field of the franchise, and put at risk whatever chance I had of helping to retain (win?) the confidence of African leaders of the future in the meantime. Well, all of these thoughts were pretty self-important and remote, and what could I say to Garfield? There were other difficulties as well, like the fact that the process of getting Scanlen & Holderness geared to meet the current demands on it was still only in its early stages. Should I have ever come into politics in those circumstances?

So I remained a backbencher, dubious virtue intact, and with freedom to make a nuisance of myself in the interests of reform — for what it was worth. And for what seemed a long time none of the relevant issues came up even for debate in Parliament. The Government had other, urgent pre-occupations. Soon after its appointment there was a strike of African workers at the vital Wankie Colliery to be dealt with. There was urgent work to be done to clear the ground for and promote economic development. Ellman-Brown and Hatty were impressive enthusiasts for economic reform, and Todd saw eye to eye with them about that. The achievement of everyone's aims, after all — including the aim of African advancement — depended upon maximising the national income. The first problem was shortage of capital. Southern Rhodesia was now in competition with all sorts of other undeveloped countries for available capital, and there had been a miscalculation, so the Government thought, in the financial arrangements connected with Federation as regards the share of revenue needed by the Territorial governments for what they had to do. A lot of capital was locked up in government-owned enterprises like the Iron and Steel Commission and Triangle Sugar Estate and the Central Mechanical and Equipment Department. Their organisation and balance sheets had got into a bad state and must be overhauled. After that private enterprise could be brought in on the first two, and capital freed for other purposes. Communications were a key to development and although trunk roads were a Federal responsibility, a host of roads essential to development were the sole responsibility of the Territorial Government. Cheap power was an essential ingredient, and it was the job of the Federal Government to see to that by setting up a major hydro-electric scheme at either Kariba or Kafue, but we must get going on housing for white immigrants and for blacks committing themselves to industry and commerce in the towns. And we must get going on increasing the efficiency of African agriculture — the part of agriculture allocated to the Territorial Government to look after.

Todd and his Government got going with such vigour — pressurising the Federal Government to choose Kariba in preference to Kafue, launching a publicity drive in England to attract industrialists to set up in Southern Rhodesia and so on — as to cause a certain resentment in Federal circles; which I thought not necessarily a bad thing. If in the eyes of Africans the Federal Government appeared to be dominated by white Rhodesian politicians of the old school, it could be desirable that the new Southern Rhodesian Government should be seen to be acting independently. It was certainly acting with enthusiasm and team spirit under Todd's leadership, and complete unanimity on economic policy seemed to exist at this stage and afterwards.

An interesting feature of the strike at the Wankie Colliery which they were faced with soon after coming into office was Todd's decisiveness and lack of inhibition in calling out Territorial Army Reservists for security duty. That was permissible under the Defence Act 'in case of emergency', and there were special reasons for doing it which he explained later when the matter was reported to Parliament as required by the Act, but one might think it would need very strong justification in the eyes of the Africans. Even Jack Keller, old and die-hard as he was in many ways, criticised it in Parliament on these grounds —

> It has been my experience in this country before with white strikers, not black strikers, that the Defence Force has been called out to intimidate strikers, and I think it is undemocratic. It is dictatorial and it must have a bad effect on the native labourers themselves, not only at Wankie but in all other parts of the country.

In the event Todd's reputation with blacks seemed to be undamaged. In the minds of most whites the action was wholly commendable, as being 'firm' action.

It was not until November 1954 that, in the field of what tended still to be referred to as 'Native Policy', anything significant came up to be debated in Parliament; and then what it consisted of was a set of amendments to the Land Apportionment Act. The Bill containing them was something falling within Ben Fletcher's portfolio as Minister of Native Affairs. The Land Apportionment Act was something he liked changing as little as possible, but events had occurred which made these changes inescapable. The first concerned the University about to be set up which, it had been agreed, should be multi-racial and built on land in the northern residential area of Salisbury which for purposes of the Land Apportionment Act was 'European' land. Without an amendment to the Act the residence there of Africans as staff or students would be illegal.

Secondly, there had begun to be official visits to Southern Rhodesia by delegations containing Africans whose residence in any of the existing Rhodesian hotels — all of them situated in the 'European Area' — constituted a breach of the Act. Thirdly, there had been an application to the Salisbury Municipality by a body called the United Club for permission to use premises which it had acquired in Salisbury for purposes of a multi-racial social club, and that too could be held to be illegal under the Act as it stood. And finally, there was the case of Herbert Chitepo. He was the first Southern Rhodesian African to become qualified to practise at the Bar, and to enable him to do so with any chance of success it would be necessary for him to take a lease of an office as his Chambers in the building in Salisbury where nearly all of the other Advocates had theirs, and where they were agreeable to make one available to him. (Manfred Hodson was Leader of the Bar at the time). But without an amendment to the Act his holding of such a lease would be illegal.

Very well, one might say, so the Act was obviously out of date, at the very least in those respects; surely there could have been no problem about the relevant amendments? In fact they caused considerable agitation, and some brief extracts from the lengthy debate which took place in the House will perhaps be the best way of conveying the nature of it.

Between them Ben and the Native Department had seen to it that the amendments to the Act were minimal and had the effect of conferring on the Minister of Native Affairs the maximum discretion. The problem of the University was to be dealt with by empowering the Minister at his discretion to grant and to revoke permits to Africans to make use of the premises as students, teachers, research workers and so on; and the problem of Herbert Chitepo similarly by empowering the Minister to grant or revoke a permit to occupy premises in the European Area if the Minister was satisfied that it was necessary to do so. To cope with African visitors to the country the idea was that a hotel or hotels would come into existence at or near an airport or airports, and the relevant amendment to the Act would permit them to reside there. And as regards multi-racial organisations like the United Club the Minister should be empowered to grant permits to ones which he approved of to occupy premises in a part of a town especially demarcated for that kind of purpose under prevailing town planning arrangements. It was about as tight as you could get but caused concern nevertheless.

Ben Fletcher, who habitually wore a lugubrious look due to the misery lines on his forehead like a Disney bloodhound, seemed more pained than usual trying to convince himself and the House that the amendments represented no departure from the principles of the Land Apportionment

Act —

> At each election that I have fought I have given an undertaking that I would never violate the principles of the Land Apportionment Act . . . (It) is the framework within which the two major races are required to work out their relationship. The need for this is quite apparent; it is not based in colour prejudice. If the races were permitted to mix unduly then the tempo of the nation would drop to some average between the two, which we are not prepared to accept, because we have set British standards as the standards of this country. We cannot permit any social system which will retard or lower the standards we have set . . . This Act through the process of evolution gives protection to both the major races alike. The member of either race has the right not to mix more than he desires . . .
>
> Its first and fundamental principle is the principle of segregation of ownership of land . . . The second is the control of the occupation of either area by the other race. Europeans are controlled in their occupation of the native area. The same applies in reverse . . .
>
> These four contentious clauses comply with all the primary and fundamental principles . . .

If Ben bore a resemblance to Dismal Desmond, Jack Keller was more like a sort of mongrel terrier, full of lively aggression but a lot of it more ragging than venomous. In this case he could let himself go in the classic manner of the champion of white labour —

> Mr Speaker, to me this Bill is the most direct step yet taken towards the African goal — and incidentally the goal of the Colonial Office — of a Gold Coast government in this country . . . It is the thin end of the wedge and its appearance marks the biggest danger to the white population of this country. It threatens the Europeans politically, economically and socially and finally, will result in the disappearance from this country of the white working man . . .
>
> Mr Speaker, I have been in this country for forty-three years and I am very proud to say so. And the Native during those years has always in my experience been happy enough; happier than those of us who looked after him, Mr Speaker, much happier very often. And he was contented enough until we started to mollycoddle him. He was at one time a law-abiding citizen, and always respectful to the Europeans. To-day he cares very little for our laws, and in our towns, I am sorry to say, but it is the truth — he is lazy, and very often insolent to the European, male and female; and all as a result of our most considerate attitude towards him . . .
>
> I am aware of course that there are natives in this country, a comparative few, I know, who have distinguished themselves in the fields of science and letters, and I say all credit to them. Personally I honour them, but I feel it is their duty to live among their less fortunate

fellows, to pass on to them their learning and experience, and so fit them to become skilled in their professions and trades, and in the responsibilities of government. It is not for us, Mr Speaker, to unduly hasten measures of this description a generation or so before their time. By so doing we are only courting disaster for both the white and the black populations of this country . . .

Ralph Palmer who, if he could not match Keller's forty-three years in the country would have been able to claim nearly thirty at that time, and who also was small statured but not so much like a terrier as like a warm-hearted gnome, took a different view —

Much of the opposition to this Bill comes from people who have very little contact with the educated African. Their only contact is with the primitive African from the kraal and they cannot realise how very much the African has developed in recent years. As a matter of fact it is fairly obvious I think, because if you go through the streets of Salisbury to-day it is very rare to see a Native wearing a sack or seeing anyone in rags. The standard of dress of our Africans has really remarkably improved. The women in the country districts you also find are reasonably clothed and a few years ago that was not the case. From the point of view of hygiene and cleanliness they are advancing. This will gather momentum particularly as the demand for education is met. It is impossible to retard education. Once you have started on that road you cannot go back and I am very glad to see it because the more educated he becomes the more useful he is going to be to the community. I myself consider that the implementation of these amendments to the Act will be an earnest of our desire to improve race relations but for many years they will not have any great impact on the life of the community . . .

Ray Stockil was too sophisticated not to see the necessity for the changes but being in effect the Member who still carried the flag of the old, right-wing Liberal Party in his hand, he had to condemn the Bill as a whole, relying on the 'no mandate' argument —

. . . This is undoubtedly one of the most important and, in my opinion, possibly the most important debate which has taken place in recent years in this Chamber. We have under consideration one of the basic principles on which past, present and future settlement is based here in Southern Rhodesia . . . This is a matter which should be referred to the electorate.

Ben Baron and Abe Abrahamson spoke as younger generation white Rhodesians, born in the country —

Baron: . . . I am convinced that the great mass of people in this country are liberal and fundamentally decent, and are completely with us in our proposals. They have demonstrated this in three recent elections. I had thought that racialism in this Colony had been crushed, but apparently it was only pushed underground and is now rearing its ugly head. We in this Parliament have the opportunity of giving it what may be its death blow . . .

Abrahamson: I approach this question as one who was born in this country whose children were born in this country and who, I hope, will continue to live in this country. I agree with the honourable Member for Victoria (Mr Stockil) when he says that he would like to see his children carrying on living in this country, and he has no plans to send them elsewhere. I approach this problem from the same viewpoint, realising also that we live in this country under the Land Apportionment Act. But nevertheless this is the country in which we employ African cookboys, a country in which the African brings us in our early morning tea, a country in which the African is permitted to look after our children, a country in which the African assists us in our agriculture, mining and secondary industries, all within the framework of the Land Apportionment Act, and with all of which we are content. All that we are prepared to tolerate, but when amendments are proposed whereby Africans will be able to advance in thought, in culture and will be able to ply their occupations if there are no facilities for them to ply their occupation or profession in the Native area, then we create a furore . . .

Humphrey Dudley Wightwick OBE (who pronounced his name WITTIK) was a post-war Rhodesian, born in Australia, and now managing a factory in Umtali manufacturing jute bags essential for the agricultural industry and in particular its staple product, maize. He was a heavy jowled, thick-set man who seemed pretty certainly to see himself as a Churchillian figure with a great political future in Southern Rhodesia, if not the Federation, and he probably occupied more of the time of the House than any other back-bencher with his oratory. (On one occasion when in full swing he looked round at the clock and Ray Stockil interjected 'You shouldn't look at the clock. You should look at the calendar'.) Liberal nonsense, Wightwick seemed to have decided, was no way to realise his ambitions —

. . . I want to state quite bluntly, Mr Speaker, at the start of this speech, that I intend to oppose this Bill.

I regard it certainly as the most serious legislation which has ever been introduced into the House and also one of the most ill-conceived pieces of legislation. It is ill-conceived and also ill-drafted and I am quite satisfied that if it passes through the House in its present form it will do almost irreparable damage to race relations in this Colony and will provide both the African and the European with endless opportunities for misrepresentation of one another's intentions and perhaps the honourable Minister's and the Goverment's . . .

I cannot . . . find in this Bill the words 'multi-racial club' which has been used frequently by the honourable Minister and by others. In fact, I appealed in the House to the honourable the Minister not to use such phrases as I considered they would bait the public and inflame public opinion . . .

There is here 'sporting activities' mentioned in the Bill. That has been interpreted as being playing fields for Native servants, domestic servants in European areas. But since the honourable the Minister has made it quite clear that the wording of the Bill itself is only euphemistic I do not see why, in the future, some less well balanced Minister of Native Affairs might not interpret 'sporting activities' as meaning multi-racial mixed bathing in the European area. There is nothing very extraordinary or exaggerated about that. Here is a design for the new University in this country, and in that design I can only find one swimming pool. What is the intention?

For some other post-war Rhodesians too, like Knight and Wrathall, the crucial question was what their constituents might think of them for supporting amendments to the Land Apportionment Act —

Knight: . . . I am concerned because I have been approached by various individuals all of whom I respect . . . They are people who have been in this country for many years, who are desirous that Rhodesia should continue along its path of racial harmony, who are not extremists in any sense of the word, but who at the same time feel extremely worried about the measure with which we are dealing to-day . . .

It is not a question of what I think would be the right thing. It is not a question of what I would like to see done. That is not the question. The question is what does the country want. I think the only way of deciding that is by approaching the country and asking them as to whether or not they approve of this particular measure. I think the way is to educate the people first, put over what you think is the right thing, see as to whether or not, having addressed them on the matter, they agree, and if they are in agreement, then I have no doubt the right thing will have been done for the country . . .

Wetter than Wightwick!

Jack Quinton was the Irish boy made good; creator of one of the most successful tobacco estates in the country and martinet instructor of a succession of 'pupils'. He did not care for Wightwick's airs and congratulated him ironically on 'the able way he presented the views of some of the new settlers'. He took a pragmatic view —

To-day the eyes of the world are on the development of Central Africa whose role, if well planned, has a great future in the development and

146

security of the Commonwealth. We, a mere handful of Europeans, have been entrusted with the work. We have got to develop a state so that all races can prosper with allegiance to the Crown. This part of the African continent has a great future and if prepared, broad minded and well planned, can go a long way to justify the ideals of our Founder, Cecil Rhodes.

Now, the confidence of world finance must be won. What comes out of this debate will prove to the world the sincerity and ability to implement our policy of progress on all fronts ...

The person who viewed the Bill with the most real hatred was Stumbles, and his second reading speech was a good example of his style and outlook —

Mr Speaker, I think it would be correct to say that this debate will go down in history as one of the most important and far-reaching ever to take place in the annals of this House ... It takes place, Mr Speaker, in an atmosphere which, by outside influences, has been charged unfortunately — and I say that advisedly — with emotion and racial feeling. It therefore calls, Mr Speaker, for the utmost tact, the utmost diplomacy, the utmost understanding, and most important of all, for the utmost tolerance of the other man's point of view ...

It is I think correct to say that partnership has become with some an ideal, political, social and economic. But, Mr Speaker, what is an ideal? An ideal only exists as an ideal or a conception. Once it becomes a fact it is no longer an ideal. So all idealists strive to attain their ideals. But I think it would be wiser for us in Southern Rhodesia to try to idealize the real than to try to realize the ideal. That may take a little explaining. Partnership as envisaged by the idealists can only be accomplished by a long, gradual and patient process, and I submit that any attempt to hasten that process is doomed to failure, and doomed to create, as it has already created in some quarters, reactionary groups ...

... We will first of all acknowledge that over the years we have introduced into Southern Rhodesia a system of education for Africans regardless of the necessity of providing an outlet for the more highly educated African. We will also have to acknowledge that we must, and we must do it soon, make every endeavour to provide that outlet. And here I may not have agreement on all sides of the House but I am sure I am right, the surest way of providing that outlet is to go out and create conditions which will establish a middle class of African. A middle class, Mr Speaker, as I have said before in this House, is the backbone of any community, and the Africans need that backbone. We will also acknowledge, Mr Speaker, that under conditions as they are to-day there are enough of these Africans, there is sufficient material in our midst to try to create conditions which will stimulate and foster that middle class, but not assimilate them, and that is one of the dangers which I foresee in this proposed legislation ...

... The effect of at least some of these amendments — and I say it without fear of contradiction — will be to isolate the educated and more cultured African from the lower school, and now I want to pursue for a little that question of the lower school ... I suggest that the amendments — or most of them — which are envisaged in this important piece of legislation purport to give privileges to the prefects in the African school ... that we are spending too much time on considering the privileges which we will accord to the prefects rather than directing the prefects to do their duty to the lower school ...

To me there was about Stumbles a combination of bombast and parochialism which seemed quite outrageous, but nobody else seemed to mind much, and to him I was just as maddening — 'emotional' was his polite way of putting it.

The Prime Minister, Garfield Todd, came in towards the end of the second reading debate and made an interesting reference to a visit which he had just made to Kenya —

I had the privilege quite recently of going to Kenya for ten days and while I was there I tried to go round and see as much as I could. I had the privilege of being shown round Kiambu and various places where a number of incidents have been taking place recently, by the Brigadier in charge of military operations. I had some idea from seeing the military organisation there just how disrupting it must be in the life of the nation, and the figures show how very expensive trouble like this can be.

I was shown round the Kikuyu locations by a young Kikuyu, and I looked at some of the housing there round the suburbs of Nairobi, inside the barbed wire area. In one place I went into there were three men, their wives, three women, and nine children living in a room which by my own measurement was 8 ft, by 9 ft. I went out to Athi River to a camp where there were 1,900 Mau Mau all of whom had been there for two years. From that 1,900 after two years work they had managed to get 300 who were co-operating a little bit and 24 who were really co-operating and seemed to have freed themselves from the influence of the Mau Mau doctrines, and I had the pleasure of spending an hour with these men.

One of them used to be a divisional commander under Kenyatta, and had 600 men under him. Another had been Kenyatta's treasurer and handled up to £20,000 at a time. Another had been one of the Mau Mau judges and sent many a man to his doom. At last these men were beginning to co-operate with consecrated Europeans and Africans who were also working in that camp and endeavouring to get to know them and get them to understand the European point of view. But it was costing a great deal of money, and the results, as far as one could see, were very small. I was taken into one barbed wire compound where there were 150 of these men who had been under psychological treatment for two years and they trusted them so little that they put five guards with automatic pistols and rifles around me while I went and talked to a number of these people who were educated and could talk English.

When I saw these things I thought we have a chance in Southern Rhodesia which the people in Kenya would give a great deal to have given back to them . . .

Mr Speaker, I believe that only if we move reasonably with the times and only if we are prepared to let commonsense and decency have its way and meet our problems one by one without leaving too big a time-lag will we be able to carry on and build up the good feeling which to-day exists between the races here. The visit to Kenya, Mr Speaker, made me more and more determined that I would leave nothing undone which I could do in my own responsibility to make sure that race relations in Southern Rhodesia and Central Africa were not only maintained but improved . . .

Todd allowed a free vote on this, as on all other issues during the lifetime of that Parliament, and as well as the four official Opposition Members Stumbles, Wightwick, Wrathall and Knight all voted against the passage of the Land Apportionment Amendment Bill.

The debate was a very important one for me, or should I say for 'us', because the speech which I was entitled to make on the second reading was, I thought, crucial; and as it turned out I found that it was possible, in a long speech containing views which to nearly all the other Members were more or less radical, to command a keen and even enthusiastic hearing.

CHAPTER 12

Select Committee Extraordinary, 1955–1956

In some ways the most challenging and interesting job tackled by the Eighth Parliament of Southern Rhodesia was one which might at first sight seem to have been technical and dull — the formulation of a new, non-racial Industrial Conciliation Act to replace the existing one which was basically confined in its operation to whites.

On the face of it there is nothing positive which legislation can do to ensure good industrial relations. It can only provide a legal framework which may or may not be constructively used by employers and employees, and there was no assurance that any change in the existing law which we made would succeed in resolving the special problem of relations between blacks and whites in industry. But there was the fascinating possibility that in designing machinery to avoid South Africa's mistakes we might at the same time provide the basis for a better and more constructive system of conducting industrial relations generally than, for example, England had been left with by its long and sometimes bitter history.

It was a long process involving two Select Committees. One started work in November 1954 and included in its programme of investigation visits to the Union of South Africa, Northern Rhodesia and the Belgian Congo, and issued a report in March 1956. The other, appointed in May 1957, by the end of that year reached substantial agreement on a new Industrial Conciliation Bill embodying the first Committee's proposals, and put the finishing touches to it in March 1958.

The immediate problem was one which the group involved in promoting the Interracial Association had had a shot at defining earlier on, in the Draft Declaration on African Affairs —

> Perhaps the most difficult problem is that of the Industrial Colour Bar, which is not clearly understood by all Africans or by all Europeans. What has happened is that the European artisan, coming to Rhodesia with a hard-won tradition of organised labour behind him, has felt his whole position to be potentially undermined by the competition of unorganised black labour. The African had nothing to

lose by accepting a wage which for a European would mean abandoning his customary standard of living. The African had not had to serve an apprenticeship; he had no system of collective bargaining; he could always go back to the Reserve if necessary, and, most important, the standard of living he was prepared to accept was far below the European's. There was therefore a real danger that he would be employed in preference to the European even though his workmanship was not up to standard. Standards of workmanship and life would fall, and the European would find himself unemployed.

To meet this danger the European artisans in a few 'organised' industries have come to agreements with the employers to the effect that within those industries nobody shall be employed on any but the most menial jobs at less than a minimum rate of pay, and Parliament has sanctioned the arrangement by allowing the agreements to acquire the force of law under the Industrial Conciliation Act. Legally this does not create a colour bar because, theoretically, anyone can be employed at the minimum rate ('equal pay for equal work'), but in practice the minimum rate is fixed sufficiently high to deter most employers from employing an African.

This state of affairs only applies to a limited extent. It only applies in the industries in which European labour is highly organised, notably the building industry; it only applies within the municipal area; it only applies to contracts undertaken by registered members of the industry as such, and, as only Europeans can be registered, it is left open to a person to employ, for example, an African builder or building contractor even inside the municipal area if he wants to. Nevertheless, it is a vitally important problem to solve because it is no advertisement for European civilisation that Europeans should have to secure themselves by preventing employees of another race from doing work which they are capable of doing. It artificially limits production and it plays into the hands of those who contend that economic justice cannot be expected from our system.

There is another aspect to the problem. Even if an African were skilful enough to warrant being employed at the minimum wage fixed by an Agreement under the Industrial Conciliation Act, an employer in the industry would not employ him for fear that the European employees would refuse to work with him. A prejudice against working side by side with an African on the same job has grown amongst the Europeans from the idea that the African is a potential enemy. Typically, fear has led to hate.

We thus have the position that in a few industries in which European labour is organised Africans can only do menial jobs. In the majority of industries, including most of the new secondary industries, in which there is no official trade union organisation the only Europeans employed are overseers at high rates of pay and Africans are used to do semi-skilled and even skilled jobs at labourers' rates of pay which it would be impossible for a European to accept . . .

Apprenticeship — the traditional means of teaching in industry and of establishing a standard of skill — is non-existent for the African in either type of industry; in organised industries due to prejudice, and in the others due to the absence of European master-craftsmen to whom to be apprenticed. So we are failing to pass on the knowledge and skill which is one of civilisation's most obvious gifts to backward peoples.

The conclusion arrived at in the Draft Declaration was that the growth of a really responsible trade union organisation was needed which would —

(a) enable Africans to be used to the full extent of their capacity in the industries which are at present closed to them;
(b) enable Europeans to enter the industries which are at present closed to them except as supervisors;
(c) establish a proper system of apprenticeship in industry and make it available to all who have the aptitude.

and that this could only be achieved by means of inter-racial trade unions.

We were under no illusion about the opposition that this would be likely to meet with, not only amongst white artisans but (for equal and opposite reasons) also amongst the champions of African advancement; and not only from the labour side but also from some employers opposed to trade unionism in general. But an impressive committee of the Interracial Association got to work under the combined leadership of Fred Lacey and Eileen Haddon who, with her husband Michael, had recently come to live permanently in Southern Rhodesia. Michael had been born in the country. His father had been one of its successful, independent miners and had sent him to Harrow and then to the Royal School of Mines. Eileen was Johannesburg born, graduate of the University of the Witwatersrand and a staunch liberal. As a couple they shared a zest for the good things of life, food, wine, argument, politics — and possessed complementary qualities — Eileen forthright, scornful of old-fashioned prejudices about women, sex and race, enthusiastic and sometimes aggressive arguer, not easy for everyone to like before getting around to recognising her underlying sensitivity and enormous courage. Michael, large, courteous, kindly, scornful of red tape. Their garden, surrounded by a dense screen of cyprus trees, with its old-style, verandahed bungalow and large but unpretentious swimming pool, were to become probably the most relaxed setting in the country for multi-racial collections of people (including academics, overseas journalists and the like) to foregather for al fresco eating and political debate.

Fred Lacey and Eileen, and with them Charles Mzingeli, somehow managed to win the confidence of enough of the relevant people to make possible a multi-racial conference on the subject of industrial relations in July 1954. It took place in Salisbury over a Saturday and Sunday under the auspices of the Interracial Association, and of the thirty-five delegates who attended seven were representatives of official, white trade unions, twelve were Africans representing unofficial African workers' organisations (including significant leaders of the future like Nkomo and Nyandoro), seven were representatives of big employers or employers' organisations (including the Federation of Rhodesian Industry), four were representatives of Industrial Councils established under the existing Industrial Conciliation Act, four were government officials (including the Chief Industrial Officer and Acting Commissioner of Native Labour), and the remaining delegate was a representative of the Salisbury African Welfare society, a voluntary organisation which had been in existence for some time and had become more or less part of the Establishment.

It was the first conference of its kind ever to take place, and I remember shaking at the knees a bit at the opening. It had been no exaggeration to say in the Draft Declaration, in relation to the attitude of white artisans to blacks in industry, 'Typically, fear has led to hate'. You could observe it, without having first-hand experience as an artisan yourself, on a building site for example: the arrogant attitude (part self-defence, part contempt) of a bricklayer towards his black labourers, and the latters' potential frustration and resentment. Was it possible that a meeting of this kind, bringing together for the first time leading representatives of both, could take place without rancour, or even perhaps an explosion of some kind? Might it end up doing damage rather than good? A fiasco?

There were five discussion points on the agenda —

1. The need for a new approach to the problem of industry and labour furthering the cause of racial harmony in the field of industry.
2. The desirability of amending the Industrial Conciliation Act to include the African as an employee.
3. The expediency or otherwise of seeking official recognition of existing African trade unions covering those fields of employment which are entirely African.
4. The advisability or otherwise of admitting the African to membership of European trade unions in those spheres of employment where there is or will be a mixed labour force.
5. The desirability or otherwise of admitting to the facilities of apprenticeship anyone possessing the relevant qualifications irrespective of race.

The discussion, well handled by Fred as chairman, was amazingly harmonious. By agreement no findings were to be published, but notes prepared by Eileen were circulated afterwards. They contained this reference to the delegates' closing speeches —

> Closing speeches from various delegates . . . expressed appreciation for the opportunity of meeting members of other races round the same conference table for a completely frank exchange of views. It was felt that all delegates had learned a great deal and it would be easier for them in the future to appreciate the other side's point of view as a result of the personal contacts which had been made. It was obvious that there was no lack of a desire to co-operate, which was most encouraging, and it was felt that definite progress had been made towards mutual understanding. It would now be possible for delegates to return to their organisations with a much clearer picture of the industrial relationships, and they would be able to formulate opinions as to the evidence it was desirable to present to the Government regarding future industrial legislation. Many delegates expressed the hope that this would not be the last meeting and that the Interracial Association would keep in touch with them and arrange further conferences on the same lines in the future.

I mentally took my hat off to Fred and Eileen and Charles Mzingeli, and to the delegates, and also to three people who, come to think of it, were quite outstanding examples of the unassuming but high quality we had in some of the civil servants of the time. These were three Labour Officers who had helped: the senior, W.F. Baillie (father of one of our Auxiliary Air Force pilots); Simon Grant (a gentle Scotsman), and Pat Bashford (who later, after turning himself into a successful farmer, was to be one of the few trying to continue the unequal battle against Smith and the Rhodesian Front).

In trying to assess the conference afterwards what seemed to be clear was that it would be bound to have had a significant influence in promoting an open-minded approach on all the issues covered by the agenda on the part of many, if not all, of the individuals who had attended as delegates, and that at least some of that influence could be expected to spread to the organisations they were representing.

Meanwhile the thinking which had been developing in government official circles, in the Department of Native Affairs, was that something would have to be done about some form of legal recognition and control (especially control) of specifically African trade unions. They were already officially recognised in Northern Rhodesia and so, with Federation, perhaps it was inevitable here. And perhaps the existence of recognised African unions would obviate the kind of difficulty that had been encountered during the Wankie strike — the problem of knowing what leaders the authorities could deal with. There had been a steady growth in the number of unofficial organisations in existence and in the number of African workers belonging to them, and there was need for a law to control them. So the argument ran, and the result was a Bill, entitled 'Native Industrial Workers' Unions Bill', ready for presentation to Parliament in November 1954.

The Bill bore all the marks of a typical Native Department product and would have been presented to the House by Ben Fletcher, but Todd decided it was time to set up a separate Department of Labour and to become Minister of Labour himself; and in presenting the Bill, instead of proceeding to a Second Reading, he proposed that it should be immediately referred to a Select Committee. As a result, the Select Committee — comprising Todd himself as Chairman, Jack Keller (doubly qualified as one of the four Opposition Members and doyen of the white labour movement), J.M. Macdonald (owner of the Matabele Steam Laundry and a former Mayor of Bulawayo, known to one and all as 'Matabele Mac'), Norman Straw (established farmer in the Rusape area), Harry Reedman (post-war Rhodesian, developer of Marlborough Residential Estate near Avondale), Abe Abrahamson and myself — found ourselves free to go outside the scope of the Bill referred to us and recommend something quite different if we should think fit.

We had evidence presented to us by people representing the whole spectrum of relevant opinion in the country, employers' and employees' organisations, officials, interested individuals (and impressively amongst them, Fred and Eileen representing the Interracial Association and Charles Mzingeli, Joshua Nkomo, James Bassoppo-Moyo and three other Africans jointly representing the African Unions), and the opportunity of putting questions to and promoting discussion with them away from the glare of publicity. In our sorties to other countries — unique for a Select Committee and in some instances dependent for its contacts on information thrown up in the course of past National Affairs Association activities — we had special access to people whom it would have been difficult to see otherwise. For example, in Elizabethville (now Lubumbashi) we saw senior executives of the immensely powerful and traditionally secretive Union Minière and, in that impressive but not particularly lovable modern city on the banks of the gigantic Congo river, Leopoldville (now Kinshasa), we saw the Governor-General M. Pettillion, who was at that time trying to promote a new and more liberal line in the wake of the recent visit to the Belgian Congo (now Zaire) by the young King Baudouin. Official attitudes were still strongly disciplinarian and paternalist in the Congo, and the most interesting thing to be seen relative to the Select Committee's enquiry was the far greater use being made there than in Southern Rhodesia of Africans on relatively skilled jobs in industry and commerce. On the social side, we did on one occasion find ourselves at an official dinner where Africans were present but we gathered that was about as much of a novelty to the Belgians as it was for most of our committee.

In Johannesburg and Cape Town we met some highly enlightened people, and also some exponents of hard-line white attitudes who made one understand that if many of the operative corpuscles had been carried from the South African into the Rhodesian blood stream, any hope we might have of promoting a non-racial set-up would be doomed. I still remember the impact made on me of the then General Secretary of the South African Mineworkers' Union which I recorded in a note made at the time —

> A crude . . . looking fellow. His main thesis was that the African was a "baboon"; incapable of appreciating the responsibilities of trade unionism and at the same time dangerous because he was not satisfied with equality; he had to be the boss; if he were allowed to advance it could only be at the expense of the European. He had to be handled 'with a knobkerrie'.

Impressive in a quite different way were three young Professors from Stellenbosch University who were core executive members of SABRA, the highly influential South African Bureau of Racial Affairs. They were purist apartheidists, accepting that the policy must be implemented morally with all the self-denial and inconvenience to whites that that would entail; and something that has struck in my memory is the answer one of them gave to a question arising from their exposition of how the Bantustan policy would work out. As I remember it the question and answer went something like this —

> Question: 'But suppose the time arrives when the Bantustans have been set up with all the genuine autonomy you have talked about, why should they then acquiesce in the dominance of white South Africa?'
> Answer: 'Well, I suppose you might think it an immoral thing to say, but judging by what we know of the Bantu, they are not an aggressive people compared with people of Eastern cultures, or even as compared with people of Western culture. They are a pacific people, and we rely on that'.

The views expressed in the evidence proper, by people inside the country, were initially so diverse, and the attitudes we members of the Select Committee ourselves started off with so different, that the chances of reaching agreement on some worthwhile recommendations must have seemed remote indeed. Garfield Todd and Abe Abrahamson and I might be able to work out something we could agree on, and Matabele Mac, who had probably been influenced by contact with the enlightened Hugh Ashton in the course of Native Administration in Bulawayo (and who, incidentally, possessed a rich and joyful fund of rude stories — some very rude — which he would deliver in his still marked Stornowegian accent) might go along with it if he could be persuaded that what it amounted to was common sense. But Jack Keller must surely adopt the kind of attitude he had expressed in the Land Apportionment debate, and Norman Straw — one of those people with an English name but of South African ancestry and hardly any experience of the world outside southern Africa — would surely be bound to adhere to the disciplinarian and paternalist point of view. Harry Reedman was possessed by a fantasy-world conviction (which, to our embarrassment, he would expound on at length in the course of ostensibly putting questions to witnesses) that the whole business of trade unions was an unnecessary aberration, and could be replaced by a sort of Guild system.

Despite all this we did, in the end, arrive at a unanimous Report containing recommendations that were not merely a negative compromise. And I think part of the reason for that was the influence of the select committee process itself. Although the committee was a sort of microcosm of the full House there was a marked psychological difference between one of its discussions and a debate in Parliament. Somehow there seemed to be a strong, underlying compulsion in select committee to look for agreement rather than party or personal advantage. Was it connected with the fact that select committee procedure had no provision for a minority report? Or that members of a select committee who belonged to the Opposition had the same access as governing party members to the background information? Anyway the whole process seemed educational and evolutionary, both for the members of the Committee and for the witnesses. And it seemed to follow from this that in the Report containing our conclusions and recommendations it would be necessary, if we were going to make them convincing to others who had not been personally involved in the process, to write in as effectively as we could manage the background reasoning which had led up to them.

The Report was quite a short document entitled —

REPORT

of the Select Committee on Subject of
Native Industrial Workers' Unions Bill
(A.B. 50, 1954)

and it was printed unglamorously on cheap paper without a cover; but I think it was important, and as it was itself already pretty condensed, that the only way of giving an adequate impression of it may be by quoting quite extensively from it — with advice to anyone not particularly interested in the subject to skim or skip.

The introduction was designed to defuse some of the strong feeling surrounding the subject —

2.   Good industrial relations are vital to our progress. The development of our natural resources is based on private enterprise and in order to attract the necessary enterprise and capital we must satisfy the industrialist that he will be working with a willing and productive labour force. Similarly, in order to attract skilled workers from abroad, and in order to provide the necessary incentive to the workers living here, we must assure labour of satisfactory living standards and opportunities to advance. In all this the relations between management and labour, and between the different sections of labour, play a vital part.

Legislation cannot of itself bring about good relations. It can, however, provide machinery which encourages their development.

A description followed of the relevant existing legislation —

The Industrial Conciliation Act
12.   The Industrial Conciliation Act, which was first passed in 1934 and last revised in 1945, provides, in essence, that if in any particular industry the employers or employers' organisations on the one hand, and the employees' organisations on the other, come together to form a joint body consisting half of employers' representatives and half of employees' representatives, that body, called an industrial council, may be registered and thus obtain official recognition. The function of the industrial council is to negotiate agreements relating to minimum rates of pay in the industry and other matters of mutual interest, and to endeavour to prevent and settle disputes.
13.   When an agreement has been reached the Minister may, at the request of the industrial council, and if he considers it is fair to consumers and members of the public as a whole, give the agreement the force of law by declaring it to be binding on all those who were represented on the industrial council which drew it up. If he is satisfied that the industrial council is sufficiently representative of employers and employees as a whole in the industry, he may declare the agreement to be binding, in whole or in part, on all employers and employees in any given area notwithstanding that some of them were not represented on the industrial council. The Act provides that in any given area there shall be only one industrial council representing any one industry . . .
15.   The Native worker is specifically excluded from the definition of 'employee' in the Act, and consequently he is not represented on the

158

industrial council and the terms of an agreement do not apply to him. The Act does, however, provide at Section 60 that the Governor, at the request of an industrial council or conciliation board, and if he is satisfied that an object of the agreement might otherwise be defeated, declare the whole or any part of an agreement to be binding on Natives in any municipality included in the area covered by the agreement . . .

The Native Labour Boards Act

17. The Native Labour Boards Act was passed in 1947 following the strike of African railway workers which occurred in 1945. Originally it provided for the setting up of a National Native Labour Board and Regional Native Labour Boards for Mashonaland and Matabeleland . . . In 1954 this machinery was changed so as to put the boards on an industrial, rather than a regional basis. . . .

19. The role of the Boards is advisory. They investigate the conditions of employment of Natives in industry and advise the Government on these matters and on the preventing and settling of disputes between employers and Native employees . . . The industrial council interested in the particular industry under investigation is consulted and, thereafter, if the Minister considers that an award should be made, he submits the report to the Governor who is empowered to make regulations fixing minimum rates of pay and other conditions of service of Native employees . . .

21. Under existing legislation, therefore, there is machinery available to Europeans based on the principle of self-government in industry and the principle of consent, and relying on the existence of organised employers' and employees' associations. There is separate machinery applicable to the African based on the fixing of minimum conditions of employment by the Government on the advice of advisory boards.

Next there was a bit about the historical background (revised version, in fact, of what had appeared in the Interracial Association's 'Draft Declaration') which ended by pinpointing what the Committee saw as the main problems arising in present circumstances —

27. . . . (a) The problem of the African worker who has become interested in and has begun to form trade union organisations.
(b) The problem of relations between European workers and the African workers who have learnt to do similar work.
(c) The problem of industrial relations on a works or factory basis as opposed to relations between employer and employee in an industry as a whole.

Then came the heart of the Report, starting with an analysis of the Bill referred to the Committee for consideration, and a tactful, initial pat-on-the-back for it —

34.   The Native Industrial Workers' Unions Bill is an attempt to meet the problem of those Africans who, having become conscious of the benefits to be achieved from some form of collective bargaining, have begun to form trade union organisations. This is done by giving legal recognition to African trade unions as such, by bringing them on to an industrial rather than a regional basis, and by controlling them. It provides for two stages of recognition: enrolment and registration. The main functions of an enrolled union under this Bill would be to report any alleged contraventions of any law relating to wages and conditions of employment, and, in association with an officer of the Department of Labour, to negotiate with an employer or group of employers in regard to conditions of employment. The registered union would negotiate direct with employers, submit a panel of names to the Minister from which members could be appointed to a Native Labour Board and make representations to a Native Labour Board. There are strict provisions relating to the supervision of activities of Native unions by the Registrar, qualifications for office bearers of unions and matters generally concerning the running of the unions.
35.   Your Committee are in agreement with the principles of the Bill to this extent: *that there should be available to Africans machinery for collective bargaining recognised by statute on an industrial basis, and subject to certain essential controls.*

Some of the principal arguments considered by the Committee were then set out —

37.   Some witnesses were opposed to trade unionism as such, feeling that it tended to create hostility between management and labour, to encourage restrictive practices and to encourage wage demands on a national or regional basis unrelated to the economics of particular industries.
38.   Your Committee realised, however, that there is no question of dispensing with trade unionism, especially as it is already an established part of our system as far as Europeans are concerned, and that it could not be confined to one section of the population. In any case African trade unions are not illegal at the present time, and no witness suggested that they should be made so.
39.   Trade unionism can certainly be misused, but your Committee felt that the only insurance against abuse is a system in which trade unions are part of a machinery in each industry designed for co-operation between management and labour, such as our industrial conciliation system, which appeared to command the support of all witnesses.
40.   The great majority of witnesses agreed that the time must come when the African would have access to trade unionism recognised by statute, but there were differences of opinion as to whether that time had already arrived. Many witnesses contended that Africans were

not yet ready for trade unionism and that nothing should be done until they had been educated to it.

41.   Your Committee concluded, however, that some Africans have reached the stage of being able to take part in trade union activities. We believe that it is essential to ensure that these Africans acquire the best traditions, and that the organisations to which they belong are responsibly run. Further, any legislation passed for this purpose should not be designed to create trade unions but only to deal with those that come into existence . . .

Then came the reasons for rejecting the Native Department's racially-based Bill —

43.   Your Committee disagree with the Bill on the ground that *any legislation of this kind should provide machinery for contact and negotiation between management and labour whereas the Bill is almost wholly concerned with the negative aspect of control.*

44.   . . . the provisions of the Industrial Conciliation Act for the establishment of industrial councils are, although only permissive, the essential part of that machinery. It is considered that this has been the principal reason for our fine record of relations as between management and European labour since the Act was introduced. By making positive use of the machinery employers and employees, with the blessing of the Government, established a system which was a distinct advance on the system in force overseas, and refuted the theory that, due to a fundamental conflict of interests between employers and labour, such an organisation cannot work effectively. Your Committee are of the opinion that any legislation embracing the African should incorporate similar principles.

45.   Your Committee further disagree with the Bill on the ground that, by providing for specifically Native unions, *it would tend to perpetuate the racial basis of the existing machinery and this, in the long run, would be detrimental to the interests of European labour, African labour and the interests of the country as a whole* . . .

47.   Your Committee felt that their fears in this regard were fully justified by the position which has arisen on the Copperbelt. There the Government was faced at an earlier date with a similar decision to the one which has to be made here and decided, not as a matter of law (which is not on a racial basis) but as a matter of administrative policy, to train and establish African trade unions which would operate entirely separately from the European trade unions.

48.   Your Committee are of the opinion that the result of this policy has been to exaggerate the sense of conflict of interests between European and African workers. Furthermore it complicates the collective bargaining problem by creating three parties to an agreement, leaving it open to any one of the parties to play off the other two against each other . . .

49.   In examining the apparent conflict of interests between Europeans and Africans your Committee came to the conclusion that in some ways it is more imaginary than real, for the following reasons:

(a)   Fundamentally it is not the ability of the African to compete for the type of work which Europeans do, but it is the lower conventional standard of living of the African which constitutes a threat to the European's position. This means that fundamentally it is in the interests of the European worker that, commensurate with increasing productivity, the standard of living of the African should increase. This is also in the interest of employers and the country as a whole.

(b)   Moreover, there is no threat to European standards in every case in which an African is employed on a job at a lower rate than the European, but only if the African is paid less than his work is worth. This means that it is in the interests of the European worker to ensure that the African is paid his full economic worth; which is also in the interests of the country since, where labour is paid less than its economic worth, the result is a misuse of that factor of production. It follows that properly worked out grading schemes will allow the African to be used on more skilled work without displacing the European.

(c)   Finally, there is a fundamental common interest between employers and all classes of labour in that the aspirations of all depend upon increasing our production per head of population.

50.   These considerations indicate that there is a real basis for co-operation and your Committee have come to the conclusion in principle:

(a)   *That as regards the fixing of minimum wages and conditions of service, and other matters which are outside the scope of management-labour relations in a particular works, the ultimate aim should be a system based on agreement arrived at in each industry by the representatives of employers on the one hand and the representatives of labour on the other; that is to say, a system comprising in each industry a single industrial council, a single employers' organisation to appoint the employers' representatives and a single employees' organisation to appoint the employees' representatives.*

Broadly speaking this would entail extending the machinery under the Industrial Conciliation Act to include Natives by extending the definition of 'employee'.

It would not necessarily mean compelling existing trade unions to accept African members, provided there was machinery whereby the constituent trade unions making up the employees' organisation could jointly appoint representatives to the industrial council.

(b)   *That, as there will for an unforeseeable time to come be industries, or sections of industries, in which those concerned will be unable to operate the industrial council system, but in which it may nevertheless be necessary to have rules governing certain of the general matters with which an Industrial Council would otherwise deal, the Government should have power to make regulations dealing with these matters, and to appoint advisory boards which would at the same time constitute a training ground for the industial council system.*

The advisory boards might be called Industrial Boards as distinct from Industrial Councils.

(c)   *That alongside the machinery for dealing with the general matters referred to above, there should be an effective system of works committees providing a means of consultation and co-operation on a works or factory basis.*

The last section of the Report described in detail the actual amendments to the existing statutes which would have to be made to give effect to its recommendations.

When the report came before Parliament in March 1956 it was received with extraordinary enthusiasm. Jack Keller could still not quite believe that the white trade union leaders would be able to get their rank and file to identify themselves with the views the leaders had finally expresed in discussion with the Select Committee; and Norman Straw was still a little stunned at having gone as far as he had in identifying himself with the Report. But even Stewart Aitken-Cade, leading spokesman for the Opposition, was complimentary —

Right through the report of this committee, Mr Speaker, it is possible to read the absolute sincerity that the members of this committee have put into their work and into their investigations . . . They have taken a basic fact, the fact of economic integration and they have worked from that . . . Their report is a model, I believe, for all other select committees that have the onus and the responsibility of such work placed upon their shoulders by this House.

And Ralph Cleveland, old Salisburian, conservative, felt that he must 'subscribe to the congratulations which have been showered on the committee for what I must call an amazing report'. Cyril Hatty, Minister of the Treasury, said —

It would not be too much, I think, to say that the report itself can constitute one of the greatest steps forward in our whole industrial development, in fact our economic development, for a good many years to come. It has already been said in this debate that in many ways this report tends to give a lead to what should be done in these matters, particularly in multi-racial countries. I myself believe that the report does do just that; it sets a lead.

The motion for the adoption of the Report was put and agreed to without any dissenting vote.

I could hardly believe it. Obviously it was not the end. The legislation we had recommended would still have to be drafted and put to the House and passed; and after that would come the need for high quality administrative effort in helping people — employers and employees, black and white — to use the machinery made available by statute. But it was a magnificent beginning. And I was especially happy to think that the efforts of the kind of liberals Pat and I had been associated with from the beginning of the National Affairs Association and then in the National Affairs Discussion Group and then the Interracial Association — and not excluding my own as a member of the Select Committee — had played an essential part in it. That was something to show for a lot of devoted and sometimes unpopular work by a lot of people.

CHAPTER 13

Bad Omens and Good Ones, 1954–1956

While the Industrial Relations Select Committee was conducting its investigation significant changes were taking place outside its committee room, some hopeful and some ominous, and some either hopeful or ominous depending on the standpoint of the onlooker.

At the level of Territorial politics there was, at the beginning of the period, in November 1954 the appointment of Stumbles as Minister of Justice and Internal Affairs, which seemed onimous, and at the end of it in June 1956 there was a Congress of the United Rhodesia Party at which African Branches were dynamically represented, which seemed full of hope. At the Federal level there was the launching of a scheme for the construction of the greatest man-made lake in the world, Kariba; the beginning of a high-grade, multi-racial university; a new international feel in the atmosphere; money from outside for investment, expertise, immigrants; a diplomatic corps; foreign journalists. On the fringe of politics the activity of the Interracial Associaion was at its height, and another organisation, the Capricorn Africa Society, was preparing for an extraordinary, multi-racial convention to be held on the shore of Lake Nyasa in May 1956.

Stumbles' appointment as a Minister was something of a shock, especially coming as it did within weeks of his having demonstrated, in the course of the Land Apportionment debate, what sort of reaction could be expected of him to even a modest move in the direction of 'partnership'. Did Garfield really think it desirable to have another ex-member of the mis-named Liberal Party in the Cabinet as well as Geoff Ellman-Brown? Did he see no danger in it? Clearly he had to get rid of the portfolio of Justice and Internal Affairs in order to take on a new Labour portfolio, and also the portfolio of African Education when that could be extracted from the Ministry of Native Affairs. But why Stumbles? If it had to be someone with legal qualifications why not a liberal-minded man like Paddy Lloyd from Bulawayo? Could it be that it was simply a geographical necessity: Todd himself, Fletcher and Hatty were all from the south of the country so the new Minister must come from Salisbury? If so, it could be said to be all my fault for having, as a Salisburian, declined Garfield's earlier invitation.

I consoled myself with the thought that it was best in the long run anyway that Stumbles should be inside the Cabinet, sharing responsibility for what had to be done rather than outside it free to appeal to the whites' fear of change. The example of Geoff Ellman-Brown seemed reassuring at that stage. In the philosophy of the Liberal (later 'Rhodesia') Party which they had both belonged to, racial segregation in land ownership had been an article of faith, and yet here now was Geoff, enthusiastically promoting home-ownership schemes for Africans on land (albeit zoned as African Townships) which was situated right in the heart of the 'European Area'. (There was an engaging amateurism in Geoff's speeches. The word 'sincerely' occurred frequently in them, and a composite word 'in-my-humbl'-opinion', and sometimes enthusiastically jumbled phrases like 'We must get down to brass . . . We must get down to copper . . . We must get down to brass bottom'. Actually the last was I think partly a fabrication of Muriel Rosin's and mine. We occupied neighbouring seats in the House and for a time kept a note of 'Geoff's malaprops'.)

The first task Stumbles set himself was to overhaul Southern Rhodesia's security legislation and present to the House amendments to the existing Sedition Act and Subversive Activities Act, a Firearms' Bill and a new Public Order Bill which contained in it all possible provisions for dealing with agitation and subversive conduct that could be gleaned from the laws of England and its Colonial Territories over the centuries. He said it was a result of a request from the Federal Government to the three Territorial Governments to review their existing security laws, and the discovery that the legislation in Southern Rhodesia 'lagged far behind'. Some of us were appalled by the Public Order Bill and Paddy Lloyd expressed this view of it —

> The Bill in itself is merely a symbol, and that is its danger. The danger lies in its symbolism rather than the intrinsic character of the provisions contained in it, and the symbolism is of a body of men who have held themselves out to this country as being of a liberal mind, without being ultra-liberal in a way that might lead to the destruction of the country, but of moderate liberal opinion, who have now decided to adopt the weapons and the measures of reactionaries . . .
>
> Mr Speaker, when this Bill becomes law the weapon which it will place in the hands of those who wish to destroy liberalism in the future is manifest. Because once you adopt weapons of this nature you have compromised yourself, and you are compelled to go on adopting them. And in answer to those honourable Members who have suggested that in the hands of such a government as ours this weapon can never be used to destroy essential rights of the citizens of this country I would say that so has many a liberal government said in the past, and it has

seen the weapons it has forged itself used to destroy that very liberal government . . .

In time to come, Mr Speaker, I think that this Bill will be referred to as a charter for martyrs. The prosecution of agitators under it will gain for them a following which, but for the existence of this legislation, they would never otherwise have gained . . .

We made some impact on the Bill in the course of its passage through the House, but not very much.

Salisbury, already the capital of Southern Rhodesia, was chosen to be the capital of the Federation as well, and in Salisbury the benefits accruing from federation seemed most obvious, especially to whites. But to blacks in Northern Rhodesia and Nyasaland the picture looked different — more like a conspiracy by whites to rob them of their promised freedom and substitute a new, and in some ways more unacceptable, form of colonialism for the old one. That way of looking at it reflected itself in some of the speeches of the black Members of the Federal Parliament from those Territories and many of the white Members were shocked by them. In the northern Territories the African National Congress movement grew, and with it an anti-Federation movement. The reaction amongst whites was to talk of getting rid of Colonial Office influence, and early in 1956 a new Opposition Party was formed, calling itself the 'Dominion Party' intended to operate in both the Territorial and Federal fields, ignoring the distinction between them which to some of us seemed sacrosanct. The leader, Winston Field, was himself a courteous and quite broad-minded man and, by current standards, no racialist; but nearly everyone else in the new party was to the right of him.

We were not unduly worried by these developments. For Africans in Southern Rhodesia the possibility of achieving progress in co-operation with whites was still credible. There was something fundamentally to be trusted about Garfield Todd which seemed more important than his complicity as Prime Minister in conduct on the part of his Government which still from time to time reflected the old, white supremacist attitude. And not only Garfield, but both him and Grace. The more I got to know them the more I learned to appreciate their complementary qualities; he basically the decisive, and in some ways boyish, man of action, and she the sage lady with intuitive foresight. Whether or not she was in agreement with all the actions Garfield felt he had to take as Prime Minister it was impossible to tell, but it seemed certain that none of the important ones would be taken without the benefit of her opinion. And when it came to the far-reaching, five-year plan for African education which emerged after Garfield's assumption of that portfolio, her technical knowledge as well as her wisdom would have been available. She was an expert on the subject in her own right and had been responsible, for example, for one of the text books still standard in that field. I am afraid this description may make them sound grave and puritan. They were in fact a happy, human partnership, respecting one another's judgment.

One of the achievements of the Interracial Association was the production of a quarterly magazine under the title *Concord*. It was an attractive publication, on good paper and with a front cover usually based on a striking and sensitive photograph by Peter Fernandes, a Rhodesian of Goanese extraction whose ancestors had presumably been involved in the history of Portuguese trafficking between Europe, Africa and the Far East. The first editor (though he avoided being described as such) was Monty Bennett, a sensitive, esoteric, Jewish man married to one of the daughters of an important early merchant family called Frankel; and amongst others involved with it at various times were Peter McKay, who had a Scots Guards background and great journalistic ability and, stronger than both, an extraordinary sense of service; and Elias Mtepuka, a gentle and talented Nyasa.

Looking through surviving copies of *Concord*, and recalling the names of the Africans mentioned in it as contributors or otherwise, what strikes me as being quite remarkable is the extent to which real friendships between blacks and whites developed over that quite brief period following the inauguration of the Interracial Association in July 1953. It was, after all, quite a big gap to bridge, and getting together for purposes of the Interracial Association inevitably had something self-conscious about it as its name would suggest. And yet real, straightforward, natural friendships developed often no less congenial, and sometimes more so, than friendships one had with other whites. I don't think I exaggerate this or only imagine it. In my case, and especially in relation to politics at that time, I think of Stanlake Samkange, Lawrence Vambe, Nathan Shamuyarira, and also, belonging to a slightly different context or period, Herbert Chitepo, Enoch Dumbutshena, Leo Takawira and others. Lawrence Vambe had a nice, lazy sense of humour and usually a cigarette hanging from his lips journalist-style: and once when we were on the way to an early committee meeting I remember his drawled comment as we pressed the button of a terrible, creaking lift that had been installed in one of the old Salisbury buildings: 'The white man's magic' he called it. Stanlake Samkange was broad, husky-voiced and highly intelligent, later to be appointed a lecturer at Harvard University.

He was a free-lance writer, and with radical potential as the son of one of the founders of the African National Congress in Southern Rhodesia and himself a Secretary of it; but he was evidently incapable of tackling any subject unhumorously. When I was dealing with private business for him as a lawyer he would typically send me a note in the despised 'kitchen kaffir' addressed to 'Baasi Holderness'. Nathan Shamuyarira, usually called 'Shamu', was a good deal younger; a long-faced, heavy-lipped young man of charm and intelligence who would listen concernedly, and then come to his own conclusions. He was a journalist and he, in his way, and Herbert Chitepo and Enoch Dumbutshena in theirs, were destined to become leading members of the Nationalist movement.

Herbert Chitepo was a more difficult proposition to get on with. He had to be, pioneering at the Bar. I had been in touch with him before his departure for England in about 1950 and afterwards about the possibility of becoming a professional lawyer in Salisbury and the best course of study to follow in England in order to do so, and had advised him that since nearly all of a Barrister's work had to come to him through Solicitors (all of whom were still white) the first African Barrister would, I thought, have a thin time for a long time. There was no opening in the public service, where Africans were still precluded from being taken on to the Fixed Establishment, and I thought the best opportunity of practising law would be to become articled to a Solicitor if that could be arranged. Things being what they were, I thought this would probably mean establishing an African department dealing with African clients and there would be various problems, such as accommodation and getting hold of an African typist; but I thought there was a real possibility of our firm trying the experiment. However, he decided to go ahead and become qualified as a Barrister in England, and then see if he could make a break through at the Rhodesian Bar after returning home. And by 1956 he had virtually achieved that, despite all the difficulties, including the Land Apportionment Act and the fact that even someone like Dendy Young, himself a Barrister and not of the old school, had been opposed to its amendment. It would have been impossible for Chitepo to have done all that if he had been too thin-skinned in the process; and so the person one found oneself dealing with had to be that much cocky and confident. And yet much of the same basic congeniality seemed to exist with him as with contemporaries of his like Shamu; and it was not long before white members of the Bar were treating him quite naturally and some (including Bennie Goldin, one of the former chairmen of the National Affairs Association) as a personal friend.

If this kind of thing could happen surely it must be possible, we argued, to make a break through in politics proper, constitutionally and without racial conflict or violence. Clearly a widening of the franchise would be necessary before Africans could hope to make any significant impact as voters in a general election, and the promised franchise commission had not been set up yet; but what about trying to make an immediate impact at party level, by becoming members of the URP, forming branches and sending delegates and resolutions for consideration to the Party Congress? There was no colour bar in the party constitution, and not even a requirement that members must be registered voters.

This was a proposition that could for the first time be considered by Africans, but of course it had its dangers. Accepting any role in white dominated institutions could imply an acceptance of the status quo and, particularly if there were any element of patronage in it, turn out to be the kiss of death. Already it looked as if that was what was happening to Jasper Savanhu and Mike Hove, the two who had accepted nomination by the Federal Party for the African seats in the Federal Parliament, and on the fringe of politics, to someone like Chad Chipunza who had become a full-time employee of the Capricorn Africa Society.

Capricorn was, like the Interracial Association, a self-proclaimed multi-racial organisation, but it was a more exotic affair, with more high-flown objectives and more money. Its leading light was David Stirling, who had achieved fame as Colonel Stirling, DSO of the Long Range Desert Group before settling in Rhodesia, and it had an impressive array of patrons and supporters locally and overseas. It had begun with the idea of promoting in 'those lands of Eastern and Central Africa which lie between the Abyssinian border and the Limpopo River' — 'Capricorn Africa' as N.H. Wilson had originally christened it — a more extensive political entity than the two Rhodesias and Nyasaland, and promoting large scale immigration to it from Britain and the West — a bastion against communism, Asian immigration, Afrikanerdom and the rest. While the Federation of the Rhodesias and Nyasaland was brewing, Capricorn found itself identified with the promoters in the minds of Africans hostile to it, and lay low for a while. After its re-emergence it adopted as its main objective the promotion of a common citizenship in 'Capricorn Africa', linked with proposals for a multiple vote franchise. Some members of the Interracial Association were members of Capricorn as well, and in fact Peter McKay, who had come to feel he wanted to be involved full-time in this kind of work, accepted full-time appointment with it. That turned out to be good business for Capricorn, for it was Peter who constituted the king-pin of the organisation of that improbable international gathering at Salima on the shores of Lake Nyasa which occurred in May 1956.

The Salima Convention was boycotted by the African Nationalists in Northern Rhodesia and Nyasaland and had no special political impact afterwards, but it was a romantic occasion. I was present as an observer and have happy flashback memories of it. The recreation area on a little plateau elevated by a small cliff from the lake, in earshot of the waves breaking on the little beach; trestle tables loaded with food and drink, surrounded by beautiful Nyasaland bush; white Rhodesians hobnobbing with black ex Mau Mau Kenyans under the stars; high-powered representatives of the Press from all over the world. The meeting hall was a thatched, open-sided structure reminiscent of Colonial days, and some of the material for discussion and speeches contained a strange mixture of looking forward to the realisation of black aspirations and looking back nostalgically to Rhodes' dream. Coming back from one of the opening sessions in which the latter element had been prominent I remember walking alongside the small-statured Alan Paton, who nudged me and in his impish way said 'Who's this fellow Rhodes they keep talking about?'

———————————

There was no damage to Peter McKay's reputation in the eyes of Africans as a result of his working for Capricorn, but with Chad Chipunza there was somehow an acceptance of patronage about it. The idea of joining Southern Rhodesia's governing party and trying to influence it from inside could hardly be said to have any implication of patronage, but it had to be thought about all the same. It would have no appeal to George Nyandoro, for example. He had become scornful of the prospect of making progress by that kind of means and, with James Chikerema, had recently started up an organisation called the City Youth League, committed to taking a defiant line in dealings with bureaucracy. But Stanlake Samkange, Nathan Shamuyarira and others were prepared to try the experiment, and they got to work in collaboration with Mike and Eileen Haddon and Fred Lacey who also decided to get themselves nominated as delegates to the Congress, and with the co-operation of Tony Pedder, a liberal-minded, young, post-war Rhodesian who was now Honorary Secretary of the URP. So when the annual Party Congress assembled in Gwelo in June 1956 it found itself with four African delegates present, representing three new branches of the party which had been established in the African Townships of Harare, Highfield and Mabvuku; and on the agenda, amongst the variety of resolutions of the usual kind, several put forward by them.

It was a novelty and no-one knew what the outcome would be, but it worked. The resolutions were not supposed to be especially important or comprehensive. They were about the effect of the Land Husbandry Act on urban Africans, the substitution in official usage of 'African' for 'Native', a rumoured intention to move Africans in Harare further out of town, the cost of transport to get to work, and an amendment to the existing liquor law to permit Africans to buy ordinary beer and wines as distinct from the 'kaffir beer' supplied by the Municipalities. All of the resolutions were presented ably, and often entertainingly, by the proposers, and all were received well, and not without a touch of wonderment, by the white delegates. It was a small, peaceful revolution and perhaps best illustrated by the resolution about liquor. If it had been left to whites to decide on the reforms which they thought would be most desirable in the interests of Africans a change in the liquor law would probably have seemed the least urgent. To Africans themselves the consequences of the existing prohibition were evident and real, and the need for a change more than mere self-indulgence. As one of them said —

> Many Africans do drink European liquor, and as many as four thousand empty spirit bottles are collected by one individual in Harare every week-end. For this liquor they pay very high prices; 30/- for a 17/- bottle of brandy; 4/- and 5/- for a quart of beer. The only people who gained were the Shebeen Queens who exploit the African in this respect. As a result Africans have taken to drinks far stronger than European liquor, which do them no good. Police are busy and people get into the habit of breaking the law. It was one of the most serious aspects of the affair that people who are genuinely law abiding and support the Police become their enemies.

An amendment was proposed 'stressing the need for enquiry' as the minutes reported afterwards 'rather than action', but a great majority of the delegates swung in favour of the original resolution proposed by the African Branches, and it was passed by a majority of 48 votes to 22. It was an enlightening experience all round, and the adoption of this and other resolutions proposed by them and passed at the meeting gave the Government both a mandate and an obligation to bring about the changes.

It was not this but another aspect of the proceedings that caught the news headlines. In dealing with a resolution submitted by one of the old-established branches Todd decided to make it the occasion to bring into the open in a forceful speech the problem of relations with the Federal Government which, it appeared, had been exasperating him and his Ministers for some time. The way they saw it, all the efforts of the Southern Rhodesian Government designed to bring about African advancement and partnership in conjunction with a programme of vigorous economic development was being jeopardised by a negative attitude on the part of the Federal Government; a negative attitude towards the raising of outside capital funds and to immigration, and also a failure to use its influence with the United Kingdom Government to counter African nationalist and anti-Federation agitation in Northern Rhodesia and Nyasaland. The Federal Government, he said —

> . . . holds that Kariba is so big that it must dominate the entire economic scene until power is flowing from it. The Southern Rhodesian government believes that the decision to build Kariba has as its corollary the necessity to press for widespread development, with such immigration as is required to make possible this development and with the provision of all the services required to absorb a rapidly growing population . . .
>
> The Federal Government states that loan funds are so difficult to obtain that it is not possible to raise the money necessary to give us a completely adequate transport system and also provide the roads, schools, hospitals, etc. which would be needed by a fast growing population. We hold that there has been lack of planning . . . that if the vision were there and the planning done then the funds could be found . . .

Politically, the underlying assumption — that you could not expect whites to accept African advancement except as part of a package of general economic development — was discernible in two examples given in Todd's speech —

> . . . we have been greatly embarrassed as a Government because of the fact that, when we launched a progressive plan for Native education it appeared concurrently with statements from the Federal Government that the Treasury could not make money available for the provision of necessary school facilities for European children. Another example of this apparent conflict lies in announcements, on the one hand from our Government of sound plans for the improvement of African farming and on the other hand from the Federal Government that European immigration must be limited, to 20,000 a year, thus implying curtailment of European progress.

On the political side the Federal Government was doing nothing to prevent developments occurring which were in conflict with the 'pattern agreed upon between the partners in federation' and 'which we had the right to expect . . . would have been the pattern for all political development in the Territories' —

> What I do object to is the political pattern in Northern Rhodesia and Nyasaland — the jockeying for seats in the legislative assemblies on

the basis of race, the continued and increasing underlining of colour . . . The background of Colonial Office experience makes it an unsuitable guide for our people in the North in the development of their political life within this Federation. The division resulting from two governments being under the Commonwealth Relations Office and the other two under the Colonial Office is not only an unhappy one but is fraught with some danger.

He appreciated that he would be accused of interfering in the affairs of Northern Rhodesia and Nyasaland, but there were many Nyasas in employment in Southern Rhodesia and he went on —

but I would remind those who would criticise us in this way that the Nyasaland Congress in particular is active throughout Southern Rhodesia. From time to time meetings are held in various places in Southern Rhodesia. At these meetings anti-Federation songs are sung and people are harangued by leaders who are not concerned with the truth, but are concerned with swaying an uncivilised people by every device they can muster . . . We have waited in vain for the Colonial Office authority to take action against Congress.

What he proposed was that the speech could be put forward as an invitation to the Federal Party to consider the views expressed and —

if in Congress the Federal Party feels there is merit in what we say, and if it is ready to improve its policy . . . then we should link up with them for the benefit of the Federation . . . but if new policies regarding immigration, economic planning and constitutional development are not advanced by the Federal Party — policies which are acceptable to us and to the great number of people in the three territories who are critical of the present Government . . . then we must seek a liaison with people of like mind to ourselves in Northern Rhodesia and Nyasaland and, together with them, challenge the Federal Government all along the line.

The approach seemed pretty clearly to be a sort of amalgam of the views of the five Ministers, although Ben Fletcher was actually absent from the Congress, and it was expressly supported by Ellman-Brown and Hatty, the latter making a spirited repudiation of allegations of financial irresponsibility which had evidently been expressed or implied by the Federal Government —

. . . this old chestnut of bringing up the amount of the national debt means nothing to me because one needs to relate the national debt to assets and I would far rather have a national debt of £500 million relating to earning assets building up inside the country than to have a debt of £20 million on paper. There are many things that we as a government have been doing over the last two and a half years, and one can sum them up in this way: we have been putting more and more value into the country's balance sheet in the same way as the manager of a successful company puts into his balance sheet. The President yesterday, in making his speech, took a particular line. First of all it had a lot of feeling behind it, and secondly, that in our own particular case we are, as my colleague said earlier on, acting as a team and there has been a lot of feeling of the team behind that speech.

The feeling behind the resolution which was the occasion for Todd's speech was an uneasy one, that the confidence of the electorate in the Federal Government was draining away and the Dominion Party, operating as one in both the Territorial and the Federal fields and appealing to the electorate on the basis that Dominion Status and an end to Colonial Office interference were practical possibilities, was cashing in. But Todd's challenge to the Federal Party was disturbing to a number of the delegates to the Congress, many of whom were active members of both parties, and some — notably Ben Fletcher's sister Pat Cooper, one of the formidable ladies of the party — took it as a personal attack on Huggie (now Lord Malvern) which, they said, was particularly reprehensible because Huggie was out of the country at the time. Huggie, in fact, was about to hand over as Federal Prime Minister to the Deputy Prime Minister, Roy Welensky; and Welensky made an immediate, and unconciliatory, statement in reply to Todd's speech which was read out at the Congress.

For me, and I suppose other delegates to the Congress with an Interracial Association connection, there were ominous aspects about all this. How could Africans interpret the strictures on the Colonial Office and talk of Dominion Status as other than confirmation of their suspicion of white intentions? Well, one must concentrate on fundamentals: and one fundamental was the Southern Rhodesian franchise. If that came out right Southern Rhodesia's good faith would be confirmed, and that in turn would be fundamental to the future of the Federation.

At a fairly lugubrious moment in the debate about relations with the Federal Government, when various delegates had been expressing grave views and lending weight to them by referring to instructions which they had received from old-established branches of the party, Stanlake Samkange got up to make an unexpected contribution, which began —

Mr Chairman, I have very clear instructions from Harare on this matter. Which is a great relief to me because it absolves me from the responsibility of doing any thinking on the subject myself . . .

It was very refreshing, and I thought a good augury for the future.

CHAPTER 14

Franchise Proposals, Miscegenation Madness, 1957

The Commission of Enquiry to advise on the franchise which had been promised in the URP manifesto at the general election in January 1954 was not actually appointed until the end of 1956, nearly three years into the life of the Eighth Parliament.

The franchise, or to put it more broadly, the whole question of the role to be played by blacks in national politics, was in a way the most obvious and critical of the issues facing the Todd Government. The means qualification for the vote had been raised by the Huggins Government in 1951, but as a temporary expedient, and the main issue had been left to be decided later. It had since become a red hot issue elsewhere in Africa. In the Gold Coast (on its way to becoming 'Ghana') Nkrumah was on his way to power by the process which he was to glorify in that profane phrase 'Seek ye first the Political Kingdom . . .', and in Northern Rhodesia and Nyasaland the leaders of the African National Congress seemed to be after the same sort of thing. It had its charms for Southern Rhodesian blacks, and its nightmare quality for whites. The franchise was really the common focal point of African aspirations and white fear of change.

The decision to set up a Commission or Select Committee had been part of the understanding arrived at by Todd before the election with the former members of the Rhodesia (previously 'Liberal') Party when they decided to pack it up and join him, but it had been left for the Government to decide after its appointment what the terms of reference were to be and (having decided on a Commission in preference to a Select Committee) who should be appointed as Commissioners. Being outside the Cabinet I could only guess what sort of battle Garfield might be having with some of his fellow Ministers over those questions but could well imagine it could be a tough one, especially after the inclusion of Stumbles, and being already stuck with what had appeared in the Party manifesto —

> To consider the qualifications for the franchise, and consider the best means of ensuring that the government of the Territory will remain for all time in the hands of responsible and civilised men.

It was eventually revealed to us backbenchers that the Commissioners were to be Robbie Tredgold (Sir Robert — Chief Justice of the Federation), Sir John Murray (Chief Justice of Southern Rhodesia) and Sir Charles Cumings (one of the early Rhodesian Rhodes Scholars who had joined the Colonial Service and been knighted for services as a legal officer and a Judge in the Sudan, now retired), and that the terms of reference were to be —

> To consider and report on a system for the just representation of the people of the Colony in its Legislative Assembly, under which the Government is placed, and remains in the hands of civilised and responsible persons, and in particular to consider —
> (a) the qualifications and disqualifications of persons who are entitled to vote at an election for a Member of the Legislative Assembly;
> (b) the qualifications and disqualifications of persons entitled to nomination as candidates for election as a Member of the Legislative Assembly;
> under the existing law of the Colony, and to make recommendations as to any changes that should be made in the law . . .

My reaction was that it would have been more consistent with the deal Todd had made for the Commissioners to be confined to proposals within the framework of a common voter's roll, but I came to feel it was probably wise of Todd to allow the terms of reference to be wider, and that one could hardly have hoped for more than the appointment of Tredgold as Chairman of the Commission and the inclusion at the opening of the terms of reference of the phrase 'a system for the just representation of the people of the Colony'. It was difficult to guess what the attitude of the other Commissioners would be. John Murray was one of that wide network of descendants of the famous Presbyterian Minister Andrew Murray, who had become a Minister of the Dutch Reformed Church in 1822, which now spread across the whole range of white political opinion in South Africa. He had recently come to Southern Rhodesia on his appointment as Chief Justice and he was a wholly lovable and civilised man, but it was difficult to tell what his attitude would be to a constitutional and political question of this kind. Charles Cumings, a more puritanical character, seemed also unpredictable.

The Commissioners did their best to make up for lost time. After considering evidence presented to them by organisations and individuals representing the whole range of relevant opinion in the country (including the newly-formed and growing Dominion Party and, even to the right of it, bodies called the Segregation Society and the League of Empire Loyalists, and at the other end of the scale, some of the African trade unions, and to the left of them the Southern Rhodesia African National Youth league —

previously the City Youth League), they had their Report ready for official release on 15 March 1957.

It was quite a remarkable document, comprehensive but not long, partly philosophical, part pragmatic, and much of it bearing the stamp of Tredgold's classical style of thought and expression. What it ended up with, in essence, was the recommendation that the country should at all costs stick to the common voters' roll and avoid adopting a system of 'group' or racial representation, and that it should substitute for the existing means test based on an income of £240 a year (£20 a month) a combined means and education test which would provide, in effect, four doorways to the franchise, three of them 'Ordinary' and one of them 'Special' —

Door One: Income of £60 a month with literacy (based on ability to complete the application form unaided)

Door Two: Income of £40 a month with Standard 6 (representing the completion of primary education)

Door Three: Income of £25 a month and Form 4 (representing 4 years post-primary education).

Door Four: (Special): Income of £15 a month with literacy.

Door Four would be special in that the votes of voters qualified by that route would be subject to devaluation, if necessary, so as to count for not more than one half of the total votes cast in a constituency by 'Ordinary' voters.

The argument of the Commissioners leading up to this recommendation, and the impact it was likely to have on Rhodesians reading the Report at the time, can best be judged by extracts from it. The first problem they had was to try to reconcile 'a system for the just representation of the people of the Colony' with one 'under which the government is placed, and remains in the hands of civilised and responsible persons', and the Report said at the outset —

> We feel that we should emphasise at the outset that, in our view the first requirement is more fundamental and more important even than the second. No system that leaves any substantial section of the people labouring under a justifiable grievance can, in the end, prevail. It must result in a sense of cleavage, which means that the consent of the governed, upon which all government must ultimately rest, is withheld. Unless the principle is accepted that all sections of a people have their highest interests in common, that people will perish. A house that is divided against itself cannot stand.

Their second problem was to justify the rejection by the Commission of a franchise based on 'one man one vote' — universal adult suffrage — so dear to the hearts of modern Africans. In the opening part of the Report they attempted to do this theoretically —

It may be accepted that the ideal system for the government of a people is democracy based on universal adult franchise, but it is open to question whether this system can function except under certain conditions. For it to operate satisfactorily it requires a homogeneous electorate, at a fairly high standard of civilization and divided by political divisions based on the policies and record of the government and opposition, and not confused by differences, such as race or colour, that tend to create artificial divisions cutting across the real issues. In a young country with a mixed population, at vastly different stages of development, it has yet to be proved that such a democracy can survive, and an objective approach to this possibility suggests grave doubts.

The concept of democracy based upon the adult suffrage has involved so much emotion, not to say passion, that we are fully aware that to challenge its efficacy, even under special conditions, involves a measure of temerity . . .

We hold that government is a man-made institution and that its prime object is to secure to the individual the opportunity to lead the good life, as he sees it. We hold that the democratic system of government can be justified, and amply justified, on the principle, itself manifestly right, that every man should have a say in his own government. But we believe that this right, like every other right, should only be exercised when it can be done without detriment to the rights of others. There is indeed a maxim accepted in all the legal systems of all civilised countries, which being interpreted means that no man should use his own so as to hurt another.

In approaching the franchise with these considerations in mind it must be remembered that even in the most advanced countries the voters only constitute a proportion of the inhabitants of a country . . . Moreover in casting their votes the voters may affect the rights of generations to come. This means that a voter's right to vote must be considered in the light of its possible effect on other voters and other inhabitants of his country born or yet to be born. Surely he should only be permitted to exercise his right if he can do so intelligently . . .

We are entirely satisfied that a country is amply justified in making an endeavour to confine the franchise to those of its inhabitants who are capable of exercising it with reason, judgment and public spirit. It is in this sense that we have interpreted 'civilised and responsible persons' as used in our Commission.

A little later in the Report the Commissioners adopted a more pragmatic justification for the rejection of adult suffrage —

. . . introduced to the Colony at this stage the effect must be to place the European minority entirely in the hands of the African majority, a majority for the most part uneducated and backward. Recent happenings in Africa must have demonstrated . . . that there is a grave danger that many Africans, on an emotional appeal to African nationalism, may sacrifice their own best interests, let alone interests apparently opposed to their own. Even if the fears of the Europeans were unsubstantial, we could not close our eyes to the fact that they exist. There can be no political peace until they have been set at rest. With them allayed the way is open to a more fair-minded approach to every problem that presents itself, for there is no greater disturber of a man's judgment than fear.

The third problem, as the Commissioners saw it, was to choose between schemes in which a franchise on a frankly racial basis had been suggested and those in which the franchise was on a non-racial basis, and the Report said —

The Commission is emphatic in its view that a franchise on a racial basis is wrong in principle and is only to be tolerated, if it is to be tolerated at all, as a purely temporary expedient, to be abolished at the earliest moment it can be replaced by something better . . .

It might be suggested, for example, that in a multi-racial community it is convenient that groups having such obvious common characteristics should be placed on separate rolls and be given separate representation; or that it is impossible in any other way to give the African adequate representation without sacrificing the European interest. Such suggestions disregard the fundamental principle that the interests of the people of the Colony as a whole are infinitely more important than any sectional interest. Moreover, these and any other arguments that we can envisage are heavily outweighed by the fact that racial representation must put a premium upon appeals to passion and prejudice. When the voters in a constituency are all drawn from one section of the community and when conflict, real or apparent, arises between the interests of that section and other sections, it is asking too much of human nature to expect that the Member for the constituency should fearlessly support the view that he knows will be unpopular with his constituents . . . Only a man of exceptional moral fibre can be relied upon to press for the long view, involving compromise and concession of immediate benefits by his group, especially as this course must lay him open to a charge of disloyalty to his group. Conversely, a member avowedly representing a racial group, consciously or subconsciously, feels himself, in a measure at least, absolved from his broader duty to the community as a whole. It is easy for him to convince himself that 'it is the other man's job to press the other side of the case'. . . .

Fourthly, in examining the existing franchise in Southern Rhodesia the Commissioners concluded that it was 'a common roll that is nominally a common roll, but in which the qualifications for the franchise are fixed so high that, in effect, the African is virtually excluded'. They said —

It is in substance, though not in name, a system of racial representation, with this to be said for it, that it does hold out hope that in the passage of time a reasonable proportion of the unrepresented sections will be admitted to the roll. It can only be supported on the assumption, which we do not believe to be true, that at the present time all but a small handful of the Africans in the Colony are incapable of exercising the franchise ... It seems obviously wrong in principle, therefore, that a Member of Parliament should be placed in a position in which he can only do right, as he sees it, at the risk of offending the overwhelming majority of the voters upon whom he depends for his seat in Parliament. This seems to us equally wrong whether the voters be African or European.... Indeed it is a tribute to the Europeans of this Colony that, placed in this situation, they have conducted the affairs of the Colony with so large a measure of fairness to all its people. This has, in part at least, been due to the moral responsibility felt, in greater or less degree, to the Africans in their constituencies even although these were virtually unrepresented on the voters' rolls, a feeling that might well have been absent had they avowedly, and not only in practical effect, represented a European electorate. Despite this creditable record a doubt arises whether, had it not been for the reservations in the Constitution, they might not at times when feeling ran high have done things they regretted in their calmer moments. However this may be, the fact that a system has worked in spite of an obvious defect is no reason for perpetuating the defect.

Amongst suggestions made to the Commission and rejected by them was a system based on proportional representation, of which the Report said —

... Serious disadvantages are inherent in it, particularly in that the size of constituencies has to be increased and a measure of uncertainty is introduced into all election results. We feel that it would tend to encourage an appeal to sections, which in this country would mean racial sections, and to block voting along the same lines ...

They did, however, recommend consideration of the single transferable vote —

This device is designed to avoid the election of candidates by a minority vote owing to the splitting of the vote between a number of candidates. In voting under this scheme a voter indicates his first and second choice of the candidates. If no candidate obtains an absolute majority over all other candidates the second votes are counted and added to the number recorded for each candidate ...

The Commission's main argument was based on principle and not on the relative numbers of white voters and black voters who would qualify in the event of their recommendations being adopted, and although statistics had been presented to them they did not think it appropriate to publish them with the Report. But they realised that relative numbers would be a major preoccupation in the minds of whites and they said —

> We have carefully examined the statistics available to us and, making due allowance for the economic advancement of the Colony, we cannot see how the adoption of our suggestions could possibly involve consequences that should cause uneasiness, even to the most timorous. Human foresight is fallible but such is our considered opinion.

And they tried to be as specific as possible about the type of African voter whom they envisaged as being enfranchised by the 'Special' qualification, their proposed fourth doorway to the franchise —

> Whilst a number of Europeans would obtain registration on this qualification in the main . . . it would apply to Africans. We have, therefore, especially studied its implications in this regard. Subject to the odd exceptions which must occur to any general rule, we are satisfied that an African who is earning £15 per month has proved himself as a citizen. Before he attains to this group an African must have acquired a certain standing, such as that of agricultural supervisor, building overseer, clerk, interpreter, Minister of religion, chief, editor or journalist, medical orderly, building contractor, artisan or farmer (but only the most advanced representatives of these two occupations). The group does not include anyone with less than ten years service in the Police unless he has been promoted to the rank of non-commissioned officer. A Native Department messenger would not qualify until his thirty-seventh year of service, or his eleventh year of service as a head messenger. An African nurse would qualify but only if she were state registered, which involves passing the necessary examinations. The group would not include unqualified teachers. A teacher who has passed Standard six and taken his primary teacher's lower certificate two years later would only enter it after some years service. To enter it at the outset of his career a teacher would have to have taken a two year secondary course plus a higher teacher's certificate. The impression created by these specific instances is confirmed by the results of an interesting survey carried out by the officers of the Labour Department. On the information before us it can be said with confidence that an African drawing £15 per month has passed well beyond unskilled labour and may be regarded as a reasonably responsible citizen. Now it would be unfair to judge the capacity of an African as a voter by the highest standard that can be expected of a European voter. If he measures up to the general average he should be entitled to vote. By this standard it would be difficult for any fair-minded person to deny this privilege to people of the types described or their equivalent. If they are literate and know English and so can follow intelligently the course of an election, we feel they should vote.

So, what did all this boil down to? There were obviously plenty of arguments against the Commission's theoretical approach to the question of 'fitness to vote', but leaving all that aside for the moment, what immediate prospects of participation in politics did their proposals offer to Africans? Assuming the qualifications for the franchise now proposed by the Commission were accepted in toto by the present Government and Parliament and made law, and that qualified Africans would be willing to register on the roll, how many of them would be on it by the time of the next election?

Without the statistics it was impossible to arrive at an estimate, but one could say, on the basis of the Commission's conclusions, that there should be a significant number, a perhaps small but yet significant proportion of the total roll. And, except for the provision about devaluation in the event of the number of votes cast by the Special Voters amounting to more than half the ordinary votes (which we could be certain would not arise, at any rate at the next election), their votes would be the same as anybody else's, and have to be sought by politicians in the same way. So surely no party would be able to ignore them? Suppose they only amounted to 10% of the total roll, their influence in some constituencies would be less than that, but in others it would be greater, and even if it was only a really significant factor in a few out of the total of thirty constituencies, must not that fact influence the whole approach of a party seeking an overall majority of seats? If Samkange, Shamuyarira and co. had been able to make the impression they made as delegates to the URP Congress in 1956, how much greater impact might African voters have on the whole approach of politicians and their understanding of the problems during and after the next general election? And would not that be the best way of proceeding even for impatient, modern blacks tempted towards an uncompromising form of African nationalism, at any rate in Southern Rhodesia where a confrontation with the whites must inevitably involve tough civil war? In their situation one would find it hard oneself to be convinced, but perhaps it would be possible if, at this moment in history and no later, the whites were to give a convincing indication of their good faith.

Parliament was not in session when the Tredgold Report first appeared, but the indications at a caucus meeting in March, when advance copies were distributed to us backbenchers, were favourable. Todd and his Ministers had already received theirs and had time to read it, and they seemed to be all delighted with it. 'This is what we have been waiting for', they said, 'this is the answer'.

183

When Parliament assembled on 23 April it had a lot on its plate including, as matters of crucial importance, the Tredgold Report and an Industrial Conciliation Bill, put together by the Labour Department officials and the law officers charged with drafting work for Parliament, which was supposed to embody most of the recommendations of the Select Committee which had issued its Report the previous year. And it soon began to emerge in caucus that a lot of Members of the governing party were in a disturbed state as a result of what they had discovered in the course of making contact with their constituents preparatory to the session. There had evidently been continuing rumblings of discontent of the kind which Todd had referred to in his controversial speech at the URP Congress: why was so much attention being paid to African interests — African agriculture, African education and all the rest of it? What about the whites? It seemed to be no satisfactory answer to point out that this was the job of the Territorial Government. And on top of all this, there had been a recent development which had aroused amongst a lot of white voters steeped in the southern African tradition a sense of outrage which defied any attempt to resolve it by appeal to reason.

A Rhodesian-born African, Patrick Matimba, who had managed to get some post-school education overseas, had recently returned to the country bringing with him a white wife who had been born in Holland and the first of their children. It was the first time such a thing had occurred, and the family were obviously going to be faced with difficulties, including problems with the Land Apportionment Act about where to live. The obvious place for them to take refuge while getting sorted out was St Faith's Mission where Matimba had been born and where Donald Stowell and Guy Clutton-Brock, uninfected by the anti-miscegenation bug, would be sympathetic. St Faith's was in the Rusape constituency represented by Norman Straw, who had as some of his most influential constituents a number of successful farmers with strong Afrikaner Nationalist inclinations, and who himself considered that Guy and Molly were in effect betraying civilised standards by living amongst Africans and sharing their kind of diet.

What members of the caucus had been coming across were accusations that this — Patrick Matimba and his white wife breeding Coloured children — was the kind of thing the URP approved of, and the inevitable result of 'partnership'. And some of them thought it was absolutely vital to do something to clear their own and the party's name. But what to do? Logically the thing to do, some argued, was to make all sexual intercourse between blacks and whites illegal; but that would hardly be practical. That was the policy of the Nationalist government in South Africa which we were supposed to have turned away from in opting for Federation. However, there was an old existing law on the statute book which prohibited sexual intercourse outside marriage between an African man and a European woman. Why not amend that, so as to 'make it equal'? There would surely be justice in that, and we would be making the political point at the same time. So the reasoning went, and they agreed between them that Max Buchan would propose, and Dr Alexander would second, the motion —

> That the Immorality and Indecency Suppression Act be amended to prohibit illegal sexual intercourse between a European.male and an African female.

and it was set down for debate on 1 May 1957.

Max Buchan was a qualified engineer who had for years been the manager in Gatooma for a leading company dealing in mining machinery. He was an active churchman, kindly and in many ways broadminded; but he had lived forty-four years in the country and in his outlook miscegenation was a self-evident evil. Once he had reconciled himself to the fact that he must confine himself to the subject of sexual intercourse outside marriage he was able to make quite an eloquent and sincere appeal on the basis of hardships encountered by illegitimate children of mixed parentage, and the vulnerability of young African women in the towns 'to fall for the monetary wiles of the unscrupulous European lacking in race consciousness'. And he claimed to have not only the written and verbal approval of all the leading womens' organisations but 'the authority of the heads of the following Christian religious orders to state that this motion has their full support: Anglican, Presbyterian, Roman Catholic, Methodist, Dutch Reformed, Seventh Day Adventist, Baptist, Congregational and Salvation Army'.

Dr Alexander spoke as if the logical course would be, not to pass the motion but to abolish the existing law —

> In my experience in medical practice over the last thirty years I have come across only four cases of European women becoming pregnant to Africans. They were all convicted and they all served terms of imprisonment; but the important point is that without exception every one of these women were of low mental development.They were mostly simple girls marooned on farms miles away from any big centre. They had no social life, and most of them had received very little education. It is submitted, Mr Speaker, that these girls would have been better off if they had been dealt with by a psychiatrist rather than by a High Court Judge.

But he seconded the motion, and voted in favour of it.

It all seemed slightly crazy, like something out of Alice in Wonderland, but one had to make a decision about what line to take in the debate. For most of us the result was, I suppose, more or less predictable. Against the motion, on the ground that the proper thing to do was to abolish the exhisting law, would be (in alphabetical order) Abe Abrahamson, Ben Baron, George Davenport, Paddy Lloyd, Ralph Palmer and myself, and possibly Matabele Mac and Eric Palmer, and of those who supported it Aitken Cade, CFS Clark (who had succeeded Williamson in the Gwelo seat), both Dominion Party, and also Norman Straw and Stumbles and Cleveland would do so for ideological reasons, and the rest if not for ideological then for strategic ones. But for Garfield Todd the motion, crazy though it might be, had critical implications. If he were to come out against it, whatever his reasons and however well expressed, it could count as an indelible black mark against him as a politician looking for white votes and as a Prime Minister depended upon by his colleagues to command them. All of them, Fletcher, Ellman-Brown, Stumbles and even Hatty, had made it clear before Garfield spoke that they would support the motion.

Garfield's speech was well researched and as conciliatory as possible, but uncompromising —

> At first glance the motion which is before us seems perfectly clear. It is concerned, prima facie anyway, with morality. It sets a high standard and it treats European men and African women in the same way as the law of 1903 treats European women and African men, and on the face of it that would seem to be fair play. I would like to be on the side of morality and fair play. But, Mr Speaker, this is frankly a racial measure and not a measure which is concerned with morality.

He explained the historical background. The Act of 1903 prohibiting intercourse between African males and European females had been passed in response to complaints from the still small population of European women that a few women, all known to the Police, who had operated in the brothels before their closure in 1901, were consorting freely with Native males and this could lead Africans to believe that all European women were of this type. In 1916 the law came up for revision because the original version had the words 'for gain' in it and this made it too difficult to secure convictions. Between 1921 and 1951 some proposal of the kind Buchan was now making had been made on a number of occasions, which Todd detailed in his speech, but on each occasion the government, on looking further into the matter, had decided against taking any action.

> Maybe it is to be wondered, if the case were as clear cut as the honourable mover has endeavoured to point out, that legislators down

through fifty-four years have turned down the suggested amendment on each occasion.

He pointed out the implied insult to the Coloured population contained in some of the statements made in the course of the debate —

Sir, much has been said about the offspring of Europeans and Africans, and it is true that many of them are being brought up in surroundings which do us no credit and do the country no credit, but if there is any suggestion that these people are of a lower breed or less capable then I would refute that completely.

It is suggested that we do not know Euro-African shorthand typists but that is only because we have had a secondary school for these people for only about four or five years. There has been a great lack of willingness by Europeans to accept the responsibility which should have been accepted long ago with regard to these Coloured children. Not only that but certain statements made this afternoon are, I think, an insult to the Coloured people in general. There are a great many other Coloured people who from legitimate marriages have produced children, one I know myself has nine children who have helped to swell the total over the years from 1,000 to about 8,000. I, myself, have many friends among the Coloured community who are worthy people. Amongst them are fully trained mechanics, teachers, transport drivers, nurses, and people in positions of responsibility and holding some place in the community of Southern Rhodesia. It was said that when these people grow up they 'reproduce people of their own kind'. What can be taken from a statement like that? We can only gather that people of their own kind are not worthy. We in this country are all against miscegenation. Under the circumstances which exist in southern Africa it is very unwise to say the least of it. But I am amazed at the action of the Churches. I also would like to be on the side of the Churches, but I wonder if the honourable Member has put before the Churches what is involved. This is not a moral question; it is a racial question.

He did his best, but when the vote was taken (and after allowing for the fact that Wightwick, who on this occasion was going to vote with 'the liberals', got himself into the wrong lobby by mistake) 9 Members including Todd were against the motion, and 15 were in favour, including all four of Todd's fellow Ministers. It seemed a lunatic anachronism.

CHAPTER 15

Franchise Reform, 1957

For a while it looked as if the kind of reactionary mood amongst whites which had resulted in the Buchan motion being put before the House and accepted by it might put in jeopardy all our hopes for the future. It seemed to infect both the debate on the Tredgold Report and the debate on the new Industrial Conciliation Bill which proceeded in parallel during the whole of May. And when one looked over the fence into the Federal field the prospect there was disturbing too.

Welensky, now Federal Prime Minister, seemed to be trying to beat the Dominion Party at their own game, talking about Dominion status and using the word 'we' in his speeches as Prime Minister to mean, not the citizens of the Federation generally, but the white ones. Our companion party, the Federal Party, was talking about making changes in the Federal constitution, including changes in the Federal franchise which, so far as one could see, seemed to be designed to go in the opposite direction to the one advocated by the Tredgold Commission, and to entrench group representation instead of getting away from it. And yet some sort of fusion between the URP and the Federal Party looked to be unavoidable. The Dominion Party was gaining ground — despite the fact that Winston Field, to his credit, refused to cash in as leader on white reaction to the Matimba affair. Amongst Southern Rhodesian Africans a movement was gathering momentum to re-establish the African National Congress on a new and up-to-date basis.

For a time the climate for bridge-building looked gloomy; but later the clouds began to disperse.

The reception of the Industrial Conciliation Bill was quite different from the enthusiastic one which had been accorded to the Report of the Select Committee on the Native Industrial Workers Union Bill, whose recommendations were supposed to be incorporated in it, and for a moment there was the spectre that it might founder and all the fruits of the Select Committee's work be wasted. But the objections in the speeches on the second reading were not all attributable to the change of mood. What had happened was that the officials charged with drafting the Bill, instead of simply taking the existing Industrial Conciliation Act and putting into an amending Bill the changes which we had been at pains to specify in the Report of the Select Committee, had decided to go further and to try to kill a number of other birds with the same stone. They had produced the draft of a complete new Act of 136 clauses in place of the existing one, and had included in it, for example, sections relating to the Rhodesia Railways which were a special case and we, on the Select Committee, had thought that it would be biting off more than we could chew to tackle at that stage. In a prominent place at the beginning of the new Bill they had put in compulsory provisions relating to Works Committees which, in the Select Committee Report, had been not much more than an afterthought. And they had put in a number of provisions giving discretionary powers to the Minister and government officials which, in a Bill confined in its operation to Africans would have seemed normal, but in this one involving white trade unions would be bound to get in their hair. In short, it was a bit of a mess, and a striking example of how different a drafting job can be depending whether the draftsman is working in close personal contact with the interested parties or separated from them by an intermediary, no matter how detailed and precise the intermediary's instructions.

Instead of letting the debate go to a vote on the second reading Todd, as Minister in charge of it, decided to propose that it should be referred to a further Select Committee, and everyone agreed. I was happy about that because I thought it was possible, given the chance, to meet most of the objections expressed in the course of the debate and, in particular, to incorporate in the legislation provision for an Industrial Tribunal or Court which had been suggested by Wightwick and supported by Paddy Lloyd. Wightwick had expressed wholesale opposition to the Bill but when you boiled it down his objections were really centred on the powers given to the Minister and officials, and if most of these could be transferred to an Industrial Tribunal there would be little left of his objections. The further Select Committee was set up and I was glad to find myself appointed a member of it, with four others who had also been members of the previous one — Todd, Abrahamson, Reedman and Straw — and two newcomers representing recent hostile opinion — Wightwick and Clark (Dominion Party).

Turning to the franchise, the proposals contained in the Tredgold Report came before Parliament on a motion by the Minister of Justice (Stumbles) 'that the House take into consideration the Report of the

Franchise Commission'; and the change of attitude towards the Report which had grown amongst Members since making recent contact with their constituencies was most bluntly expressed in the course of the debate by Matabele Mac —

> The honourable Member for Railton was not alone in his views when he expressed the opinion that a great many of the European population were apprehensive of the forced pace of African development. That, Sir, is no exaggeration. I discount entirely the extremist when I say that there are two strands of thought in the reasonably minded European to-day. On the one hand we have the element who, with the present pace of African development, foresee a complete African domination in the near future, and when one considers the amount of legislation under discussion in this very session combined with the incessant demand of some African leaders, they may feel that they have reasonable grounds for that fear. We have, on the other hand, the European element who feel that if we do not take the 'moderate' African with us we may drive him into underground channels where he becomes a subversive element.
>
> 'Moderation' is a term which the average African does not understand. You only have to listen to the utterances of the more responsible leaders, in and outside of Parliament in another House not far from here, to realise this statement is no exaggertion ... No sooner was the report of the Franchise Commission ready than we have a demand from the Southern Rhodesian African National Congress for universal adult suffrage. The Pass Laws Amendment brought forth a violent opposition from a body styled the African Youth League who, according to press reports, will oppose it tooth and nail. I would warn these people that they are doing their cause incalculable harm ... They are forcing the moderate minded European to align his thoughts along the racial pattern in the Union of South Africa ...

Sixteen Members — more than half the total membership of the House — took part in the debate, and the key issue was the Special Qualification for the franchise proposed by the Commission, described earlier as 'Door Four': income £15 per month with literacy and the provision for devaluation in the event of the number of special votes cast exceeding one half of the ordinary votes cast in any constituency. It presented everyone with a dilemma. No one now, it seemed, wanted to abandon the common voters' roll, to exchange a system which was non-racial in principle for a racial one, and the Tredgold report said that if the existing income qualification of £240 per annum (equivalent to £20 per month) was maintained it would be a common roll only in name and not in practice. But to agree to a reduction to £15 per month could be courting condemnation by the white electorate on the ground that it constituted a 'lowering of standards' — a phrase which had come to have a potent, political significance. On the strength of the sixteen speeches it looked as if a 2:1 majority would be opposed to the Special Qualification suggested in the Report, and only five of us — Todd, Davenport, Ralph Palmer, Ben Baron and myself — would be prepared to accept it. The only two Ministers to speak were Stumbles and Todd. Stumbles, while heaping fulsome praises on the Commission and quoting a large part of the report verbatim, let it be known that he was 'not necessarily wedded to that income bracket'. Garfield spoke in conservative terms but indicated pretty clearly that, so far as he was concerned, whatever formula did emerge should be such as to make eligible for the vote at least the kind of people the Tredgold Commissioners had in mind in proposing the Special Qualification. Wightwick had evidently decided this was the time to disassociate his image from any taint of liberalism. 'We should reject the Special Qualification and the fractional vote altogether', he said, 'and deal with the problem of political representation for people who are not yet fully civilised' in a Second Chamber and not in the Legislative Assembly.

It was clear that my view of the matter would be the most radical, and I thought I might as well express it if only to give other relative liberals something to be to the right of —

> . . . personally, Sir, I would have been happy with a much lower qualification than is recommended by the Commission, and an unconditional one. As a European who was born in the country and who has my future and that of my family committed to it, I would have been happy with a much lower qualification. For leaving aside the fears that some people have of being swamped, and of a lower standard of voter being susceptible to appeals to racialism, it seems to me that the qualification which a person needs to vote is a very simple matter . . . What he does is, not himself to govern, but to make a choice between alternative candidates for Parliament, and what we want him to do is to choose the type of candidate who will exercise his function in a civilised and responsible way . . . In order to do that I suggest that what the voter needs in the first place is a 'nose for integrity', so to speak, and secondly, a sufficient understanding of affairs to be able to tell whether a candidate is talking realistically or bluffing. As regards the first quality, one grown-up man is likely to have as good a nose for integrity as the next. As regards the second, the voter must have been educated up to a certain point, either at school or by life. And I think the alternative requirement of his having attained a certain standard of formal education or a certain earning power is the best.

I had come across in the Parliamentary Library a speech which had been made by a famous Chief Justice of South Africa, Sir James Rose-Innes,

191

in 1929 and quoted it in my speech —

> At that time, as honourable Members will remember, the Cape Province had a great many Africans on the common voters roll — it still had a common roll and the qualification was very low. It was about this time that the iron men from the highveld were making a really serious bid to abolish the common roll, not because the Africans of the Cape Province had done wrong but simply because these men had a bigoted feeling that it was wrong for black and white to vote together. This is what Sir James Rose-Innes said —

>> The argument is sometimes heard that, no matter how great the intelligence of the individual civilised Bantu, yet the race still lacks certain qualities of stability and balance which in the European have been evolved through the centuries, and which are necessary to the successful working of constitutional government. And much is made of instances where Negro communities, left to themselves, have disappointed the hopes of their well-wishers. But the circumstances in the Union of South Africa are widely different from those which prevail in Haiti or Liberia. We have to do here with a section of the Bantu race which in actual capacity for affairs is remarkable.

>> The native is a born politician, and even in his uncivilised state is well accustomed to debate and to decide communal concerns. And the Cape natives for three-quarters of a century exercised their electoral privileges in a manner which now is not called in question. I venture here to bear my own testimony on this point. More than forty years ago I represented a country constituency, one third of whose electors were natives. Making every allowance for unconscious partiality due to the fact that they gave me unwavering support, I should like to say that they took an intelligent interest in all questions which affected them, and debated them keenly and with great pertinacity. The dignity and restraint, as well as the ability with which the proceedings of the Bunga in the Transkei are conducted afford another proof of the political capacity of the Bantu . . .

My speech concluded —

> . . . another reason which I would have for accepting a low and simple qaulification is that I am confident that an act of faith in this country at this time would give the lie to the contention that the Africans would vote in a block against the Europeans. And I think the experience in England in 1867 and 1925 does support that. But of course, Sir, you cannot leave aside the factors which for the time being exist — the fear of being swamped and of appeals to racialism. The most we can hope for at this stage is a formula which will be acceptable to honourable Members of this House and to the voters of this country which will produce a sufficient number of Africans on the roll for two purposes: first to convince them, the Africans, that there is real hope of

achieving progress through the Party system and secondly, sufficient to give Europeans the opportunity of satisfying themselves as to whether the Africans will vote in a block or not.

My greatest doubt about the recommendations of the Commission is that the effect may not be to bring on enough for these purposes. On the other hand, I think that the fears of the Africans that they will bring on too few are exaggerated, and sometimes based on a lack of knowledge as to how minorities may have a real influence in the system . . .

My firm conclusion on the matter is this: that although the recommendations of the Commission could be described as 'universally unpopular' they are certainly the best we are likely to get, and . . . I think we should accept them as a whole and 'give it a go', on the basis of the recommendations.

As well as the 'no lowering of standards' argument there was an objection to the Tredgold special qualification in the speeches of Members ranging from Wightwick to Paddy Lloyd which I thought was good, and might even be promising in that, if we were able to meet it, we might find ourselves with a number of converts. It related to the 'fractional' or devaluation aspect suggested by the Commission. Ben Baron dealt with it best, and made a constructive suggestion in what seemed to me to be an endearing speech —

The report of the Franchise Commission is therefore, as it must inevitably be, a compromise between the maintenance of the common roll on a high standard and the other principle of ensuring the just representation of the people. It is in effect a compromise. It is a sincere and courageous attempt to preserve the principles of the common roll which are dear to us all and to adapt such principles to local conditions. It is an attempt to allay and dispel the fears of the Europeans of domination by Africans, and to give expression, on the other hand, to the growing demand of the African for representation.

Other countries very near to us — Northern Rhodesia, Nyasaland, Kenya, Uganda — have effected the compromise in another manner; that is, by giving direct representation to Africans in their Legislative Assemblies. Our Federal House has done the same; but this is not to our liking, and rightly so. . . .

But, Mr Speaker, there are in my submission very considerable objections to the fractional vote as propounded by the Commission.

He listed a number of objections, including the following:

That although it was a vote it might not always be a full vote;
That the value of the vote might vary from constituency to constituency;
That there would be considerable difficulty — if not impossibility — in delimiting constituencies to give effect to the Commission's

recommendations;

That special voters would start with a grievance because their votes might not count as full votes;

That the special voters would have to be on a separate roll, and vote with different coloured voting papers;

and he concluded:

I have worked out an alternative scheme which I offer with due deference and which I hope may commend itself to honourable members . . . Briefly this scheme is: let us decide on the maximum number of special qualification voters we are prepared to accept on the roll. Let us say there are at the moment in round figures 60,000 voters on the roll. They will remain as ordinary voters. According to the Tredgold basis we would then be prepared to accept one half of this figure, that is 30,000 as special voters. The present 60,000 would become the ordinary voters and any persons who qualified in the ordinary way of whatever colour would continue to come on as ordinary voters, but we would close the list of special voters at 30,000 . . . These special voters would be able to come in on the same qualifications as are proposed by the Tredgold Commission, that is a salary of £15 a month and knowledge of the English language. I would not change that, and they would still be called special voters. But the position is, once having been enrolled, they would come on to the ordinary roll . . .

Having heard the sixteen speeches the Government decided to withdraw the motion and turn the problem over to the caucus to see whether governing party members could arrive at some agreement, and in caucus a sub-committee was appointed comprising two Ministers, Stumbles (Chairman) and Ben Fletcher; two of the strongest opponents of the Bill on the back benches, Wightwick and Straw, and, as in effect the representatives of the left, Ralph Palmer and myself.

The sub-committee spent nearly two full days battling over the Special Qualification. By this time there had been more or less general agreement that instead of making the special vote a reduceable one we should make the special door to the franchise a temporary one, to be closed once a substantial number of special voters had come on to the roll through it. And nearly the whole of the sub-committee debate was concentrated on the question of what the special qualification should be, and at what point the door should be closed. The probable effect of each proposal in terms of relative numbers of white and black voters was a fundamental consideration. It was no good pretending otherwise, and all possible figures and estimates were obtained from the relevant Government Departments.

There was powerful resistance to anything lower than the existing income qualification, and Ralph and I felt that it was only by a pretty skilful bit of team work on our part that we managed to block the adoption of a formula which would have amounted to a rejection of the most enlightened of the Tredgold Commission's proposals and a reversion to what they described as a common roll which was in substance though not in name a system of racial representation from which 'the African is virtually excluded'. The sub-committee reported back to the full caucus without agreement but recording four of the proposals we had discussed, including two which Ralph and I would have thought passable.

At this stage *The Rhodesia Herald*, adopting the tone of a righteous supporter of liberal causes which it was not, came out with a leading article attacking Todd. It accused him, not of going in the wrong direction (which would have opened it to the charge of being illiberal), but of failing to command the united support of the party in the matter of the motion on miscegenation, and on the Industrial Conciliation Bill, and now the franchise. And Wightwick, in a pompous letter to 'My dear Prime Minister', marked 'Confidential to URP Members' and with a copy to each of us, gave it as his belief that Garfield no longer commanded the support of the country and ought to recommend to the Governor 'someone who is not regarded as quite so extremely liberal as yourself'.

Garfield called a caucus meeting for 19 June and set out in a letter to Members the conclusion which he had arrived at after considering the report of the caucus sub-committee —

> ... The Committee agrees that there should be a special category of voters as an interim measure.
>
> I suggest as an alternative, Standard 8 and no monetary qualification. This would mean that only people who have had ten years' schooling could qualify — not, e.g. a literate wife of a man who has Standard 8.
>
> As for the influence this group would have, it appears to me that the simplest and fairest way would be to allow registrations, on a country-wide basis, up to 20% of the total and then close down this avenue of entrance ...

The letter was despatched on the 11 June, and Garfield must have had strong indications soon afterwards that he was going to be faced with serious opposition in the caucus and even, perhaps, in his own Cabinet. On 15 June he was due to fulfil an engagement to address the Fourth Annual General Meeting of the Interracial Association of Southern Rhodesia. I was no longer chairman of the Association. If I had been I would perhaps have felt reluctant to embroil him, knowing now more from the inside of politics what sort of political psychology amongst his colleagues he had to cope with, and what sort of reaction they had to something like the Interracial Association. Eileen Haddon had taken over from me as chairman and, partly at least due to her courageous and forthright approach, it continued to comand support amongst leading Africans. I was present at the meeting in my more nominal role of President, and in greeting Garfield and Grace I remember having a private word with her, and her saying something like this: 'Gar is really going to say something to-day, and' (with a mixture of excitement, humour and foreboding) 'the future is anyone's guess'.

Todd made a stirring address, reported matter-of-factly in the Association's minutes afterwards as follows:

> About 170 people were present at the Meeting when the Guest Speaker, the Hon R.S. Garfield Todd, MP, Prime Minister of S. Rhodesia, was welcomed by the Chairman, and after congratulating the Association on their work on investigations and memoranda on many subjects addressed the meeting on the following lines:
>
> For many years there did not seem to be much progress for the African, but since 1950 there had been tremendous changes in S. Rhodesia. Secondary Industry, last year valued at £100,000,000 employs more than 60,000 Africans and 70,000 Europeans. Expanding national income had made development schemes possible, such as the Land Husbandry Act. Already 3,400 houses had been completed in Highfield Township where more than 16,000 people now live and where Salisbury Africans can buy their own homes. It was remarkable that so far the Government has not needed to station one single policeman there. Mr Todd said he agreed completely with the Tredgold Report where it says that we must make it possible for every individual to have a place in the sun. This did not mean that what we call European standards would be lowered, but that opportunity to work for and attain those standards must be given to all Rhodesians. Tolerance, understanding and more of the vision of Rhodes, who abhorred race antagonisms, was needed now, and unless racialism was banished from Government policies, franchise proposals and the minds of people the spirit of Rhodes would pass from the land.
>
> We were in danger of becoming a race of fear-ridden neurotics. Rhodes felt that when a man had so far accepted civilisation as to be a working, wage-earning citizen, sufficiently educated to read and write, he was entitled to a voice in the government of the country. The Federal Goverment to our great disappointment announce the continuation of the racial pattern. S. Rhodesia must uphold Rhodes' liberal dictum of equal rights for civilised men, regardless of colour, and if legislation further to implement that policy when introduced to our House in July was so changed as to continue to keep off the rolls our 6,000 Africans who have had 10 years education and who work as teachers, medical orderlies, and so on, we would be so betraying the

spirit of Rhodes that, said Mr Todd, he would not continue to lead his party. However, he was confident that our legislators would meet the spirit of the challenge of the Tredgold Report.

Mr Todd's speech was greeted with great enthusiasm, and he was several times interrupted by applause.

At the caucus meeting four days later it was apparent that the blockage had been cleared, and agreement was quickly reached on changes to the franchise substantially the same as the ones recommended by the Tredgold Commission, but with this modification: that instead of a single 'Fourth Door' giving special access to the common roll there would be both a Fourth Door, requiring £240 per annum income with literacy, and a Fifth Door, requiring Standard 8 education without any minimum income; and instead of providing for the votes of specially qualified voters to be reducible, the law would provide for Doors Four and Five to be closed when the number of votes registered on those qualifications reached 20% of the number of ordinary voters.

After the caucus meeting Todd embarked on an exhausting campaign to sell the new franchise to the electorate, personally addressing large and small meetings all over the country, inviting questions on it from farmers and others disposed to be hostile and dealing with them himself; and the actual legislation was passed at the next sitting of Parliament on 21 August 1957.

Looking back now it appears a modest enough reform, but it was something of a triumph relative to the realities of white politics at the time. Relative to African opinion it was, of course, minimal compared with 'one man one vote'. But there was obviously a limit to what Todd and the white liberals could be expected to achieve; and the fact that he had been prepared as Prime Minister to put his head on the block to achieve this much, and even chosen to do so at a meeting of the Interracial Association, was substantial evidence of good faith.

CHAPTER 16

ANC Revival,
Industrial Relations Reform, 1957

During the second half of 1957 I was so heavily involved with the work of the Select Committee on the new Industrial Conciliation Bill, and so convinced of its importance as a companion piece to the now established franchise, that I suppose I tended to discount the significance of other events taking place at the same time; like the decision of the Federal Party and URP to merge, and the decision by the Federal Party nevertheless to go ahead with a Constitution Amendment Bill quite inconsistent with the spirit of the new Southern Rhodesian franchise, and the rebirth of the Southern Rhodesian African National Congress and its impact on white opinion.

I have no personal record of what moves towards rapprochement between the Federal Party and the URP were made following Todd's exposure of the differences between them at the URP Congress the previous year. It must have resulted in some clearing of the air surrounding economic and financial policy, and that, so far as Todd's Ministers were concerned, would have been the main obstacle to 'fusion' (as the proposed party merger was termed). For Garfield himself I suspected that the continuing difference in outlook epitomised by the attempt to establish a genuine, non-racial common voters' roll in Southern Rhodesia, on the one hand, and the determination of the Federal Government, on the other, to continue and entrench the principle of racial representation in the Federal Parliament, must seem to be a fatal obstacle. But speaking to Grace on some occasion she told me in confidence, and with some foreboding, that Garfield had agreed to fusion. There had been no alternative. And at a Congress of the URP in 1957 a Resolution was passed agreeing in principle to fusion with the Federal Party under a Constitution which was to be adopted at a Congress of the Federal Party in November. It would then cease to be the Federal Party and become the United Federal party (UFP) and it would only remain for individual branches of the URP to convert themselves into Territorial branches of the UFP.

The inaugural meeting of the new Southern Rhodesian African National Congress was arranged to take place on 12 September, the day when the whites would be commemorating the arrival of the Pioneer Column in 1890, known as 'Occupation Day' until its recent change of name (in deference to Federation) to 'Pioneer Day'. It must have been a stirring occasion for those present, with speeches and songs carrying a feeling of solidarity with African nationalists elsewhere in the sub-continent, including an address by Dauti Yamba, leading member of the Congress in Northern Rhodesia, and that moving and beautiful song 'Ishe Komborera Africa' (God Bless Africa) which had first been heard in South Africa earlier in the century and had since become a sort of African National Anthem. Joshua Nkomo was elected President, and James Chikerema and George Nyandoro (of the City Youth League, now superseded) Vice-President and Secretary-General respectively.

To whites having even the limited contact with African leaders that Pat and I had it was no surprise that some of them should feel it necessary to revive Congress at that stage. What did seem in a way extraordinary was the nature of the manifesto adopted at the meeting, entitled 'Southern Rhodesia African National Congress Statement of Principles, Policy and Programme', and the fact that a white man had been intimately involved in the formulation of it and was present as one of the speakers at the meeting. St Faith's Mission Farm, with its experiment in community co-operation promoted by the 'C-Bs' (Guy and Molly Clutton-Brock), had become a meeting ground for the kind of ideas Guy believed in and ones which people like George Nyandoro would find themselves formulating when they looked beyond the abolition of white supremacy to the positive policies which they would like to see implemented; and Guy had been entrusted with the main drafting of the Statement of Principles and Policy.

It was anything but a racialist or anti-white or inflammatory document, and not even particularly revolutionary. In fact the middle section of it headed 'Political Programme' was quite similar in its approach to the kind of thing the Interracial Association had tried to do, offering constructive proposals under various heads — in this case twenty-one of them including Land, Agriculture, Urban Areas, Local Government, Education, Industry and Trade Unions, Taxation, Foreign Investment, Immigration, Political Representation and Foreign Affairs. And while the abolition of racial discrimination was a consistent theme, the acceptance of current realities and the need to convince the existing establishment of the need for change was conspicuous. For example, concerning 'Land', it was emphatic that land reform was of the utmost importance and the Land Apportionment Act 'must be repealed' but it also put the point in another way saying —

> Government must promote the fullest freedom for the use of land by competent people regardless of race, and must provide for this now largely through the system of freehold land tenure. It is, however, both uneconomic and also socially undesirable that land should be apportioned racially.

On 'Agriculture' —

> Agriculture will benefit greatly if racial restrictions are removed and the large and small farmer are permitted to farm side by side to their mutual advantage.

As regards economic policy, there was none of the hankering to retreat from industrial revolution which had been characteristic of much of the labour movement in England in the first half of the nineteenth century —

> Congress believes that in the whole of Eastern and Southern Africa there are three outstanding needs which it is supremely important to meet:-
>
> (a)   the standard of living of millions of people must be raised in a short space of time through their rapid social, economic and political advancement;
>
> (b)   this is only possible with the aid of skills, techniques and capital from overseas. These must be attracted to this country not only by the offer of material advantages but also by appeal to altruism and the sense of service prevalent in the world. This is a challenge to the more advanced and privileged people in the world whose help is required in the interests of world peace and the total development of mankind.
>
> (c)   in view of the inevitable uprising of national feeling among the people of Africa and the need to enlist the co-operation of the mass of the people in this great enterprise, full participation of African people must be provided for in Government, and the legitimate political aspirations of the people be thus fulfilled.

The nearest to being revolutionary the document got was in regard to Political Representation —

> Congress can see no justification for continuing any limitation of the franchise on grounds of either income, educational standard or race. The only form of government acceptable to the vast majority of peoples in the British Commonwealth is parliamentary democracy based on universal adult suffrage, since this alone can produce a government responsible to all inhabitants of the country and aware of the needs of all. Further, only by this system can the enthusiasm of the whole people for government enterprise and national development be evoked; and only by this system can we arrive at that fully representative government which, in the eyes of the United Kingdom

and the world is the condition of complete national independence. The real danger to future stability lies in keeping the majority of the people voteless, not in extending the franchise.

Congress believes that the present electoral arrangements are designed to keep political power in the hands of one small racial section of the population, and the continuation of a racial alignment of political forces will be disastrous. The vote must be cast for the good of the whole country, not to promote the sectional interests of any one race. Racial politics will be disastrous for all. They can be avoided by universal suffrage NOW.

But the next section — 'Political Programme' — seemed to make it clear that what the document meant by 'universal suffrage NOW' was really 'universal suffrage as soon as possible' —

Congress ... believes that the country can only develop peacefully as a society in which the different races become increasingly integrated in social, cultural, economic and political life . . .

The opening part of the document, headed 'Principles and Policy', began —

The African National Congress of Southern Rhodesia is a people's movement, dedicated to a political programme, economic and educational advancement, social service and personal standards.

Its aim is the NATIONAL UNITY of all inhabitants of the country in true partnership regardless of race, colour and creed. It stands for a completely integrated society, equality of opportunity in every sphere, and the social, economic and political advancement of all. It regards these objectives as the essential foundation of that partnership between people of all races without which there can be no peaceful progress in this country.

Congress affirms complete loyalty to the Crown as the symbol of national unity.

It is not a racial movement. It is equally opposed to tribalism and racialism . . .

The closing sections read —

SOCIAL PROGRAMME

Congress encourages hard voluntary work for the development of community life. It will attempt to promote the following social organisations and will co-operate in their formation with all other bodies interested and devoted to non-racial principles:-
COMMUNITY ASSOCIATIONS, NEIGHBOURHOOD CENTRES and SETTLEMENTS to develop improved facilities for education, recreation, housing, health and social, moral and intellectual advance in co-operation with local authorities and voluntary organisations.
ADULT EDUCATION facilities including literacy classes, evening classes, courses and discussion groups.

PUBLIC LIBRARIES and READING ROOMS to make available good books, periodicals and general information to local committees.
MENS' and WOMENS' Clubs for educational, social and recreational purposes.
YOUTH CLUBS and YOUTH ORGANISATIONS for the provision of healthy leisure ocupation for young people.
CHILDRENS' NURSERY SCHOOLS and PLAY CENTRES to aid people in the upbringing of their children and to provide facilities for early education and play for children.

PERSONAL PROGRAMME

Congress encourages all members in their daily lives to offer to all people, regardless of race, colour, creed, class or political affiliation, a good example in habits of —
FRIENDSHIP, COURTESY, GOOD MANNERS and RESPECT in all dealings with individual people.
HONESTY in all dealings with other people and in all money transactions.
HARD WORK with hand and brain in industry, agriculture and all services of benefit to the community.
TEMPERANCE, ECONOMY and SIMPLICITY in personal living.
AVOIDANCE OF VIOLENCE or provocation to violence in all relations with other people or organised bodies.
VIGOROUS EFFORT to promote the social, economic and political welfare of all men and service to the community as a whole.

I was familiar with the contents of the document because by this time Elspeth and I were seeing quite a lot of Guy and Molly, and enjoying 'corrupting' them occasionally when they were in town by putting at their disposal the facilities of our little establishment in Orange Grove Drive which, though quite modest, were luxurious compared with their chosen standard of living at St Faith's. But we would have been amongst a very small handful of whites who had studied the document; and the reaction of the great majority of whites, including most officials of the Ministry of Native Affairs (about which the manifesto said that it 'must be abolished and government by Native Commissioner and the Native Affairs Department must give way in all areas to a system of local government authorities elected on a democratic franchise') was to see the revival of the African National Congress simply as a deplorable development, and Clutton-Brock not as a bridge builder but an agitator 'putting ideas into the minds of the Natives'. That was certainly the view of Stumbles, Fletcher and Ellman-Brown, and some of my time in caucus was spent crossing swords with them on the subject of Guy's intentions and influence.

The job of the second Select Committee on industrial relations — appointed to consider amendments to the new Industrial Conciliation Bill — turned out to be just about as formidable as the task of the first Select Committee which had issued the Report recommending what the Bill should contain. But it was all worthwhile because what it meant was that the revised Bill which emerged in the process was one which we could be sure carried the maximum agreement of the Committee itself (including the members who had not been involved in the original investigation), and would have a smooth passage through Parliament, and after that would have the maximum chance of being understood and used to good effect by employers and employees in industry.

Between the end of May and early October we had sixteen meetings, some of them lasting all day; more than fifty memoranda containing written evidence were submitted to us, and we had discussions with witnesses resulting in verbatim reports covering more than six hundred pages of typescript. By 10 October we had reached broad agreement on the changes to be made in the Bill, and it was resolved 'that at the conclusion of the present deliberations Mr Holderness, in conjunction with the Parliamentary draftsmen, prepare the first draft of a new Bill to be circulated to members of the Committee before the next meeting'. Intensive sub-committee meetings followed, and on 25 October we got authority from the Cabinet for the Parliamentary draftsman to give absolute priority to the work. By 8 November we had ready for consideration by the full Select Committee a twenty-nine page memorandum detailing the proposed amendments to the Bill, and after three further full meetings the stage had been reached when virtually all that remained to be done was a fresh printing of the revised Bill and its formal endorsement by the Committee.

What we ended up with was pretty well exactly what the first Select Committee had recommended in its Report, worked out in detail and with the rejection of one of the Report's subsidiary suggestions and the adoption of another. The suggestion that the establishment of works committees might in certain circumstances be made compulsory turned out to be much more troublesome than it was worth, and we abandoned it on the ground that the success of a works committee depended on the spirit in which it was set up and operated, and any element of statutory compulsion would probably do more harm than good. But the suggestion that 'consideration should be given to the setting up of an industrial court' which was related in the Report to the fact that its recommendations involved giving a number of new discretionary powers to the Minister and Government officials, turned out to be valuable not only in itself, but tactically, in winning Wightwick's support. The Dominion Party member of the Select Committee, C.F.S. Clark, had turned out to be no problem, and by mid-November only Wightwick's agreement was still outstanding. So I was relieved to get a letter from him, in my capacity as member in charge of the drafting, which began —

> My dear Hardwicke,
>
> I shall be unable to attend the meeting of the Select Committee on the 20th and 23rd and I am therefore writing to you to comment on your Re-Draft of the Bill.
>
> May I first start by congratulating you upon this Draft. You have certainly done a very good stout bit of work.
>
> I find myself substantially in agreement with the new Draft which you have got out, largely for the reason that an Industrial Tribunal has been introduced.
>
> The only things I am still not sure about are as under . . .

The points which followed were ones which we were able to satisfy him about without any difficulty.

In essence, this was the effect of the revised Bill —

It enabled trade unions and employers' organisations conforming to certain requirements to get official recognition by registering with the Industrial Registrar. The body concerned would apply for registration in respect of a particular industry and a particular area and the interests of people engaged in specified kinds of work (in the case of a trade union) or employers engaged in specified classes of enterprise (in the case of an employers' organisation). If its membership was not confined to the industry concerned it must have a separate, autonomous section for members within the industry, and the registration would apply to that section. On the contentious issue of race, the relevant provision was to the effect that the Constitution of a registered trade union or employers' organisation might provide for its membership (or the membership of the autonomous section confined to members within the industry) to be divided into branches on the basis of the kind of work or enterprise or the place of work or business or the sex or the race or colour of the members, but it must not contain any provision whereby any person was excluded on grounds of race or colour from membership of the body itself (or the autonomous section confined to members within the industry).

It provided that where in a particular industry one or more employers' organisations and one or more trade unions set up an Industrial Council conforming to certain requirements, it could be registered as the Industrial

Council for that industry in a specified area; and it defined as the main functions of an industrial council the negotiation of agreements prescribing minimum rates of pay for different classes of employees and other matters of mutual interest, and the prevention and settlement of disputes in the industry.

It empowered the Minister, at the request of the Industrial Council and after taking into account 'the interests of consumers and members of the public as a whole', to declare the terms of an industrial agreement to be binding on all the members of the employers' organisations and trade unions represented on the Council and, if he was satisfied that the parties to the agreement were sufficiently representative, on all employers and employees in the industry whether or not they were members.

It empowered the Minister to appoint an Industrial Board to act as a sort of substitute for an Industrial Council in any industry or area where none existed, and after considering its recommendations and the interests of consumers and members of the public as a whole, to make regulations governing minimum rates of pay for different classes of employees in the industry.

It contained elaborate provisions for mediation, conciliation and arbitration in dealing with industrial disputes, and it prohibited employers and employers' organisations from taking part in any lock-out, and employees and trade unions from taking part in any strike, until after the fulfilment of certain defined conditions, including the following:

> In the case of matters covered by an agreement of an Industrial Council or by an employment regulation made following an enquiry by an Industrial Board, until the expiry of the period of the agreement or employment regulation.
>
> In other cases if an Industrial Council or Industrial Board was in existence in the area, until after the dispute had been considered by it, and otherwise until after the dispute had been considered by a Conciliation Board provided for in the Bill.
>
> In other cases, until after the dispute had been considered and reported on by an arbitrator or arbitrators and an umpire provided for in the Bill, or by the Industrial Court.

It set up an Industrial Court as a body to which appeals could be made from a wide range of decisions by the Minister and decisions of the Industrial Registrar, and to play a part in the machinery for mediation and conciliation.

An interesting aspect of the approach contained in the new Bill was the criticism which it attracted, not from locally based whites or blacks, but from some left-wing critics steeped in the English tradition of industrial relations. The concept of joint councils comprising employers and employees in particular industries, and the principle of prohibiting strikes until after the trial without success of elaborate conciliation procedures, were things which Southern Rhodesian whites had got used to because they had been embodied in the original Industrial Conciliation Act of 1934. But some critics were sceptical. They saw it as a kind of conspiracy against blacks — a price which white labour had been prepared to pay for a deal with employers designed to ensure that blacks would only be employed in the most menial jobs. Some of that criticism continued despite the fact that the new Bill applied equally to whites and non-whites; but I thought myself it was probably as enlightened legislation in its field as one would be likely to find anywhere in the world — and possibly more so!

CHAPTER 17

Stocktaking, December 1957

Taking stock of the situation at the end of December 1957 it was impossible not to be aware of some threatening aspects, but they seemed unimportant compared with the brilliant prospect opened up by the new Southern Rhodesian franchise and the Industrial Conciliation Bill, with the best part of a year still to go in the life of the Eighth Parliament.

Todd was away 'at the coast' (to use a traditional expression). It had been a tough year for him, acting not only as Prime Minister but also as Minister of Labour (including taking the chair at meetings of the industrial relations Select Committee), Minister of Social Welfare and — until about October — Minister of Native Education. There had been abnormal pressures involved in the battle over the franchise, the anxieties over fusion and, more recently, the growing sense of outrage in the Cabinet and caucus over the revival of the African National Congress and official reports of activities of some of its members — including Clutton-Brock. Garfield had been under pressure to take some drastic action against them, and his response had been contained in a public speech delivered shortly before his departure for the Cape.

The occasion was one which, owing to the prevalence of Scots in Rhodesian society, had come to be regarded as appropriate for the making of Ministerial pronouncements — the annual St Andrew's Night banquet, where he had been invited to reply to the toast 'Southern Rhodesia'. His strategy was to give vent to the feelings of outrage felt by whites and talk of the possibility of further, tough security laws, but at the same time to create an opening for the African leaders of the movement, and for Guy, to clear themselves of the charges levelled against them. Copies of the speech as released to the press were circulated to members of the caucus, and here are some extracts from it.

The opening thesis was that the various achievements of the Government during the four years of its existence had had the effect of adding to individual liberty — freedom in the economic sense (dear to whites) or in the political sense (increasingly the obsession of blacks) —

The Southern Rhodesian Government has pursued a vigorous programme designed to extend the influence of private enterprise, and to provide an increasing degree of liberty for the individual . . .

In the wider view, the denationalising of the steel industry, the sale of the State sugar industry, have brought new freedom, fresh opportunity, and a great deal of new capital flowing into the country. The setting up of various courts and boards, for example in Town Planning, has taken power from officialdom and placed it increasingly in the hands of local residents. The introduction of the Land Husbandry Scheme promises to three hundred thousand African peasant farmers a greater degree of freedom than had ever been contemplated. The immediate results of giving ownership and dignity are seen in a doubling, and even a trebling, of production per acre. Another example of the policy is the granting to Africans of ninety-nine year leasehold of land near industry and the provision of such assistance as had already made it possible for thousands of Africans over the past eighteen months to acquire their own homes in town . . .

In line with such a policy has been the introduction of legislation to ease the Pass laws and allow greater freedom of personal movement . . .

A far-sighted plan for the extension of a sound and practical education programme was introduced two years ago, and the African people as a whole responded splendidly to the challenge . . .

(The franchise and new industrial relations draft legislation were of course included in the list of achievements).

But we all know, Todd said, 'that if freedom-loving people wish to keep their liberty they must be eternally vigilant', and over the last three months the Government had had to concern itself with the preparation of further security legislation — 'legislation which could be used to restrict the freedom of individuals and organisations'. This had been made necessary by developments that had occurred since the revival of the Southern Rhodesian African National Congress, and he set out in the speech what they were as seen by the Government and its officials —

Some months ago, when the African National Congress was formed, I was asked for my views on its significance and for the reactions of the Government. I said we would wait and take careful note of what happened.

At that time there were one or two matters which concerned us, but Mr Nkomo, to whom had been given the leadership of Congress, was known to be not only well educated and capable, but a responsible person. The choice of the name 'Congress' was not reassuring for its popular appeal was likely to be on the lines of the northern Congresses whose influence in Southern Rhodesia has grown. The Constitution which was accepted was a reasonably responsible document, but we did not know whether Mr Guy Clutton-Brock and the others who helped frame it meant it to be a rule of conduct for Congress members in Southern Rhodesia, or propaganda to place in the hands of the Africa Bureau and other friends overseas. We did not know what influence Mr Clutton-Brock would be able to exert, or how responsible other leaders, official and unofficial, would be.

The best thing to do was to wait and see the kind of fruit the tree would bear, and here are some of the fruits . . .

Mr George Nyandoro has in effect supplanted Mr Nkomo in effective leadership and, with other Congress members, campaigns against those Africans who wish to take their place amongst the civilised and responsible community which governs Southern Rhodesia. Africans who join the present political parties are termed 'sell-outs', 'Judas Iscariots', 'foolish people' and they are warned that they will be dealt with in due course.

A leading member of the African Congress inferred in Salisbury last week that the Congress would determine what is in the African interests, and that 'those who pursued courses which were detrimental to the African interest should be dealt with accordingly'.

At a recent meeting in the Native Reserves another leading Congress member instructed that European store-keepers in the Reserves should be approached for financial support and that if they refused they should be reported to Congress. 'I will know what to do with them', said the speaker.

At recent Congress meetings held in the Reserves near Salisbury the Chiefs have been flouted and members of the Police force have been humiliated. There are no laws governing such matters and there should be no need for them. African people have very strong traditions of courtesy, but what shocks them to-day in the undignified and irresponsible conduct of some Congress leaders could very well attract them to-morrow.

So what it looked like was that Congress 'does not concern itself with voters, but is endeavouring by its actions, and in conflict with its Constitution, to discipline a mass-machine whose powers would not be exerted through the vote but through some type of mass action'.

This part of Todd's speech was prefaced by his saying —

What follows is said in the hope that public opinion, both European and African, will be so roused in support of freedom for the individual and the maintenance of good relationships between the races and between the forces of law and order and the people themselves, that we may yet be able to refrain from bringing our new security measure before Parliament in February next.

And the speech ended —

What lies before us — co-operation or unrelenting racialism? It is the first duty of the Government to provide protection for all our people, and this we will continue to do, even if it means introducing further legal restrictions. If, on the other hand, leaders in Congress and particularly Mr Clutton-Brock and Mr Nyandoro would throw in their weight with the forces of law and order, if they would give their support to the cause of racial harmony, we could in the next three months halt the erosion which has started and make further restrictions unnecessary.

Times of change, of development and adjustment are always fraught with danger, and in such time powerful emotions can easily be stirred. May I give the solemn undertaking that the Government recognises these things, and that we can be depended upon to keep firm control and not delay decisions when the security of the country may depend upon our action.

We later learned that soon after making the speech, on his way to the Cape, Todd had had a good meeting with Nkomo in Bulawayo (arranged, not through the Native Department but direct, since he knew Nkomo personally as a former pupil of the Dadaya Mission School), and there were constructive meetings too with Guy and, I think, with George Nyandoro.

In the matter of the Federal franchise, there had been a joint meeting of governing party Members of the Southern Rhodesian and Federal Parliaments to discuss changes in the set-up of the Federal Parliament which had now been worked out by Greenfield and approved by Welensky and others of the Federal Government. Without going into all the complexities of the scheme, what it involved was an increase in the size of the House to 60 Members (including the Speaker), the continued existence of different categories of member, and the establishment of two voters' rolls — an 'A' and a 'B' roll — for federal voters to take part in the election of most of them. The qualifications for 'A' and 'B' roll voters respectively were broadly the same as the 'ordinary' and 'special' qualifications recently adopted in Southern Rhodesia, but there the similarity ended. In the new Federal Parliament 44 'Ordinary' Members would be elected by 'A' roll voters only (almost exclusively white), 8 specifically African Members would be elected by voters on both the 'A' and 'B' rolls (predominantly white), 3 white Members for African Interests would be nominated by the Governors of the three Territories, and 4 Specially Elected African Members would be elected by the African Representative Councils in Northern Rhodesia and Nyasaland. I was quite amazed to find at the joint meeting that even Jasper Savanhu and Mike Hove, the African Members of the Federal House from Southern Rhodesia, were quite prepared to go along with this, and I felt that, in view of the fusion or impending fusion of the URP and the Federal Party this could cause great damage to the position of vitally important supporters of the URP like Samkange and Shamuyarira.

I thought someone should hold up some sort of flag of protest and perhaps it should be me, so I wrote a letter to *The Rhodesia Herald* which I mention here because it gave rise to some comment afterwards. It referred to the qualifications proposed for the Federal A roll and went on —

> ... for the present and for many years to come it will be inaccurate, if not downright dishonest, to describe the Federal 'A' Roll as truly a common roll. In the meantime — and it is in the meantime that the confidence of the African population in the Federation will be won or lost — the Ordinary Member of the Federal Parliament will find himself in a position, as the Tredgold Commission puts it, 'in which he can only do right as he sees it at the risk of offending the overwhelming majority of the voters upon whom he depends for his seat in Parliament'.
>
> Most of the African Members, on the other hand, will find themselves answerable to an electorate predominantly non-African, i.e. to the voters on both the 'A' and 'B' rolls. The Federal Government tells us this is a good thing because it will produce members who are 'moderate' and 'responsible'. Africans say it will produce 'stooges' and will never prove to them that the so-called 'extremists' are useless, as the Government says, because they will never have the chance of putting extremists to the test. And 'what damage would a few extremists do anyway?' . . .
>
> It would certainly have been possible to devise a Federal franchise which would have given to the African population at this stage some real influence in the election of Ordinary Members, and to the European population an equivalent influence in the election of African Members. That would have been a just and sound step towards the abolition of racial representation in the Federal House; it would have strengthened the Federal Parliament as a legislative body; it would have done much to win the confidence of the African people, without which the Federation cannot succeed, and it would have been acceptable to the European voters . . .
>
> Many who count themselves Rhodesian patriots are gravely disturbed about the repercussions of this Bill, and — let there be no mistake — at least as much for the sake of the Europeans as anyone else. Is it too much to ask the Federal Government, at the eleventh hour, to have the courage to change its approach and do what is right?

There was obviously no real hope of an eleventh hour change of approach, and I knew the publication of the letter would infuriate many leading party members involved in the process of fusion to form the United Federal Party; but I hoped it would help to save the credibility of at least the Southern Rhodesian Division of the party in the eyes of Africans. One had perhaps to write off the Federal franchise for the time being, but in Southern Rhodesia we had the genuine article and genuine participation by blacks in politics could still become a reality in 1958. And if that happened the whole situation could be transformed.

The confidential statistics and estimates which had been presented to our caucus sub-committee considering the franchise indicated that in 1958 the number of voters on the voters' roll, excluding any who might come on to it through the special doors provided by the new franchise, would be about 50,000, including about 1,000 Africans registered under the old qualifications. (The number actually registered was always substantially less than the number eligible for registration). The number of Africans who would be eligible to come on to the roll through the two new, special doors could be about 12,000. Assuming that only 8,000 out of the 12,000 actually registered, that would give a total roll of 58,000 of whom about 9,000, or 15.5%, would be Africans. (With the total figure of 50,000 'ordinary' voters the maximum number permitted through the special doors would be one fifth, i.e. 10,000). If Southern Rhodesia could get 15% of Africans on to its common roll, or even 10% for example, we calculated that it would be sufficient to bring about the transformation. A fundamental cause of mistakes in the past had surely been bad intelligence, resulting from the lack of first-hand contact with blacks, combined with excessive exposure to the influence of white die-hards. A simple case in point had been the reaction to the Matimba affair, with a kindly and decent man like Max Buchan proposing, and all Todd's Ministers supporting, a ridiculous motion, basically because none of them was in sufficiently close contact with any African or 'Coloured' to be able to look at the situation from their points of view. If a substantial number of blacks were to come on to the voters' roll and begin playing a significant part in party politics personal contacts would be established, and people would find, as we had found on the industrial relations Select Committee by a more difficult route, that there was common ground where previously only conflict of interests had been thought to exist. And the Government, instead of being at the mercy of the white right every time it did something to benefit blacks, would stand to gain black votes to compensate for the white ones it had lost in the process.

Any African presented with the cold figure 10%–15% as the potential enrolment of Africans in 1958 might be tempted to think it derisory, but it would be a misleading indicator of their potential influence, even at the first stage. The influence which the African delegates had brought to bear at the URP Congress in 1956 had been based on a mere handful of registered voters; and besides, the 10%–15% would be spread unevenly over the various constituencies, with the result that in a few — two or three, say — it might constitute a very significant influence. No governing party concerned to win a majority of the thirty seats in Parliament could afford to ignore two or three constituencies; and it could hardly have one policy for two or three and another for the rest. The Southern Rhodesian common roll was a genuine one, and while the fourth and fifth doors might be special in that there would come a point when they would be closed, voters who came on to the roll through them were exactly the same, and had votes of the same value, as other voters. The Southern Rhodesian Parliament was a homogeneous parliament, with each Member having an obligation to the country as a whole as well as to his constituency and none of them having special responsibility to people of a particular race (with corresponding irresponsibility for others). Each voter, irrespective of race, had an equal say with other voters in the constituency in the choice of a Member of Parliament, and an equal right with others to have his interests looked after by his MP.

Once politicians began to take Africans seriously as voters all sorts of other things would fall into place. Only then would it become psychologically possible for the traditional 'Native Department' attitude to change. The traditional role of the Native Commissioner was, when you came to analyse it, a pretty impossible one in the contemporary context: being answerable to a white government, itself only answerable to whites, not only for the welfare but also for the discipline of blacks becoming daily more politically conscious and intolerant of paternalism. Only if blacks began to have some direct political influence with politicians could the traditional Native Commissioner be expected to relax, and to see the new African leaders as people rather than as a security risk. Similarly with immigrants. The tendency which we had seen demonstrated amongst immigrants — and even in the case of an enlightened man like Cyril Hatty — was to conform to traditional white attitudes, or at any rate to go along with them, rather than to stick their necks out. So even in cases where the natural outlook of immigrants was broad-minded and liberal, the country would only get the benefit when the excessive influence of white reactionaries on government policy was counterbalanced by the influence of blacks with voting power.

Turning from politics to industrial relations, one of the benefits that could be expected from the new Industrial Conciliation Act would be in the field of that trickiest of relationships — the relationship between the less well-endowed whites and talented and up-and-coming blacks. South Africa had got itself stuck with the policy of job reservation, partly because of the prevalence of 'poor whites' in South African society, but it was a dead-end policy which resulted in two artificially separated scales of pay, one for whites and one for blacks, with a vast gap between them. What our new Industrial Conciliation Act could be expected to bring about, once it was implemented, was a non-racial wage ladder with the intermediate steps filled in. One could illustrate, as it were diagramatically, what one visualised occurring by imagining an industrial council for a particular industry, represented by Employer A, white worker B and black worker C, debating the minimum rate of pay to be fixed for a particular class of work comprising certain processes and involving certain skills. One could visualise an argument between the two employee representatives —

> Employee B: I must insist on at least 10/- per hour for the work.
> Employee C: But at that rate Africans wouldn't stand a hope of being employed. We can't do the whole job or achieve that level of skill. We should be permitted to do the part of it we can cope with at a minimum rate of, say, 2/- per hour.
> Employee B: If I were to agree to that employers would find ways of using only blacks and doing without white labour altogether.
> Employee C: Very well then, what about 3/- per hour?

and so on; with the result, at the end of the process, of a new category of work being established with a minimum rate of pay attached to it, acceptable to Employee B and Employee C and also to Employer A. That kind of outcome would obviously be to the benefit of blacks, but it would also be to the benefit of whites and of industry as a whole because it would allow the best use to be made of talents available in the labour force. And it would be to the benefit, incidentally, of less talented whites because, short of racial job reservation, their chance of being employed would depend on space being available for them on rungs of the ladder below the top one, and this would be the only effective way of ensuring that the rates of pay available there were reasonable. It would allow whites to get gradually accustomed to blacks working alongside them on relatively skilled jobs, and it would open the way to apprenticeship for blacks.

It seemed wonderful, at the end of 1957, to have got as far as this. There was a next, vital step still to be taken. In the case of the franchise there would have to be a dynamic campaign to get the maximum number of voters, and particularly Africans, on to the roll before the next election; and there would have to be vigilance to ensure that the qualification tests, like

policy became one of undisguised white supremacy.

In 1965, despite being in possession of total de facto power under the existing Constitution and security laws inherited from Whitehead, the Rhodesian Front government made its illegal declaration of independence — UDI. The blacks, reluctant revolutionaries we thought, were left with no alternative but guerilla war. When it came they found themselves up against an official military force which was probably more efficient in its way than any in the world except possibly the Israelis' (and like the Israelis' consisting largely of part-timers drafted from civilian life). But they managed to win in the end.

The Smith Government held power for fifteen years until the changeover from Rhodesia to Zimbabwe in 1979. There was economic progress of a kind, despite sanctions. They inherited from the past an impressive infrastructure and fund of business and financial knowhow, and an economy of just the right size to be ideally manageable. Many business leaders were opposed to the Rhodesian Front at first, but at the first board meetings after UDI when the directors asked themselves where to go from here they inevitably found themselves concluding that their first duty was to the shareholders, and that demanded compliance with government directives. Opponents of UDI in the public service found themselves having to serve the RF government or else emigrate and try to find some way in some other country to support their families. The white population increased to nearly 300,000 and some of the economic prosperity rubbed off on Africans.

But it was tragedy nevertheless. The Smith Government's propaganda methods and control of information seemed to Pat like a kind of replay of what he had seen going on in Nazi Germany. The disregard for the rule of law and perpetration of brutalities in the name of law and order seemed to us almost like a deliberate attempt, in a country with a relatively innocent past, to build up for the future the kind of legacies of hatred that places like Northern Ireland had to endure.

Pat kept on battling, and in particular in the capacity of chairman of the Constitutional Council established under Whitehead's 1961 Constitution, which was supposed to provide some protection for fundamental human rights. A fruitless task, as it turned out, since every adverse report of the Council on legislation proposed by the RF Government was either ignored or over-ridden. In 1975, when Pat was dying of cancer, his elder son returned to the country and stayed too long. He was one of the younger generation whites who could not be brainwashed into accepting the Smith Government's image of itself as custodians of 'Western Christian civilisation' and of black guerilla fighters as sub-human terrorists to be hunted like game. He heard that call-up papers were about to be served on him, and tried to escape; but too late. He was caught before reaching the border and forced into the Army. Elspeth and I were about to leave the country at the time, and later we heard that he had shot himself — at the very place in Alexandra Park, as it turned out, which had seemed to me to have a nightmare quality about it when I was a child and it was still called Hartman Hill.

Could it, in reality, have worked out otherwise in Southern Rhodesia? My answer is yes, I think it could.

As at the end of 1957 there was one fundamental pre-requisite: that a substantial proportion of the Africans made eligible for the vote by the new Electoral Act should be registered as voters in time for the next general election. That was a practical possibility before the repudiation of Todd by his Ministers, because the Eighth Parliament still had more than a year of its maximum five year life to run then. But it would still have been a practical possibility even after that if Whitehead, when he received the last-minute invitation to stand against Todd at the special congress early in February, had been able to understand the full implications of it — and his own limitations — and had refused. The tacticians who thought up the scheme would hardly have been able to find another suitable candidate. Todd would have come through as the elected leader of the territorial division of the United Federal Party (successor to the United Rhodesia Party in Southern Rhodesia), and continued to be Prime Minister. The Cabinet he then appointed would have been one which could be relied on to encourage, and not obstruct, the registration of the new voters, and to get the new Industrial Conciliation Act through Parliament and under way.

There would have been a problem about elections for a new Federal Government, also in the offing: how to reconcile pressures from many whites in the party to give maximum support to Welensky in those elections with the necessity, relative to African opinion, to maintain Southern Rhodesia's independent position on matters such as the franchise and dominion status. But Todd, with his position as leader confirmed, would have been able to keep the Southern Rhodesian Division sufficiently distanced from the Federal Government; and would have been able to revive the dialogue with the Southern Rhodesian African National Congress which he had, in effect, invited them to enter into in his St Andrew's Night speech before leaving for the Cape. Africans, including members of the ANC, would have found it possible to work constitutionally with the franchise provided by the 1957 Electoral Act.

That franchise itself would probably not have endured for ever. At the next general election — held in January 1959, say — it would have had the effect of bringing on to the roll sufficient African voters to set in train a transformation of party politics; but African nationalist ambitions would have continued to grow. Meanwhile the break-up of the Federation would have taken place, and Southern Rhodesia would have resumed responsibility within its borders for the functions previously handed over to the Federal Government. (Paradoxically enough, the chance of the Federation continuing in some form would have depended on Todd distancing himself enough from Welensky, but that would probably have come too late in any case). At some time — perhaps the very year in which the country found itself in actuality resorting to an illegal form of independence — the necessity would have become apparent for a fresh review of the Constitution and franchise.

In those circumstances I think the business of constitution reform would have been tackled in a much more enlightened way than on the various occasions when it actually happened. The body of people appointed to go into it would not have had to start with something already prepared, taken off a peg, re-hashed and presented as part of some tactical package deal — as in 1961, and for that matter in 1979. They would have been widely representative and with a wide-ranging brief — like the body which was appointed in Switzerland in 1848 with the apparently impossible task of devising machinery that would enable twenty-two historically disparate cantons to come together as a single, modern state. I think they would have been struck with how, under the Westminster system, the governing party, however small its majority, controls all the decision making, and how in a situation where maximum reconciliation is a priority need (and in this case particularly as between black and white interests) participation must be provided as far as possible at an early stage in the process. For example, in the case of a new piece of legislation it must occur at an early stage in the drafting process and not only when the draft Bill is virtually a fait accompli. (In our little Eighth Parliament we were able to achieve an extraordinary degree of consensus in contentious matters, partly by extensive use of select committees and partly, come to think of it, by being for the moment a kind of one-party set-up — having an overwhelming majority in the House and a wide range of views and interests represented amongst ourselves).

I think the review body would have concluded that while the system prevailing in Britain tended towards decisive government and the avoidance of deadlocks, it tended also to promote confrontation rather than conser. is politics. And they would have come up with original proposals based on the maximum search for consensus consistent with decisive governm nt. The country would then have been able to give a demonstration — of value particularly to places like South Africa and Northern Ireland — of how such a system could work.

By this route the African Nationalist ideal of majority rule would have been achieved perhaps earlier than 1979, the actual year of the changeover. But it would have been achieved without the creation of legacies of hatred, bloodshed and the destruction of valuable resources, and without continuing over-dependence on white skills; and without the whites having established terrible precedents, like imprisonment without proper recourse to the courts and UDI itself which, if any subsequent government were to copy, they would be the first to denounce to the world as examples of uncivilised government. In the civil service and in industry there would have been substantial numbers of Africans trained and experienced, and in the governing party with its black leaders there would have been a substantial number of whites able to identify themselves with it and its policies.

I see no reason why the setting in train in Southern Rhodesia in 1958 of this kind of pattern of events should have been any more impossible than the transformation of the Tory Party in England by the Disraeli franchise reform of 1867.

We whites missed out on a great opportunity in Rhodesia/Zimbabwe in the end. But I find it difficult to blame personally individuals who were involved, like Todd's Ministers for example. Their effective leader Geoff Ellman-Brown was no doubt less ingenuous than he appeared, but what he thought he was doing in repudiating Todd was to help save Southern Rhodesia (and/or the Federation) from politicians to the right of him — then the Dominion Party; and looking only at the orthodox barometer — the state of opinion amongst registered voters — that is what we all ought to have been doing. I am tempted to blame Whitehead because somehow he should have known better, and yet he had special reasons for being insulated from reality. Even Ian Smith, when he found himself chosen by the die-hards to be the leader of their last-ditch movement, could hardly have done other than he did at that stage. Presumably what he thought he was saving the country from was the kind of black politician that Idi Amin later turned out to be in Uganda.

What has to be blamed, I think, was our collective failure as a community to understand a simple constitutional fact: that having been given by the 1923 Constitution virtually total power it was vital in our interests, as well as in the interests of the black majority, to find a way of sharing it and putting ourselves in direct touch with the people we were supposed to be dealing with.

Now it is the turn of the black Zimbabweans, who during the lead-up to and since the guerilla war have shown great political sagacity; who ought to have our good wishes, and who may perhaps find something to learn from our constitutional mistakes.